'The definitive history of telecommunications reform in Australia … provides a unique window into the tensions between good policy and hard politics across the governments of Whitlam, Fraser and Hawke. Essential reading.' **George Megalogenis**

'A fascinating example of policy history that tells an unfamiliar story about Australia's past, explains peculiarities of our landscape in the NBN era, and contains clues about the nation's telecommunications future.' **Frank Bongiorno**

'A fascinating study in how, and how not, to make public policy. John Doyle gives us a meticulous analysis of the politics, personalities and industry pressures at work during the most critical years in the development of the modern Australian telecommunications system.' **Gareth Evans**

'John Doyle has written the definitive account of Australian telecommunications policy. He brings to life the key figures, the passions and the deep complexities that played into pivotal decisions … offers invaluable insights into what developing and implementing policy reform is like in the real world, and how this has changed over time.' **Kim Beazley**

'The most comprehensive and balanced account written on this crucial policy matter … Doyle shows how policy reforms central to Australia's economy can be progressed while also taking account of those disadvantaged by such change.' **Graham Evans**

'Rigorous, insightful and balanced … provides a penetrating analysis of the multi-faceted politics of a leading driver of the tech revolution.' **Richard Alston**

'*Crossed Lines* provides invaluable insights into the complexities that lay behind the development of Australia's telecommunications policy and the difficult trade-offs made to meet competing interests … mandatory reading for anyone interested in telecommunications policy or in policy development more generally.' **Tony Shaw**

'A fascinating and carefully researched account of a period in Australia's telecommunications history that to date has not received the focus it deserves.' **Paul Fletcher**

CROSSED LINES

DISRUPTION, POLITICS AND
RESHAPING AUSTRALIAN
TELECOMMUNICATIONS

JOHN DOYLE

AʃP

First published 2022 by
Australian Scholarly Publishing Ltd
7 Lt Lothian St Nth, North Melbourne, Vic 3051
Tel: 61 3 9329 6963 / enquiry@scholarly.info / www.scholarly.info

ISBN 978-1-922669-62-9

Cover design: David Morgan

For Aneetha, Tom and James

Contents

Abbreviations   *viii*

Introduction   1

1   A Vast Concern   6

2   Reform and Renovation   23

3   Escalating Challenges   40

4   A Fast-changing Area   56

5   Blue Sky Dreaming   68

6   Intractable Conundrums   79

7   Turning Back the Tide   97

8   Imperatives for Change   109

9   A New Agenda   122

10   Creating Momentum   137

11   Competitive Influences   157

12   A National Champion   167

13   Lessons and Legacies   195

Acknowledgements   *212*

Notes   *214*

Bibliography   *245*

Index   *259*

About the Author   *274*

Abbreviations

ABC	Australian Broadcasting Commission[*]
ACCC	Australian Competition and Consumer Commission
ACOA	Administrative and Clerical Officers' Association
ACTU	Australian Council of Trade Unions
AEIA	Australian Electronic Industry Association
AGPS	Australian Government Publishing Service
AIIA	Australian Information Industry Association
ALP	Australian Labor Party
APTU	Australian Postal and Telecommunications Union
APWU	Amalgamated Postal Workers' Union
ASTEC	Australian Science and Technology Council
ATEA	Australian Telecommunications Employees' Association
ATUG	Australian Telecommunications Users Group
Austel	Australian Telecommunications Authority
BCA	Business Council of Australia
BTCE	Bureau of Transport and Communications Economics
BTS	Business Telecommunications Services
CPD	Commonwealth Parliamentary Debates
DOC	Department of Communications
DOTAC	Department of Transport and Communications
DURD	Department of Urban and Regional Development

---

[*] Australian Broadcasting Corporation from July 1983.

EPAC	Economic Planning Advisory Council
ERC	Expenditure Review Committee
GBE	Government Business Enterprise
GPO	General Post Office
GDP	Gross Domestic Product
ICVTS	Interdepartmental Committee on the Vulnerability of the Telecommunications System
IWGCI	Interdepartmental Working Group on Recommendations of the Australian Post Office Commission of Inquiry
NAA	National Archives of Australia
NBN	National Broadband Network
OECD	Organisation for Economic Cooperation and Development
OTC	Overseas Telecommunications Commission
PABX	Private Automatic Branch Exchange
PM&C	Department of the Prime Minister and Cabinet
PMG	Postmaster-General's Department
PREIA	Professional Radio Employees Institute of Australasia[†]
Reps	House of Representatives
ROSA	Review of Structural Arrangements
SAC	Structural Adjustment Committee
SSWG	National Communications Satellite System Working Group
TFCEP	Task Force to Inquire into the Continuing Expenditure Policies of the Previous Government
WGCR	Officials' Working Group on Communications Regulation

[†] Professional Radio and Electronics Institute of Australasia, 1975–92.

Introduction

The provision of the means of communication within and beyond continental Australia has been an abiding matter of national concern from the earliest colonial days. And it still is.

Michael Kirby[1]

On a late spring afternoon in Canberra, a youngish communications minister announced an ambitious infrastructure project that would 'bring major benefits to millions of Australians' and 'weld our scattered population into one nation'.[2] Widely known as a political numbers man, the minister was enthusiastic about technology's capacity to improve people's lives.[3] He declared that the government would utilise the 'latest knowledge' from around the world to create a new, state-of-the-art national network to meet Australia's 'burgeoning demand for communications services'. It would be 'the best system that money can buy'. The network would deliver high-quality communications and broadcasting services to Australians outside of the major cities for the first time, he said. It would stimulate innovations across health, education, science, business, and more, and would 'encourage people to live and work in remote areas'. Demand would 'spread like wildfire'.[4] The project would be developed and run by a new government-owned enterprise, which was flagged for later privatisation.

The cost would obviously be huge, but Australia's prime minister and key government and industry figures were convinced of the project's promise; it would be a game-changer, showcasing the nation globally as sophisticated and modern.[5] Australians were 'on the threshold of a great new era in communications', the minister pledged; they were to 'join in one of the greatest technological innovations in communications history'.[6] The project was about 'vision', said a top official.[7] The media was mostly on side. A leading national newspaper lauded the project's 'plain common sense' for 'a land as vast as Australia', while the *Age* in Melbourne foresaw advantages for 'a great many Australians'.[8] The opposition walked a fine line, targeting the government on costs and planning deficiencies while trying to avoid being cast as anti-progress.

Later, a new government with a new agenda substantively changed the project's policy and operating parameters. There were cost blowouts, revenue shortfalls and rollout delays. As early promises failed to eventuate, contention grew. Fingers were pointed and conflicting perspectives passionately debated. The ultimate resolution satisfied no-one.

This account will seem familiar to the contemporary reader with a passing interest in national affairs. Yet it does not refer to the Rudd government's portentous announcement of the National Broadband Network and NBN Co in 2009, but to the Fraser government's establishment of the National Communications Satellite System and Aussat thirty years before. The youngish communications minister in question was Liberal MP Tony Staley, not Labor's Stephen Conroy.

The point of this is to highlight the recurrent patterns of Australian tele-communications policy and remind us that today's NBN does not represent some sort of technological end of history. Rather, it sits comfortably on a continuum of interrelated political and policy decisions, actions and institutional arrangements. Aussat illustrates this neatly, as I discuss in this book. Through many twists and turns under two governments and seven ministers, Aussat came to play a pivotal role in shaping the telecommunications reforms of the Hawke government, a core outcome of which was a lopsided market structure dominated by a vertically inte-grated state-owned colossus, Telecom (later Telstra). While we cannot reasonably claim a direct causal link between this structure and the later NBN Co, it is assuredly the case that had Labor taken different decisions then, we would not have the NBN we have now.

There is no shortage of commentary and analysis on the NBN—the politics of network structures, technology choices and financial governance, and the decade of debate that preceded it. That is not the focus of this book. My aim has been to uncover and unpack the deeper rhythms of Australia's telecommunications reform history, from the late 1960s, when Gough Whitlam, newly elected as the Labor opposition leader, fractured a long-standing bipartisan consensus about how best to deliver services, to the still poorly understood Hawke reforms of the late 1980s and early 1990s.

During this period, Australia underwent a revolution in how telecommunications services, always vital for commerce and communities, were provided and perceived. This was an intensely contested process, involving generations of politicians, government and party officials, unions, business groups, state enterprises and local, mostly rural, communities. The outcome was that the nation moved from an era of rigid, centralised controls to one in which the dynamic forces of competition between rival companies were envisaged as unlocking new economic and social benefits for the country. It is impossible to understand how we got to where we are today without exploring this earlier period. The decisions taken then remain relevant now.

In seeking to identify the key factors that underpinned this long transformation, I have considered a number of questions. How did successive governments and the major opposition parties respond to the challenges in this policy area, particularly when they involved technological, social and economic forces largely outside their control? How did they balance the national interest with vested interests and those of their core supporters? Did some groups play a more significant role than others? And why did particular reforms occur when and how they did?

My research draws on personal interviews with key decision-makers and advisers, including former communications ministers from the Fraser and Hawke governments, Tony Staley, Ian Sinclair, Neil Brown, Gareth Evans and Kim Beazley, former prime ministers Fraser and Keating, and former top officials including Graham Evans, who was Bob Hawke's first principal private secretary and subsequently secretary of the Transport and Communications Department from 1988 to 1993. Extensive use was made of previously unexamined cabinet and ministerial papers held in Australia's national archives. I have also been informed by my own professional experience of working on strategy and regulatory policy from the late 1990s to the early 2010s in the telecommunications sector that came out of the reforms discussed here.

The book opens with a survey of the political, social and institutional context of Australia's telecommunications arrangements since federation. It draws out the key factors that were placing the system under severe strain by the 1960s and identifies the legacy issues at play in the debates that erupted from 1967 between the Liberal-Country Party Coalition government and the Whitlam-led Labor opposition. The principal focus is the five years preceding Whitlam's election win in 1972, a time when Labor committed to making fundamental changes to

Australia's telecommunications (and postal) system that went well beyond the ad hoc measures the Coalition was willing to consider.

One of the Whitlam government's first major reform programs was focused on telecommunications. It culminated in the establishment of Telecom shortly before Whitlam's dismissal in 1975. This policy aligned with Whitlam's long-standing support for user-pays principles in telecommunications, largely by reducing rural subsidies, and his aim to make Australia's arrangements more financially self-sufficient in order to free up government funds for other Labor priorities. I show that although Labor and the Coalition collaborated in the shift from the Postmaster-General's Department (PMG) to Telecom (and Australia Post), they both struggled to reconcile the forces pressing for change with their own ideological and political blind spots and the interests of their core supporters.

When the Fraser government came to office, it had given little consideration to Australia's new telecommunications arrangements, but ultimately it set the parameters of how they came to work. For much of its tenure, the government faced a rolling series of unanticipated, complex and interrelated issues that gave rise to fundamental political and policy conundrums that the Coalition was unable to settle. A particularly important issue was the government's decision to establish a new state-owned company, Aussat, to develop and run Australia's national satellite system. This presented political and policy challenges for Labor and came to play a critical role in shaping policy and reform under Hawke.

I frame the Hawke government in two parts, the first running from Labor's election in 1983 to mid-1987 and the second from then until 1991. During 1983–87, the government barely engaged with the challenges that were being thrown up by technological change and economic pressures for more flexibility in Australia's telecommunications system. Policy was left to a junior minister focused on rolling back Malcolm Fraser's market liberal baby steps. Cabinet decisions paid little heed to officials' advice to start opening up the sector, or at least avoid closing off options for later reform.

In addressing the years from 1987 to 1989, I unpack the key elements—contextual, political and structural—that saw the Hawke government's dramatic shift to an agenda of telecommunications liberalisation in the face of fierce resistance from Labor's federal caucus and the party's support base and deep ambivalence from Telecom. I argue that the most important results to come from the early competition and corporatisation changes developed under ministers

Gareth Evans and Ralph Willis were those that set the stage for further reform. Most crucial was showing for the first time that full competition was compatible with immutable bipartisan social policy objectives about ensuring universal access to affordable services.

In September 1990, cabinet agreed on a new framework for Australian telecommunications that had been developed and skilfully prosecuted by Kim Beazley. It was based on a strengthened Telecom and a privatised Aussat competing within a heavily regulated duopoly, and it ushered in a new era. Though the shift to full service competition was likely, perhaps inevitable, from the late 1980s, its timing was not; nor was the precise model settled on by Labor. Intense debates preceded cabinet's and Labor's key decisions; these combined policy principles, political self-interest, deeply held Labor sensibilities and other political dynamics playing out at the time, including tensions between Hawke and his treasurer, Paul Keating.

A consistent theme throughout the book is the important role played by particular interest groups in shaping the dynamics of telecommunications policy in Australia, especially rural interests, the large Labor-affiliated unions, business groups and the state telecommunications enterprises themselves. Beyond telecommunications, it offers a case study of 'real world' policy-making over three decades and challenges our conventional views about the Whitlam, Fraser and Hawke governments.

The book also shines a light, for the first time, on behind-the-scenes consideration of policy options not pursued, such as Telecom's structural separation, that retain strong resonance for our contemporary NBN world. In my final chapter, I draw together the disparate threads of Australia's long reform era and seek to pull them through to the present day. This account is a tale of competing community interests—city and country, unions and business, consumers and producers—wicked policy conundrums, political challenges and relentless, disruptive technological change, all carried out in the service of a universal, fundamental human need, the need to communicate and connect.

1

A Vast Concern

The [Postmaster-General's] Department comes more intimately in contact with the home life of every person in the State than any other institution can possibly do.

Anderson report, 1915[1]

Through the nineteenth century and well into the twentieth, direct action by successive colonial and state governments played a leading role in Australia's economic development.[2] Large, isolated and sparsely populated, lacking local capital and skills and heavily reliant on primary industries such as wool-growing, farming and mining, the nation imported money and people to build infrastructure in essential sectors such as transport, power utilities and communications. In all these sectors, services were provided through government monopolies.

Within two months of Australia's federation in January 1901, the new nation's six postal and telegraph departments came together to form the Postmaster-General's Department. From its birth the PMG, or Post Office as it became known, was a colossus, dwarfing every other enterprise in Australia and accounting for nearly two-thirds of the new commonwealth government's departmental expenditure.[3]

Setting the scene

The PMG faced major challenges from the outset. Its operational span was vast, encompassing the complex, capital-intensive engineering work of constructing new communications infrastructure, the myriad logistical tasks of managing a national postal service and the retail functions associated with supplying customers with services. National coordination was complicated by a decentralised organisational structure, which was set in legislation substantially drafted by the heads of the PMG's colonial predecessors, who had been keen to protect their autonomy.[4]

The PMG's activities also sat awkwardly with its status as a conventional government department subject to ministerial direction and standard public service administrative arrangements. The Public Service Board was responsible for wages, employment terms and public service staffing levels. There was a constant undercurrent of friction between the PMG and the board: from the former because its activities did not readily fit with the rest of the public service; and from the latter because the PMG's sheer scale meant that any uplift in its wages or staff conditions materially affected the rest of the public service and, ultimately, the wider economy.[5]

Successive governments also set the PMG conflicting objectives: the department was to supply essential services at affordable prices to all Australians wherever they lived, but it was also required to operate like a business. This policy tension was apparent from the beginning, including within the governing Protectionist Party of early prime ministers Edmund Barton and Alfred Deakin. During a Senate debate in June 1901, for example, a call by the postmaster-general, James Drake, for the PMG to operate on 'business lines', balancing expenditure with revenue and making up any shortfall with interest-bearing loans, was countered by his colleague Robert Best, the chairman of committees, who preferred a 'service-orientated' approach that would assure country people of receiving the services they required to achieve an 'agreeable' lifestyle.[6]

Between 1908 and 1921, the PMG was subject to three inquiries, each of which recommended it be granted more autonomy, balanced with stronger accountability, to promote greater efficiency and better service standards, and specifically to be released from centralised public service controls.[7] The first inquiry, a royal commission established by the Deakin government after negative press coverage about service delivery, concluded that if the PMG operated 'on business lines' it could be 'self-supporting' without any 'lessening of facilities'.[8] In 1915, the issue was revisited by a Labor government-appointed inquiry led by Robert Anderson, a timber and shipping-industry figure who was also reviewing the Defence and Home Affairs departments and was shortly bound for Egypt as deputy quartermaster-general of Australia's expeditionary forces in the First World War.[9] Anderson found that the 'indefensible system' of external controls had to go.[10] His recommendations aligned with the earlier royal commission, as did a subsequent royal commission into commonwealth expenditure that was set up by Billy Hughes's Nationalist government after the war.

The recommendations from these inquiries were resisted by key stakeholders and ultimately ignored by governments of all political persuasions. Treasury, Home Affairs and the Public Service Board wanted to maintain their controls over the PMG's finances and staffing; the PMG's senior state officials wanted to protect their autonomy; politicians cherished the political kudos they received for bringing new telephone and postal facilities to their electorates (Billy Hughes declared it their 'dearest wish') and rural communities dependent on commercially unviable services feared the consequences of a more businesslike PMG.[11]

Under direct ministerial control and parliamentary oversight, the PMG's pricing model was inherently political. There was a weak relationship between costs and revenues. For many years, telephone line rentals in country areas were kept below those in the cities, despite the much higher costs of providing them, and residential telephone services were cheaper than business services. This reflected a bipartisan commitment to using telecommunications policy as a tool for national progress. Successive governments focused on expanding the provision of affordable universal telephone services, which were seen as critical to Australia's economic development and to spreading sustainable, decentralised communities throughout the continent.

An increasingly complex and opaque web of politically infused cross-subsidies evolved. In general, the city subsidised the bush, business subsidised households and the PMG's telecommunications activities subsidised postal services. Uneconomic pricing distorted service demand, which in turn shaped network design and expansion, technical priorities and the allocation of capital.[12] But governments still wanted the PMG to conduct itself in a businesslike manner by matching revenues to costs and efficiently utilising resources. This was partly because politicians recognised the commercial characteristics of the PMG's activities, and also because the department's consistently high level of capital expenditure made huge demands on the federal budget.

The PMG was also tightly woven into the social and economic fabric of country life. Telecommunications and postal services, while considered essential utilities, were unlike other state utility services such as electricity, water and roads because they went to the heart of social relationships and facilitated country people's connections with each other and with the wider Australian community.

Many thousands of country people worked for the PMG, and in country towns the local post office also facilitated wider federal services such as pension payments and banking.[13] As Anderson had observed, the PMG was 'intimately in contact' with people's daily lives.[14]

From this arose a government enterprise that was unique in Australia for its scale and scope, for the technical and logistical complexity of its operations and for the intricate interplay between the structural, financial, commercial, political and socio-cultural factors embedded in it. Until at least the mid-1960s, all Australia's main political parties sustained and supported this system, with the Country Party being its most vigilant and energetic champion and, until the long-running Coalition government lost office in 1972, the greatest obstacle to meaningful reform.

Rising pressures for reform

During the 1960s, the widening scope and accelerating pace of technological change, combined with a sustained growth in demand that was well beyond the PMG's capacity to satisfy, made it clear that changes were needed to the federation-era system. This put the PMG under greater operational and financial stress and placed direct strain on the administrative arrangements within which it existed. This in turn intensified the political pressure for reform.

Technological advances meant that the quality of telephone services improved during the 1960s, and the PMG's product range expanded from voice and telex to include new data services. From 1960, the department methodically implemented a massive network upgrade program to enable a national direct-dial system with greater 'local call' distances, simpler pricing and lower connection waiting times.[15] Within a decade, the proportion of long-distance calls that could be direct-dialled across Australia rose from 2 per cent to more than 80 per cent. The proportion of telephone services running over automatic exchanges (enabling connection and transmission of calls) passed 90 per cent.[16] At the same time, large, geographically dispersed organisations such as Australia's two domestic airlines were integrating new data transmission systems into their operations.[17]

Demand for new telephones was surging. In the ten years to 1972, the number of services in operation increased by more than 70 per cent to exceed three million. Over the same period, the number of local calls rose by about 70 per cent and long-distance calls were up by more than 220 per cent nationally. Quality improvements were a factor in this increased traffic, though long-distance calls in particular were expensive and of poor quality, and demographic shifts contributed to demand as Australia's cities expanded and the number of larger-scale businesses increased. Rising community expectations about telephone ownership also played a role, as did the fact that charges for new connections were set well below cost. The fee for a new telephone in 1971, for example, covered between 0.25 per cent and 3 per cent of the average connection cost.[18]

By the Coalition's latter years in office, the PMG's scale and its relentless calls for more capital were becoming increasingly problematic. It was by far Australia's largest enterprise, the value of its assets having passed those of the New South Wales and Victorian state railways in the early 1950s. In the quarter-century since the end of the Second World War, its employee numbers and assets value had doubled.[19] With 112,000 permanent staff by the early 1970s, the PMG employed more than twice as many people as Australia's largest company, BHP, and its $3 billion in fixed assets dwarfed BHP's $1.8 billion.[20] The telecommunications and postal giant accounted for nearly half of all commonwealth public service staff, and it was Australia's largest single employer of engineers. Its capital expenditure, which was mostly spent on telecommunications, represented more than a third of the federal capital budget and was allocated to thousands of projects all over the nation, from laying suburban cables to linking Mount Isa and Darwin by microwave radio.[21]

The combined effect of these technological, operational and commercial dynamics placed intense pressure on the PMG's administrative arrangements. The operating environment was faster, more fluid, more technically complex and more capital-hungry, but the administrative model was inflexible, inefficient and subject to arbitrary political interference. Compounding this, the gulf between telecommunications and post was widening. The former was characterised by rapid growth, technological innovation and high capital intensity, the latter by less-skilled labour and economic stagnation. Year-on-year, the PMG's financial surpluses in telecommunications were used to subsidise postal losses.[22]

The Public Service Board's jurisdiction over the PMG's wages and employment conditions, especially regarding role classifications, promotions, internal organisational arrangements and recruitment, cut across senior PMG officials' efforts. Even when the board approved PMG proposals, their implementation could be delayed by upwards of a year. PMG officials could not negotiate directly with their staff (in practice with the telecommunications and postal unions) or represent the PMG in industrial arbitration hearings.[23]

The block on PMG–union negotiations also frustrated the unions and was a key factor in the industrial disputes that racked the PMG during this period.[24] While the number of working hours lost to industrial action by PMG staff was consistently less than the Australian national average, the resulting business and community disruption underlined the centrality of telecommunications and post to Australia's economic and social life. In early 1972, for example, a Melbourne shop manager told the *Bulletin* magazine that for several months, including during the Christmas rush, he had 'set up office each day in a St Kilda phone booth' because he could not get his telephone repaired. Even the prime minister, Billy McMahon, found himself unable to get a telephone connected to his beach house.[25]

In the more operationally complex and capital-intense context of the 1960s, the arrangements governing the PMG's financial affairs also worked against the efficient delivery of telecommunications services. For funds, the PMG was dependent on service revenue and Treasury appropriations, both of which were heavily influenced by political considerations. Telephone service fees and charges required parliamentary approval, making price-setting not just political but also subject to the parliament's schedule rather than to commercial imperatives. Many politicians, especially those from the Country Party, cherished this control. Ian Allan, a fierce defender of rural prerogatives, spoke approvingly in the late 1960s of how the PMG had been 'persuaded to reframe' a plan to substantially raise telephone line rentals that, if implemented, would have reduced the pro-country pricing bias.[26]

The PMG's appropriations were decided annually by parliament. This meant that the amount of funding approved each year was principally a function of contemporary political considerations and budgetary trade-offs. It also locked the PMG into short-term, rigid capital planning and expenditure cycles. This was a constant source of frustration. The department's director-general, Trevor Housley, publicly alluded to this in 1966 when he called for 'a more forward-reaching approach' that would enable Australia to 'realise the full potential of the Post Office as a dynamic force for better co-ordination of government through communications'.[27]

By the latter 1960s, the raft of operational and financial pressures being driven by technological changes and sustained high demand was making it plain that Australia's telecommunications arrangements were no longer fit for purpose. Along with related changes being made in Britain, these factors gave fresh impetus to reconsidering what historian W. K. Hancock termed the 'awkward dilemma' of public administration: how to balance direct controls over state enterprises with the autonomy they need for efficiency.[28] These underlying dynamics underpinned the respective policy positions taken by the Coalition and Labor between 1967 and 1972.

Incremental adjustments

The key figure overseeing Coalition government policy on telecommunications was Alan Hulme, who was appointed postmaster-general by the prime minister, Robert Menzies, in 1963 and retained this role under Menzies's successors Holt, McEwen, Gorton and McMahon before retiring at the 1972 election. An accountant and company director by profession and a prominent founding member of the Liberal Party's Queensland branch, Hulme had a strong affinity with country Australia and represented an outer-Brisbane semi-rural electorate. He was a diligent minister; even Gough Whitlam publicly praised him as 'a man of very great skill and experience'.[29]

Hulme supported the PMG's traditional dual objectives: the provision of affordable universal services and businesslike commercial operations. He recognised the inherent tension between these objectives and accepted that the department's operating procedures were too restrictive for a 1960s context, but was convinced that direct ministerial control remained necessary to ensure delivery of commercially unviable services to the bush. He was also committed to maintaining the PMG as a government department subject to conventional public service controls and jointly responsible for both telecommunications and postal services.[30]

In Hulme's view, the challenges confronting the PMG could be addressed through incremental adjustments to the status quo. Amid sharp price rises for telephone and postal services in 1967, for example, he supported joint recommendations by the PMG and Treasury to grant the department more financial flexibility, to facilitate greater commercial efficiency, and, as a corollary, to require from it greater financial transparency to improve accountability. These steps aligned with earlier changes to Britain's General Post Office, undertaken by the Conservative government in 1961, though by 1967 the caravan had moved on and a new Labour government-led bipartisan policy was in place to reconstitute the GPO as an autonomous statutory authority.[31]

The Coalition's decision was announced during Billy McMahon's budget speech in August 1967, and the proposed legislative amendments were introduced into parliament the following April. From 1 July 1968, the PMG's forecast annual expenditure requirements would not be segmented into individual items and voted on by parliament as line-by-line appropriations. Rather, the entire budget would be passed as a single appropriation and paid into a PMG 'trust account', with interest payable on Treasury funds as they were drawn. Telecommunications and postal revenues would also be paid into this account rather than going into consolidated revenue.[32] Hulme made great play of the PMG's new financial freedom, declaring that the department, 'like all business undertakings … must react quickly to variations in demand for its services [and plan] its expenditure with an eye to the revenue and the net financial out-turn it will yield, as well as to the service rendered to the community'.[33]

Hulme distinguished the commercial orientation of the PMG's activities from the operations of conventional policy departments, but he made clear that it would remain a government department. To emphasise the need for accountability, the PMG was to provide more detailed annual reporting, to be tabled in parliament, on its revenue, expenditure and capital program. Hulme correctly believed that this obligation would focus officials' minds as they exercised their new financial liberties. He specifically assured parliament that the changes would result in tighter, rather than lighter, controls over the PMG.[34]

Hulme's legislative bill also provided for the postmaster-general and treasurer to jointly set financial targets for the PMG, but the Coalition never utilised these powers.[35] This was possibly due to the PMG's growing financial difficulties as the 1970s dawned, but was also indicative of the Coalition parties' failure to grapple seriously with the inherent tension between its commercial objectives for the PMG and the subsidies it provided to its rural constituency. The government's cautious steps implicitly acknowledged that the status quo was unsustainable, but they also revealed the limits to the Coalition's willingness to consider more substantial changes even within the existing institutional framework. As we shall see, the

Whitlam-led Labor opposition was already advocating for more fundamental structural reform.

Hulme received reform proposals from his senior officials, which he rejected. In early 1968, for example, he knocked back a proposal by the PMG's director-general, Trevor Housley, to establish a 'Post and Telegraph Service'. Under this plan, the new organisation, to comprise 83,000 of the PMG's 99,000 staff, would operate telecommunications and postal services as functionally separate divisions and be freed from Public Service Board jurisdiction. At about this time, Housley's immediate predecessor, Frank O'Grady, was publicly calling for Australia to follow Britain's lead and establish the PMG as a statutory authority. And Housley's successor as director-general, John Knott, later claimed that he had wanted to split the PMG's telecommunications and postal operations into separate organisations but kept his thoughts to himself because of Hulme's open hostility to such a move.[36]

The political and policy tension within the Coalition was centred on the age-old dilemma of where to draw the line between ensuring affordable universal service provision and facilitating commercial efficiency. The government was prepared to give the PMG more tactical financial freedom but unwilling to take the next step and loosen ministerial or public service controls. This was despite expecting the PMG to 'conduct its affairs on a business basis'.[37] As one rural Liberal MP expressed it, a principal advantage of the existing model was that it made the PMG more 'susceptible to pressure' from politicians pushing for better country services.[38]

Hulme was possibly prepared to go further in the direction of efficiency, but he bowed to pressure from Country Party and rural Liberal MPs for ever more subsidies to rural telephone subscribers. To the Country Party, the PMG was 'an instrument of national development'; the portfolio had long been a party fiefdom, with senior figures Larry Anthony and Charles Davidson (a Second World War veteran who travelled with a suitcase made from the aluminium of a downed Japanese fighter plane) overseeing the department's rapid postwar expansion.[39]

In August 1970, despite his personal reservations, Hulme introduced an uncapped and open-ended rural subsidy program, backdated by eighteen months to replace an earlier program announced less than two years before, in which the PMG would absorb almost all the costs associated with upgrading country telephone lines between private properties and their local exchanges as part of the department's national exchange automation project. This subsidy cost $5 million in its first full year (1971/72). The PMG forecast that by 1983/84 the annual cost would increase sixfold.[40]

Another factor working against more substantive changes to the arrangements governing Australia's telecommunications system was the Coalition's generally lacklustre approach to administrative reform. Other than the 1968 reforms, it made only two other policy adjustments to the PMG. From the mid-1950s, the department was obliged to report annually on its revenue and expenditure, and from 1960, it was required to pay interest on all Treasury funds accessed since federation. The latter move ended the PMG's run of financial surpluses and precipitated contentious price rises in 1967 that were subject to much political debate.

During his final year in office, Hulme worked to implement an 'area management' strategy for the PMG. Like the earlier financial measures, this was based on advice from the PMG, which on this occasion had worked with the Public Service Board and sought to replicate a concept being considered in Britain and Sweden. The plan was to devolve operational decision-making and financial accountability from the PMG's six state directors to thirty-two 'area managers', who would be responsible for all technical, commercial and customer service functions in their areas. As in 1968, Hulme argued that the changes would drive 'a more effective and business-like basis for our telecommunications operations'. The plan, however, would be 'phased over a period of several years'. This suggested a completion target in the latter 1970s, again underlining the Coalition's unhurried approach to telecommunications reform despite the sector's increasingly dynamic and complex operating environment.[41] As it was, area management was killed off just before its launch in late 1972 by the newly elected Whitlam government.

In the absence of drive within the Coalition for more significant changes to the telecommunications system, there was simply no compelling pressure on the government to do any more than it did in the years from 1967 to 1972. The reforms cautiously proposed from time to time by the PMG, the periodic calls from business groups such as the Victorian Employers' Association for the PMG to be freed from Public Service Board jurisdiction and permitted to operate more commercially, and the consistent urging by Labor for more substantial reform were no match for the Country Party's vehement resistance to change in conjunction with Hulme's unwillingness to countenance anything more than cautious, incremental adjustments to the status quo.

The government argued, with some foundation, that Australia's arrangements, while imperfect, operated reasonably well. The telecommunications network was expanding, and service quality and range were improving. During the Coalition's last decade in office, the number of people waiting for new telephones declined from 45,500 to 13,250, although the total number of services increased by 1.4 million.[42] And from the limited benchmark data available, it seemed that Australia was performing acceptably with respect to services per hundred people, especially when the nation's difficult geography was taken into account: it ranked seventh in the world.[43]

This business-as-usual approach was underlined at election time, with Coalition leaders having little of substance to say about telecommunications. The subject did not come up in Gorton's or McMahon's prime ministerial policy speeches when they stood for re-election in 1969 and 1972. The Country Party leader and deputy prime minister, Jack McEwen, was similarly silent in 1969. Three years later, McEwen's successor, Doug Anthony, was content to restate his party's traditional aspirations for 'good telephone communications for all Australians' and a transition 'towards a single unit charge for telephone calls in Australia'.[44]

Yet when the Coalition lost office in 1972, Australia was drifting ever further away from fulfilling the dual objectives of delivering affordable universal services in a commercially efficient manner. In early 1973, the economist and public service mandarin H. C. Coombs reported to the new prime minister, Gough Whitlam, that unless there were changes to the PMG's pricing structure and capital program, its need for appropriated Treasury funds would more than double over the next three years to reach $652 million by 1975/76, with a commensurate drop in its proportion of self-financed expenditure from 41 per cent to just 14 per cent.[45]

Fracturing the policy consensus

Under Gough Whitlam's leadership, Labor's approach to the PMG and telecommunications also reflected the broad dynamics of the 1960s. But the new policies the party adopted in 1967 and developed during the next five years in opposition represented a significant departure from notions that had held since federation about how best to deliver essential telecommunications services. They also provided the basis for subsequent actions by the Whitlam government. The immediate trigger for Labor's policy shift was the convergence of two unrelated factors: first, a reinvigorated political and industrial campaign by the powerful Labor-affiliated Amalgamated Postal Workers' Union (APWU), and secondly, Whitlam's rise to Labor's leadership.

The APWU was the largest of the twenty-eight unions and staff associations that represented PMG employees. It had about 40,000 members, divided equally between telecommunications and postal services, and was led by Frank Waters, a famously hard-drinking former state Labor politician from Queensland who had been state secretary since 1946 and federal president since 1961. The institutional tension between the PMG and the Public Service Board was mirrored in the APWU. The union considered the board a block on its ability to win higher wages and better employment terms for its members through direct negotiations with the PMG.[46] This tension intensified after 1956, when APWU members went on strike for the first time, and it continued throughout the 1960s and into the 1970s as strikes and other industrial actions (mostly by postal workers over pay, but also over new automation technologies) became frequent events.[47]

In the wake of its maiden strike, the APWU sought two changes to Labor's platform at the party's 1957 federal conference: that 'the control of the PMG's Department should be vested in a Commission, and removed from any control of the Public Service Board'; and the repeal of laws that enabled striking public-sector workers to be sacked. The latter resolution was adopted but the former was not. From then on, freeing the PMG from Public Service Board jurisdiction and reconstituting it as an autonomous statutory authority became a key union objective.[48]

The APWU's campaign gained traction in the latter 1960s as the times came to suit it. The British announcement in 1966 that the GPO would become a statutory authority energised the union. At its conference shortly afterwards, it resolved that 'the Post Office should be transformed into a Public Corporation similar to the proposed Corporation in the United Kingdom'.[49] The following year, two APWU state branches took resolutions to Labor's federal conference calling for the PMG to be 'divorced' from the Public Service Board and become a statutory authority 'on the lines of the Post Office Corporation established by the Wilson Labor [sic] Government'.[50] This was well timed. Whitlam had just become Labor leader and his top priority, other than internal party reform, was developing a modern, pragmatic and politically appealing platform. The APWU offered a ready-made policy position that was consistent with Whitlam's own long-held policy views and political objectives.[51]

Whitlam had a voracious appetite for comprehensive policy reform and was contemptuous of what he considered the atrophy of Australia's administrative structures after eighteen years of Coalition government. Of the PMG, he asserted in early 1968: 'Technically there is no field of government in Australia which is so advanced as the Post Office. Structurally there is no field of government in Australia that is so archaic as the Post Office. What substantial business in Australia would have changed its structure so little as the Australian Post Office?'[52] Regarding the delivery of telecommunications services, Whitlam had long believed that the PMG's chronic dependence on Treasury funding and its inability to satisfy demand was due principally to the Coalition's direct intrusion into its operations. He considered that government enterprise inefficiency was caused by political interference rather than any inherent weakness in public administration.[53]

As deputy opposition leader in 1965, Whitlam had stated that he did not consider telecommunications policy 'as a philosophical or ideological issue'; while agnostic about the organisational structure of the PMG, he wanted direct political intervention in service delivery to be ended and service provision instead to be guided by what would come to be known as user-pays principles. Whitlam's view was that 'the persons who use the service should pay for them. They should pay for the capital and pay for the running of the service.'[54]

Whitlam did not initiate Labor's policy shift over telecommunications and postal arrangements, but his election as party leader in February 1967 threw open the door to new policy ideas. At Labor's federal conference in August, the party accepted a proposal from its Economic Planning Committee, which included Whitlam and an ambitious young union official, Bob Hawke, that Labor adopt as policy the 'severance of the Postmaster-General's Department from the Public Service Board and the Department to be controlled by a Corporation'.[55]

Some Labor politicians were already advocating this course of action. In parliament three months earlier, Western Australia's Harry Webb, a former state Labor president and a prominent participant in debates on telecommunications and post, called on the Coalition to remove the PMG from the Public Service Board's 'heavy hand' so that it could be 'run as a business undertaking, on business lines'. By this, Webb meant freeing the PMG to employ more staff in response to surging demand for telephone services and permitting direct industrial negotiations between PMG officials and unions.[56]

Labor's policy rationale was that better telephone and postal services would flow directly from industrial harmony. This relied on the questionable premise that the PMG and unions, despite operating an essential-services monopoly, would reach amicable and commercially responsible agreements that would not simply see the costs of featherbedding passed on to Australian households and businesses. PMG officials broadly welcomed Labor's new policy, although, like other informed observers, they were concerned that such an arrangement could strengthen the telecommunications and postal unions and result in more industrial disputation.

Although Labor's 1967 policy reflected its union and industrial origins, by the following year, as the government and opposition debated the Coalition's planned changes to the PMG's financial controls, Labor's advocacy for releasing the PMG from Public Service Board jurisdiction revealed a broader perspective. Labor grappled directly with the strategic issues that were undermining Australia's ability to provide telecommunications services in a financially sustainable way. Industrial concerns remained central, but the opposition also focused on the inadequacy of the PMG's financial governance arrangements, its exposure to direct political intervention, the web of opaque and substantially unaccountable subsidies that this spawned, and the need for greater nimbleness in the telecommunications sector at a time of rapid technological change, especially given telecommunications' important enabling role in economic and social development. Intentionally or not, Labor was addressing points that had been made by others on different occasions; its proposals drew heavily on an official British report that detailed the Wilson Labour government's plan to reconstitute the GPO as a statutory authority, but its arguments also reflected Whitlam's own long-held views.

Labor was prepared to give parliamentary backing to Hulme's financial reforms in 1968, but it strongly criticised them for being too little too late. The opposition asserted, as at times did the PMG, that the postmaster-general had failed to address a principal structural flaw: the department's financial dependence on annual Treasury appropriations, which forced it into inefficient short-term capital planning and implementation cycles.[57] Assuming that Australia's long postwar economic expansion would continue, and focused only on the financial supply side, Whitlam's argument was that a new statutory authority empowered to borrow its own funds would be 'freed from the tyranny of the Budget' and able to plan its network and services over a longer timeframe in a way that 'might result in really significant improvements in the quality of Australian communications'.[58]

Labor asserted that telecommunications services would be delivered in a more commercially rational manner by an autonomous statutory authority. This position was consistent with Whitlam's conviction that government enterprises could be just as efficient as private-sector companies as long as they were left to operate without political intrusion, and that telecommunications pricing should be set so that it more closely matched underlying provisioning costs.[59] The bipartisan policy objective of affordable universal service provision was not in question, but Labor argued that where commercially unviable services were provided in fulfilment of public policy, such as services supplied to country areas, they should be funded through direct and explicit government subvention. Whitlam stated that a statutory authority would be less vulnerable to 'direct political manipulation [and] could begin to follow a pricing policy geared to international criteria and to insist that where communication subsidies are judged desirable they should be provided by open rather than covert means'.[60]

Labor further argued that the accelerating pace and scope of technological changes, and the telecommunications sector's critical role in social and economic development, meant that Australia's telecommunications and postal system required fundamental reform. The Coalition's incremental adjustments to the status quo were insufficient. In parliament, Labor's Harry Webb contrasted the speed of technological advances with the 'snail like pace' of the PMG and asserted that with the Australian population and economy continuing to grow, the 'old established system ... will not meet the complexities of the future'.[61] Whitlam accused the Coalition of 'betray[ing] its professed loyalty to the values of enterprise and efficiency by hesitating and procrastinating'. He proclaimed that even 'Britain's socialist government has recognised the futility of administering the Post Office as a department of the Crown and has re-established it instead as an independent statutory corporation'.[62]

In May 1968, Labor sought agreement from the Coalition to establish a joint select parliamentary committee with wide-ranging terms of reference and a mandate to call expert witnesses to 'inquire into the desirability of removing the Australian Post Office from the administrative influence of the Public Service Board and of establishing a public corporation to control the business of the Post Office'.[63] The opposition's proposal, which was framed as an amendment to a government bill to enact the PMG's more flexible financial controls, was advanced amid heated parliamentary debate and took Hulme by surprise. But it was a genuinely bipartisan plan. It was also consistent with Whitlam's call for an 'analytical approach to the problems of the Post Office' and earlier steps taken by the British parliament.[64] Labor explicitly pointed out that the Coalition would have a majority on the proposed committee and acknowledged that it would entail working through significant policy, administrative and logistical complexities.[65]

The Coalition government was uninterested in Labor's proposal. Though Hulme conceded that at a 'point in time' he might consider such a review, this lay in the unforeseeable future. He was resolutely opposed to opening the Pandora's box of complexity, contentiousness and disruption that Labor's inquiry would entail. His own view was that existing institutional arrangements had the capacity to meet Australia's needs, pending some incremental adjustments from time to time.[66]

The sheer scale of such a root-and-branch review into Australia's telecommunications and postal system gave pause to some Coalition MPs. Bob Cotton, who would later leave parliament for a diplomatic posting in the United States, criticised those who 'talk about how they would run the Post Office if they were given the job … They fail to realise the immensity of the task of changing a public enterprise as large as the Post Office'.[67] Throughout the remainder of Labor's period in opposition, its MPs pushed consistently but unsuccessfully for a bipartisan inquiry into the PMG, sometimes attacking the government for its intransigence and at other times bending over backwards to be conciliatory. One of the Whitlam government's earliest acts was to establish a royal commission to inquire into the PMG and provide recommendations for a path forward.

During 1970–71, Labor developed further its policy position. It began suggesting that telecommunications and postal services might be better delivered by two separate organisations. Labor's thinking was in part a response to the Coalition's legislating increased telephone charges in 1970 and 1971 to offset postal losses. While the government blamed the PMG's financial problems on rising labour costs, Labor blamed them on the requirement that it pay interest to Treasury for appropriated funds. But Labor's core argument was that these policies were yet another manifestation of a system that enabled unaccountable and politically motivated subsidies.

Labor suggested that splitting technologically advanced and commercially viable telecommunications services from labour-intensive, loss-making postal services would mean that uneconomic services provided in fulfilment of social policy could be funded directly through explicit government subvention. Labor also sought to wedge the Coalition parties, with some success, by arguing that a profitable stand-alone telecommunications enterprise would be better able to hold down prices and realise the Country Party's key aspiration of concessional telephone rates in rural areas.[68]

In his campaigns for the 1969 and 1972 elections, Whitlam presented the PMG as a key exhibit in Labor's case against the Coalition government's poor industrial-relations performance and, by extension, its poor economic management. The PMG also featured in Whitlam's drive to increase Labor's appeal to white-collar middle-class professionals. In 1969 he asserted that 'most industrial unrest over the last two years has been among the higher skilled and government employees' and that 'continuing provocation and consequent disruption has occurred in Australia's largest business undertaking, the Post Office'. Whitlam promised that under a Labor government 'the Post Office will be established as a statutory corporation'.[69]

In his renowned 'It's time' campaign speech for the 1972 election, Whitlam promised that 'Australia's largest employer—the Post Office—will be severed from the control of the Public Service Board.'[70] Within weeks of victory, the new Whitlam government was executing its plan.

2

Reform and Renovation

*I do not approach this as a philosophical or ideological issue ...
we all ought to be concerned with the fact that this government
monopoly is not meeting the public demand.*

Gough Whitlam, 1965[1]

On 2 December 1972, Gough Whitlam became the first Labor leader to win
a federal election from opposition since Jim Scullin in 1929. With a sweeping
program and hungry to start, Whitlam and his deputy, Lance Barnard, governed
as a duumvirate for two frenetic weeks; Barnard's fourteen portfolios included
that of postmaster-general. After four rounds of caucus voting on 18 December,
Labor's ministers-designate gathered outside Whitlam's office waiting to be
summoned and allocated their portfolios. By the time Lionel Bowen, a Sydney
backbencher elected in the final ballot, received Whitlam's call, there were few
options remaining. Bowen wanted housing but instead was offered Papua New
Guinea or the PMG; he opted unenthusiastically for the latter.[2]

First steps

A former local and state representative of modest beginnings, Bowen was almost
fifty when sworn in as postmaster-general. His father had deserted the family in
inner-suburban Sydney while Lionel was still a boy; his mother worked as a cleaner
to support an extended family household. Bowen had to leave school at fourteen
but later completed his secondary education at night school. He served in the
army during the Second World War, then enrolled at the University of Sydney as
a returned serviceman and graduated in law.[3]

Unassuming yet ambitious, Bowen eschewed having a ministerial press secretary (unlike most of his cabinet colleagues) but kept an eye out for 'the next highest thing'.[4] As postmaster-general, he hit the ground running. Within two weeks, he was urging cabinet to establish an inquiry into the PMG. This was consistent with party policy, but also, having spent time with his senior departmental officials, he realised that the PMG was in such a 'financial mess' that it risked undermining the government's first budget, in which Labor's new spending programs were to be set out.[5]

Bowen's concerns were threefold. First, the PMG's business plan proposed politically unwelcome price rises for the next three years and forecast increasing postal losses, declining telecommunications surpluses and a bare break-even position. Second, the PMG's liability for interest payments to the Treasury, a policy opposed by Labor, had quadrupled between 1959 and 1972 and was expected to nearly double again within four years. And third, the financial impact of some Labor policies threatened to compound these inherited problems.

Bowen warned cabinet that, even factoring in higher price revenues and assuming a 4 per cent productivity improvement, the government's plans to increase public-service leave entitlements and implement a 35-hour working week would add $50 million to PMG costs and push the department into the red.[6] Around this time, the treasurer, Frank Crean, was also warning cabinet of 'a conflict developing between our spending programs and economic objectives' and a looming budget deficit 'very much larger than ever before'. Whitlam, however, was not for turning; by the time Crean delivered Labor's first budget in August 1973, spending was up nearly 20 per cent.[7]

On 9 January 1973, cabinet established five standing policy committees; at Bowen's request, he was appointed to chair an ad hoc committee to 'investigate and report' on 'all aspects of the operation and administration' of the PMG. The committee comprised Don Willesee, the special minister of state and former shadow postmaster-general, who was Whitlam's representative; Tom Uren (minister for urban and regional development); Lionel Murphy (attorney-general); Clyde Cameron (minister for labour); Jim Cairns (minister for secondary industry); Bill Hayden (minister for social security); and Crean.[8] The ministers met immediately after cabinet and agreed, in short order, that the inquiry be a fully empowered royal commission, but with a 'minimum of legal formality' to expedite progress; that it be run by three commissioners possessing, respectively, 'extensive business or industry' experience, technical expertise and a 'liberal attitude in worker/employer relationships'; and that its formal terms of reference be substantively the same as those Bowen had proposed.[9] Cabinet endorsed these recommendations on 30 January and Whitlam announced the government's plan later that day.[10]

The Commission of Inquiry into the Australian Post Office would investigate the PMG's 'organisation, administration and operations' and provide recommendations to ensure it fulfilled Australia's 'present and future needs'. The commissioners were granted wide discretion, though cabinet specifically asked them to address the central question of 'whether the Post Office should be a statutory corporation', and the terms of reference drew attention to other matters of particular concern for Labor. An especially critical issue was 'the financing of recurrent and capital costs'. This reflected Whitlam's long-held views about administering government enterprises and applying user-pays principles in telecommunications. It also recognised cabinet's immediate focus on the PMG's perilous financial situation, which was threatening the government's plans to redirect spending towards Labor's priority programs in areas such as health, education and social security.

The terms of reference addressed rural Australia by citing 'urban and regional development', but the particular interests and anxieties of country people were not acknowledged. In contrast, the 'jurisdiction of the Public Service Board', 'management/staff relations' and the PMG's use of contract labour, all sensitive issues for Labor and the unions, were highlighted.[11] Also sensitive, and bearing the fingerprints of the PMG officials who had spent the new year working on Bowen's first cabinet submission, was an instruction to the commissioners to investigate 'the division of functions' between the PMG and the Overseas Telecommunications Commission (OTC), the statutory authority responsible for Australia's international communications services.[12]

Tensions between the PMG and OTC had existed since 1946, when, following bipartisan agreement, OTC had been established in preference to expanding the remit of the PMG. Though the organisations collaborated closely on policy and operational matters, and senior PMG officials comprised the core of OTC's board, jurisdictional disagreements were regular and sometimes fiery events. A fight over global satellite governance arrangements in 1964, for example, which included a renewed push by the PMG to incorporate OTC, had required personal mediation by the postmaster-general. From around this time the already profitable OTC also became spectacularly more so.[13] This deepened PMG frustration that the international services organisation was, in the words of one official, 'wallowing in money', while the PMG was chronically constrained for capital.[14]

Whitlam's evidence-based and non-partisan drive for a more financially sustainable and self-sufficient framework for telecommunications and postal services was reflected in the government's appointment of James Vernon to chair the royal commission. Vernon, in his early sixties, was a pillar of Australia's business establishment; he had recently retired as the long-serving general manager of the Colonial Sugar Refining Company and had led a major economic inquiry for the Menzies government in the mid-1960s. Whitlam considered him a 'patriotic and public-spirited' Australian and was unruffled by Vernon's private comment to him in a congratulatory letter sent just after his election win that 'as you may probably guess, I did not vote for your Party at last Saturday's elections'.[15] The commissioner with technical expertise would be Bernard Callinan, a decorated veteran of the Second World War who was already balancing a number of private-sector and statutory appointments. The commissioner with a 'liberal attitude in worker/employer relationships' was James Kennedy, a young, wealthy Brisbane entrepreneur and former state Labor candidate.

The Vernon commission

From autumn to spring 1973, the commissioners received 482 written submissions; conducted public hearings with 130 witnesses; investigated telecommunications and postal arrangements in the United Kingdom, Sweden, the United States and Canada; and visited PMG sites in Sydney, Melbourne, Brisbane and Perth.[16] Parties whose livelihoods depended directly on the PMG engaged most strongly with the Vernon commission. Nearly a hundred submissions were received from telecommunications and postal unions, staff associations and individual employees, equipment suppliers, contractors and, from the PMG itself, a six-volume magnum opus produced by a team that included two future Telecom managing directors (Jack Curtis and Bill Pollock) and a subsequent four volumes prepared in response to others' submissions.

The next largest community of interest was rural Australia, with around eighty submissions from shires, regional city councils, chambers of commerce and other parties representing local regions, particular agricultural sectors and assorted community groups such as the Country Women's Association and the Darling Downs Housewives' and Homemakers' Association. The Country Party lodged a submission and its deputy leader, Ian Sinclair, appeared before the commissioners. Various government departments and agencies expressed their jurisdictional interests in the PMG's future. Many of the 200 individual submissions were short letters of complaint, which were subsequently forwarded to the PMG's director-general, Eber Lane. Notably uninvolved in the inquiry were the general business sector and the Liberal Party.[17]

The perennial dilemma about balancing government enterprise autonomy with the administrative controls needed to maintain accountability, and the enduring tension between telecommunications policy's economic and social elements, were central to discussions precipitated by the Vernon commission. Rural anxieties about a more commercially orientated approach to telecommunications were forcefully represented by the Country Party, which displayed a robust sense of entitlement. The party explicitly rejected the notion that a 'statutory trading corporation' should be responsible for telecommunications. It called for a 'constant increase' in better-quality rural services, higher concessional rates, and greater support for domestic telecommunications equipment manufacturers by way of a rolling three-year procurement program for the PMG. Any associated commercial losses should be met by Treasury subvention. The Country Party's preference for central planning made way for flexibility, however, when it came to labour: it wanted more contractors engaged to install and repair telephone services.[18]

Within the bureaucracy, the Whitlam government's newly created Department of Urban and Regional Development lined up with the Country Party and other rural interests. Citing regional business complaints that telecommunications costs were their 'second most disadvantageous factor' after transportation, the department wanted the PMG to become, in effect, a subordinate delivery agency. It stated that the PMG should 'integrate' its planning with that of Urban and Regional Development, provide a full range of metropolitan-standard services at concessional rates to designated growth areas and, 'as a matter of principle', relocate its offices and workshops to regional areas as far as possible.[19]

The PMG rebuffed these sectoral demands, arguing that telecommunications arrangements were already 'more generous … than can be justified on an economic basis' and asserting that the financial measures introduced by the Coalition government in 1968 'clearly established the department as a government business undertaking, albeit with some social responsibilities'.[20] The PMG specifically rejected claims that rural concessions were necessary to maintain national decentralisation. It pointed out that telephone line rentals in country areas had for years been much lower than in cities, but this had had 'little if any influence'. And, in a precursor to later debates about telecommunications cross-subsidies, the PMG noted that providing concessions to particular areas or classes of customers placed an inequitable cost burden on other subscribers that should be 'rightfully shared by all taxpayers'.[21]

The Public Service Board was in a particularly difficult position. Labor had campaigned at the last two elections to remove the PMG from its jurisdiction, but the board's institutional integrity relied heavily upon its remit continuing to cover the PMG, because the PMG employed nearly half of the commonwealth public service. Thus the board argued at length that 'centralised co-ordination arrangements' did not undermine the commercial efficiency of the telecommunications system; it was imperative that they stay in place regardless of the Vernon commission's recommendations about future institutional structures.

There was a stark incompatibility between the Public Service Board's centralising function and the push for greater autonomy in Australian telecommunications, notwithstanding the PMG's commitment to work collaboratively with the board come what may.[22] For its part, the PMG complained that its 'recruitment, establishments and organisation ... [were] restrained in its options [and] constrained in time by the lengthy delays and administrative effort required to obtain Board approval'.[23] Concurrently, the PMG and Treasury debated the extent and nature of the financial controls that should apply to the PMG: the former argued for less and the latter for more.[24] This debate would continue through the 1970s and 1980s.

The telecommunications and postal unions and staff associations were generally united in wanting the Public Service Board off the scene so that they could negotiate directly with the PMG. Confidence within the APWU was high. Its president, Frank Waters, and general secretary, George Slater, already enjoyed ready access to the new postmaster-general and had won Bowen's support for union meetings on PMG premises during work hours and for union officials to address new PMG staff.[25]

The APWU condemned the board's 'impracticality, ineptitude and poor sense of industrial relations', blamed it for every major industrial dispute the union had engaged in over the past decade and accused it of forcing the PMG into 'many uneconomic' agreements with contract labour. On this last point, the PMG retorted that engaging contractors for specific tasks had in fact reduced costs by up to 40 per cent without 'detectable difference in the standard of departmental and contractor finished works'. The APWU also 'reminded' the Vernon commission of Whitlam's public commitments to end board jurisdiction over the PMG, and briefly threatened to boycott the commission in response to a scheduling mix-up over public hearing arrangements.[26]

On the key question of whether telecommunications and postal services should be delivered by statutory authority, the APWU's position changed fundamentally in the course of the commission's inquiries. Although it had campaigned since the late 1950s for the PMG's reconstitution as a statutory authority, and was pivotal in Labor's adoption of this as policy, the union now concluded that its interests were better served by the PMG remaining a department, albeit one that was independent of the Public Service Board.

Most likely the APWU's volte-face was a reaction to its review of the PMG's own analysis of departmental and statutory authority structures, which made clear that a statutory authority would have a stronger operational efficiency orientation than a government department. In a quickly penned supplementary letter to Hugh Payne, the commission's secretary, Slater argued that 'independence of the Post Office in matters of salaries and staff' could be effected by 'straightforward [and] practical' legislative amendments to simply free the PMG from Public Service Board jurisdiction. He also claimed that the APWU's new policy aligned with 'the implication in the Post Office submissions'.[27] The PMG explicitly rejected this.[28]

OTC's independent existence was imperilled by the Whitlam government's royal commission, and the organisation fought a fierce and increasingly politically partisan battle against being subsumed by the PMG or its successor. In essence, OTC argued that the flow of easy money to government depended on its remaining a nimble and businesslike agency; its earnings would be jeopardised were it absorbed into a lumbering telecommunications bureaucracy. The PMG, for its part, adopted a posture of formal neutrality, noting pointedly that it would be inappropriate for it 'to express strong support for, or opposition against' amalgamation. At the same time, the department made it abundantly clear that it wanted OTC's rivers of gold redirected to its capital works programs to offset the cost of 'uneconomic facilities in country areas'. Appearing before the commissioners, PMG's director-general,

Eber Lane, suggested that it would be 'fairly hard' to argue credibly against merging Australia's national and international telecommunications services.[29]

The Coombs taskforce

Having been warned about deteriorating economic conditions and the impact of the PMG's financial problems on Labor's first budget, and also intent on identifying 'the widest possible options available' for the party to pursue its policy priorities, Whitlam asked H. C. Coombs to lead a review of the government's inherited expenditure commitments and to identify potential areas for cuts.[30] Members of the Coombs taskforce included a rising Treasury official, John Stone, later secretary of the department, and Whitlam's youthful adviser Jim Spigelman, a future chief justice of New South Wales.

The taskforce reported promptly in June 1973, providing Whitlam with 141 'items for consideration'. These traversed a raft of issues including rural assistance programs, many of which the taskforce considered ineffectual and without policy merit, and financial governance and pricing arrangements for commonwealth enterprises, the 'wide disparity' of which taskforce members found 'striking'.[31] The PMG and OTC illustrated their point. Whereas the former lacked any financial objectives, despite being Australia's largest enterprise, and its prices were 'determined by government', the latter was obliged to 'pursue a policy directed towards securing sufficient revenue to meet all its expenditure … and to permit payment to the Commonwealth of a reasonable return'.[32]

Regarding the PMG's voracious appetite for capital, almost all of which was spent on telecommunications, the taskforce called out the 'close relationship' between price-setting and investment decisions. It explained that the PMG's capital expenditure level was a function of subscriber demand, and that subscriber demand was a function of pricing—especially for telephone connections and line rentals—and that pricing was set too low. This was a crucial point for Whitlam because the PMG's trading results underwrote its capacity to self-finance and thus impacted directly on its demand for Treasury funds, which Whitlam wanted to spend elsewhere.

In a blunt warning, cabinet was advised that 'in the absence of "holding" action of some kind', the PMG would require an additional $96 million for capital expenditure from Labor's first budget, over and above the $288 million provided in 1972/73, and that these figures would rise by 35 per cent in 1974/75 and a further 30 per cent in 1975/76. The taskforce suggested that Labor place an 'admittedly arbitrary' limit on the PMG's Treasury borrowings and require it to increase revenues through higher prices. The 'most immediate and effective way' to take the heat out of 'buoyant demand' was by raising telephone connection charges.

Coombs's taskforce also took aim at the practice, in place since federation, of charging less for telephone line rentals in the bush than in the city. It noted that if country rental charges, which were between half and two-thirds of those in metropolitan areas, matched the city rate, telecommunications revenues would rise by about $10 million in 1973/74 and by $14–18 million per year thereafter. The taskforce was especially critical of the indirect and disguised nature of this non-means-tested form of social policy. Such programs should be 'a clearly revealed subsidy to non-metropolitan dwellers, rather than being concealed in the overall accounts of the telephone services of the Post Office'. Even if country line rentals were raised to city levels, rural subscribers would still receive a 'significant subsidy' because of the much higher provisioning costs in the bush.

Labor was also advised to wind back the former Coalition government's program to heavily subsidise the cost of constructing telephone lines to rural properties. The program's cost, which was buried in the PMG's accounts, was placing 'a severe strain on the capital and other resources available to the Post Office. It diverts capital resources from growth centres, where unsatisfied telephone demand is growing rapidly, and from other forms of telecommunications investment.'[33]

Whitlam's speechwriter, Graham Freudenberg, has characterised the Coombs taskforce's findings as a 'shopping list in reverse' for the Whitlam government, offering a range of spending cuts that Labor could target in order to free up funds for other policy priorities.[34] Its advice also aligned with Whitlam's long-held antipathy towards industry protection and other measures that he dismissed as 'producer appeasement' for favouring larger producers over smaller ones and consumers. Whitlam made no sectoral policy distinction between city and bush, though he later defended his government against charges of anti-country bias by citing the introduction of rural allowances as part of Labor's needs-based education policy and the promotion of regional hospitals and community-based health services. Whitlam also noted that nearly half of Labor's social welfare budget went to rural areas.[35] Nonetheless, the Country Party and other rural interests considered Coombs's taskforce to be a direct attack; its report became, in Freudenberg's words, 'a political time-bomb'.[36]

Tackling hidden subsidies

Immediately after Frank Crean's first budget speech on 21 August, Bowen moved to bolster the PMG's financial position. Though the challenges he faced were in principle the same as those of his Liberal predecessor, Alan Hulme, and, like Hulme, he raised charges to lift revenues, Labor's underlying approach contrasted with that of the former government. Drawing heavily from Coombs's report, Bowen began the process of re-orientating Australia's telecommunications charges so that prices bore a closer relationship to costs. Consistent with Labor's arguments from opposition, Bowen rejected the Coalition's continued focus on labour costs as the cause of the PMG's financial predicament; instead, he blamed the 'hidden subsidies and misallocation of resources to uneconomic areas of investment' perpetuated by successive Coalition governments.[37]

Bowen announced that most price rises would come from 'concessional and uneconomic areas', in keeping with Labor's position that 'there should be no hidden subsidies and that assistance should be given in a direct form where such assistance is justified ... in keeping with proper business principles'.[38] As such, rural line rental charges would rise to the city rate. This meant that the charges paid by nearly 850,000 country people would either double or increase by half. Bowen accepted that lower line rentals in rural areas had historically been justified in part by country Australians' greater reliance on timed long-distance calls, but the 'great difference' between city and country provisioning costs had to be faced. Striking at the heart of rural special pleading, Bowen said that telephones were 'valued by all sections of the community and it is not appropriate to perpetuate this difference in rentals'.[39]

The rural telephone line construction subsidies introduced by the Coalition in 1970, which by then had cost $30 million in capital expenditure and $1 million in additional annual interest payments to Treasury, were to be scaled back to a still considerable $8 million per year. Charges for complex telephone connections would also increase by 20 per cent, although at $60 the cost was less than 4 per cent of the average connection cost. Bowen also announced that Labor wanted to 'narrow the gap' between long-distance and local calls. The price of long-distance calls would drop by between 20 and 33 per cent. This move aligned with a core Country Party policy objective, and it was also increasingly an issue for outer suburban residents of Australia's major cities.

Nevertheless, there was a vituperative response to Labor's moves from the Country Party and some Liberals from country areas. Rural people were increasingly convinced that the Whitlam government was gearing up for a full-frontal assault on them. Debate in parliament was particularly heated, inflamed by some Labor ministers gratuitously rubbing salt in Country Party wounds and revealing their indifference to rural sensitivities. The minister for tourism and recreation, Frank Stewart, for example, taunted the 'bovine, bucolic members of the Country Party' for defending 'concessions that should never have been granted'. Fred Daly, the father of the house and minister for services and property, also went in hard, exclaiming that the cost of rural telephone connections was so high it would be 'cheaper to buy the farm than to connect the phone'. The Country Party, he declared, had 'bled the nation with bounties and subsidies and uneconomic proposals for a generation or more'. In response, the Labor government was variously charged with launching a 'direct attack on policies which have endured since Federation'; denounced for mounting 'the most vicious, vindictive and savage attack ever on any section of the Australian people'; and warned that country people were 'poised for vengeance against their betrayers'. Struggling to control proceedings, Deputy Speaker Gil Duthie threated a mass ejection of members.[40]

Although in government the Coalition had consistently rejected Labor's calls for a bipartisan inquiry into the PMG, Coalition politicians now sought to use the Vernon commission as a shield against any 'drastic policy changes', calling for Labor to wait for the commissioners' final report. In the end, though, the government was able to legislate its package, thanks largely to Bowen's methodical and reasoned engagement with opposition MPs and his agreement to soften some cuts to postal concessions and lessen some price rises.[41]

The Vernon report

By April 1974, the Whitlam government's legislative program was imperilled. The Senate had twice rejected ten Labor bills, including some that provided the grounds for a double dissolution. With the Coalition threatening to block supply and half the Senate due to expire soon, Whitlam announced a double-dissolution election for 18 May. Labor was in the throes of this intensely fought campaign when Vernon produced a meticulous 340-page report that sought to square all policy circles and provide the government with a detailed blueprint for significant reform.

A key recommendation was to separate telecommunications and postal services and replace the PMG with two new statutory authorities. The commissioners argued that telecommunications and post were so different 'in respect of technology, capital investment requirements, growth rates, and employment characteristics' that housing them together could 'only be assumed to have been a matter of history rather than of deliberative choice'.[42] It was also 'beyond the capabilities of any one person' to manage them both.[43] Moreover, the continuous technological advances, increasing market demand and large capital investment that characterised telecommunications meant that those in charge needed the freedom to make 'important judgments' that would impact 'the range and quality of services for decades ahead'.

The statutory authority model was favoured for three overarching reasons, each grounded in the truism that telecommunications and post were 'essential community services [with] the basic characteristics of commercial enterprises'. First, the Public Service Board imposed a level of conformity that was incompatible with the need for commercial flexibility. Second, too much of the 'day-to-day effort' of a government department went on bureaucratic liaison and coordination rather than 'the making and taking of the decisions essential to the efficient management of a commercial enterprise'. And third, the expertise and experience of departmental officials differed significantly from the 'talents and skills necessary to operate a successful business undertaking'.[44]

Whereas Labor and the unions had long argued that removing Public Service Board jurisdiction over the PMG and permitting direct industrial negotiations would result in less disputes and better service, the Vernon commission did so for quite different reasons. The commissioners stated that the mooted authorities must 'be seen to be the employers' and able to set their own staffing arrangements 'as responsible entities'. They considered that a formal obligation on the new authorities to coordinate with the board would go against the principle of granting day-to-day autonomy; and the sheer scale of a new telecommunications authority would in any case make such an obligation 'so formidable as to raise serious doubts' about its practicability. But the commissioners wanted both authorities to engage meaningfully with the board, with formal financial objectives to act as a check on financially irresponsible labour agreements.[45]

The commissioners also wanted greater decentralisation in rural telecommunications arrangements and proposed a turbo-charged version of former postmaster-general Alan Hulme's area management plan, which Labor had aborted. This would see a new telecommunications authority create around one hundred rural districts to facilitate 'true management' devolution in which all technical, operational and customer-facing functions would be the responsibility of one manager who, significantly, need not be an engineer.[46]

When it came to recommending an appropriate division of functions between Australia's national and international telecommunications operations, the commissioners differed. James Kennedy and Bernard Callinan sided broadly with the PMG, and Vernon with OTC. Having concluded that telecommunications and postal services were too disparate to stay together, Kennedy and Callinan considered that national and international telecommunications operations were too interrelated to stay apart. They asserted that 'divided control and conflicting objectives' had underpinned nearly thirty years of policy and operational strains and inefficiencies between the PMG and OTC and that this state of affairs could be resolved with minimal disruption by simply joining OTC's 2000 staff with the PMG's 90,000 telecommunications employees in a new telecommunications authority.

Vernon was initially on the same page and reportedly shocked Kennedy and Callinan when he then dismissed the synergy argument as an 'attractive simplification'; he stated that any issues between the PMG and OTC could be resolved at the board level or, failing that, by the responsible minister. Vernon's change of mind apparently followed intense lobbying by senior OTC executives, with whom he had personal links, and by Gregory Kater, chairman of the Commercial Bank of Sydney. But Vernon's revised view was also consistent with his experience as a senior executive who had run large businesses: he probably understood better than his colleagues the level of disruption that would result from transforming the PMG into two new statutory authorities. Vernon considered OTC a 'well-developed and compact organisation, strongly market-orientated [and] showing good performance' and saw a risk of it being 'destroyed' if forced into this restructuring process. He recommended leaving OTC alone, at least for the time being.[47]

The commissioners noted that the expectation, which had held since federation, that the PMG fulfil the telecommunications and postal needs of Australia's 'entire population' while also operating 'with maximum business efficiency' had placed it in a perennial lose-lose position, where financial surpluses and deficits each attracted criticism, albeit for different reasons.[48] They also acknowledged that the intimate role played by telecommunications in community life meant that it was 'more than a commercial activity'. Taken together, this meant that 'special principles' were needed to govern a new telecommunications authority.[49] The commissioners sought to construct a set of financial, operational, policy and political checks and balances that would provide for performance consistent with both 'accepted principles of business administration' and the fulfilment of public policy objectives.

It was proposed that the new telecommunications authority be required to self-fund all operating expenses and half its capital expenditure, which was forecast to increase by 90 per cent to $878 million within four years. Australia's telecommunications pricing structure should also continue to be rebalanced so that prices more closely matched costs. Price-setting decisions were to reflect commercial conditions rather than political agendas or parliamentary schedules. However, the commissioners recommended that ministerial approval still be required for strategic matters, including significant borrowings and changes to 'basic or standard' service prices. In the telecommunications context, these services included those that generated the most revenue and accounted for most capital expenditure, such as line rentals and local and national long-distance calls.

On one hand, the commissioners were alive to the risk that a new telecommunications (or postal) authority might meet its financial targets by simply raising prices to offset the costs of operational inefficiency or industrial featherbedding. On the other hand, they accepted that ministers and governments would continue to carry 'a degree of political responsibility' for basic service charges. This meant that commercially reasonable price adjustments could be blocked for political reasons. The commission therefore recommended that a minister be required to give 'proper and due regard' to an authority's formal financial objectives when considering basic price changes. To impose a political cost on them for saying no, it suggested that a minister who withheld approval should be obliged to seek parliamentary approval for a Treasury subvention to cover the authority's financial shortfall. As a quid pro quo, the authority would need to keep its minister 'informed generally about corporation activities' as well as about specific matters such as operational and revenue plans and capital works programs.[50] In practice, it was highly unlikely that a minister would be able to second-guess the reasonableness or otherwise of proposed price changes. Nevertheless, the commissioners were trying to raise the accountability bar for both governments and the mooted authorities by tipping the scales towards customer service and commercial efficiency and away from sectoral patronage and pork-barrelling.

On the fraught matter of cross-subsidies, the commissioners focused, by practical necessity, on customer segments rather than specific services. They were troubled by the extent to which some customers, such as those in cities, subsidised others, such as those in the bush, and also by the unaccountable and politically infused nature of the cross-subsidy system. While they acknowledged that cross-subsidisation could be a legitimate commercial tool to 'keep faith with customers, to retain custom, and to attract further custom', there was a point 'beyond which cross-subsidisation of a minority of customers at the expense of the majority users should not be extended'.[51] The commissioners could not unscramble this egg; they were reduced to reiterating the 'general principle' that cross-subsidies should not cause a 'gross distortion' in favour of some customers over others and that, looking ahead, the new authorities should try to 'minimise' them.[52]

The response

The political response to the Vernon commission's report was rapid and inevitably superficial, given its length and the fact that all major parties were in the middle of an election campaign. Recalling his 1972 election commitment to remove the PMG from Public Service Board jurisdiction, Whitlam announced just five days after receiving the report that the government would establish two new statutory authorities with responsibility for telecommunications and post, each with 'independent' control over its 'organisation, staff, pay and the conditions of its employees'.[53]

He also committed Labor to rolling OTC into the new telecommunications authority. This move triggered a bitter political conflict that would compound his government's woes and continue to simmer into the 1990s. In a major policy speech the following week, Whitlam linked Labor's reforms of telecommunications and postal services to its 'reforms in the structure of the government itself' and highlighted them ahead of all other policy areas apart from the economy, taxation and consumer protection.[54]

The Coalition's reaction to the commissioners' report came within hours of Whitlam's announcement. It set the parameters of the forthcoming debate between government and opposition and also revealed policy differences between the Coalition parties. Opposition leader Billy Snedden said that the Liberal Party was in 'basic agreement' with the commission's 'reported recommendations' but backed Vernon's view that OTC should remain a stand-alone enterprise. Blithely airbrushing out the Coalition's earlier refusal to countenance an inquiry into the PMG, Snedden claimed that the Liberal Party had for some time supported the establishment of two new statutory authorities and described it as 'pleasing that this assessment has now been endorsed'.[55]

The Country Party, however, was concerned by the proposed changes; when the Coalition's telecommunications policy was released shortly afterwards, the rural influence was clear. The Coalition committed only to 'study' the commissioners' recommendations. It reasserted the Coalition's traditional aspirations that 'every Australian, wherever he lives, may have the means of communicating with his fellow Australians by telephone', and that telecommunications 'be developed as a uniform service available to all Australians' with 'uniformity in the quality of service' and 'a gradual equalising of the cost of the service [until] all calls will be charged at the same basic cost'.[56]

The media response reflected a consensus that the proposed changes were a step in the right direction, but there was little confidence that real improvements would follow. An early editorial in Melbourne's *Age* captured the mood. The PMG's customer service was condemned as 'lamentable' and its 'most glaring problem' was identified as the 'multiplicity of bloody-minded union bosses ... who please themselves as to what services shall be provided, when these shall be available, and who shall be allowed, on a test of political acceptability, to receive them'. The newspaper suggested that the Whitlam government's proposed reforms offered 'the hope, but not necessarily the certainty' that 'two, more independent, specialist authorities can provide a more efficient, economic and attractive community service than the present monolithic, bureaucratic department has been able to maintain'. The British moves to establish a new telecommunications and postal authority five years earlier gave commentators particular cause for concern because, as the *Age* observed, it seemed that in Britain the level of 'political inter-ference' and industrial disputation had remained the same as before.[57]

The Public Service Board was disappointed, though clearly unsurprised, by the government's decision to effectively halve its jurisdictional territory. Board officials soon joined their PMG colleagues on the dozens of working groups formed to sort out the myriad personnel issues associated with pulling apart a seventy-year-old government department with 120,000 staff. The Department of Labour was also unimpressed, predicting presciently that a wave of pay rises would surely follow the establishment of the new authorities and stating that this would put pressure on the wider economy. Among PMG officials, the response was generally positive—particularly from those looking forward to moving to a new, profitable and high-tech telecommunications enterprise.[58]

The telecommunications and postal unions' delight at the sidelining of the Public Service Board mirrored the disquiet that was felt just about everywhere else. The APWU leadership promised its members that the board's 'annoying delays' would soon be over; 'pay increases will be processed more promptly; appli-cations for leave will receive quicker attention [and] staff vacancies will be filled more rapidly'.[59] Union and PMG officials were soon negotiating the 'house rules' to govern future consultative mechanisms. One unionist later recalled the belief at the time that they were embarking on an era 'with no restrictions … it was to be a wonderful fairytale land, not inhibited by government. It was a real world of optimism we were moving into.'[60]

For its part, OTC was appalled by Whitlam's edict. Under its 'energetic and mercurial' general manager Harold White (as historian Ann Moyal describes him), OTC geared up for a bare-knuckle fight. White led an aggressive campaign against OTC's abolition, and against the Whitlam government. The campaign united its largest union, the Professional Radio Employees Institute of Australasia (PREIA); the Liberal Party, with which White had some personal links; the chambers of commerce in Sydney and Melbourne; and the great majority of OTC's large institutional customers. About a hundred of these customers formed a pressure group, the Overseas Telecommunications Users' Association, headed by a former OTC chairman, Bert Chadwick, and was soon shaping up to Labor via mass meetings in Melbourne and Sydney. The stage was set for an almighty showdown that would have long-term political and policy ramifications.[61]

3

Escalating Challenges

The great theme of our legislative program ... has been one of reform and renovation ... to reform and restructure institutions and systems whose inefficiency or antiquity impose a tremendous burden on the Australian economy and the Australian society.

Gough Whitlam, 1974[1]

On 18 May, Labor was re-elected with a reduced majority in an enlarged House of Representatives. The Senate returned another non-Labor majority, with the balance of power held by a conservative independent who soon joined the Liberals and a former premier of South Australia, Steele Hall, who had broken away from the Liberal Country League to form the centrist Liberal Movement. In Whitlam's post-election reshuffle, Lionel Bowen became special minister of state with responsibility for public service matters and Reg Bishop, a well-regarded and politically moderate former railway worker and union official, moved from the reparations portfolio to become postmaster-general.[2] Like Bowen before him, Bishop immediately focused on advancing the government's telecommunications and postal reform agenda, but was mugged by the PMG's financial plight.

With respect to reform, Bishop and Bowen made a joint submission to cabinet on 28 June seeking 'urgent' agreement to establish an interdepartmental committee of officials to advise on the Vernon commission's recommendations, and to appoint interim boards for the new telecommunications and postal authorities. The ministers observed that 'significant policy issues' were raised in the commissioners' report, particularly regarding the new authorities' financial arrangements and formal objectives, the respective ministerial and board responsibilities and powers over price-setting, and the employment rights of PMG staff who were transferring into the new organisations. The 'sizeable task' of replacing the antiquated and much amended Post and Telegraph Act also had to be tackled. Bishop and Bowen wanted legislation before parliament in time for the authorities to be up and running 'no later than 1 July 1975'.

Envisaging that the interim board members would remain in place once the mooted authorities were established, Bishop and Bowen wanted appointments to be made quickly to ensure that members had 'direct and early involvement' in planning and decisions and gained 'a background in policy matters'. To this end, Vernon was invited to chair his choice of authority, but he 'regretfully declined', said the ministers, 'because of the pressure of other commitments'. Bernard Callinan also declined to chair the new telecommunications authority.[3] Instead, the job went to Bill Gibbs, who had recently retired as managing director of Holden and was praised by Bishop as 'an outstanding Australian industrialist with great business and executive abilities'.[4] Gibbs was prominent in Victorian Liberal circles and his appointment was yet another example of Whitlam's non-partisan approach to telecommunications reform and his aspiration for greater financial self-sufficiency and 'businesslike' management in service delivery.[5]

Rising financial difficulties

Immediately after Labor's re-election in 1974, however, cabinet's attention was on Australia's rapidly deteriorating economy rather than on telecommunications. Bishop and Bowen's 'urgent' submission was bumped from consecutive meeting agendas; it was eventually agreed to on 5 August.[6] Business activity was slowing, days lost to industrial action were at a 45-year high, and wages were up nearly 19 per cent. The annual inflation rate had passed 14 per cent by September and the unemployment rate had risen by more than half. Within his portfolio, Bishop's focus shifted from major structural reform to the dire financial situation. The PMG's position was made worse by industrial disputes and the Whitlam government's own public-sector labour policies, which had flow-on implications for the wider economy because of the PMG's immense scale. Bishop put forward a cabinet submission on 18 July; it was discussed four days later.[7]

Bishop told cabinet that the PMG's forecast revenue growth of 10 per cent for 1974/75 would likely be outstripped by a 17 per cent increase in costs, driven mostly by wages and other input costs rising at 'unparalleled levels'. Though a $70 million provision was in place to hedge against further wage rises and inflationary pressures, Bishop warned that this would probably be 'inadequate'. The government was committed to applying a working week of 36 hours and 45 minutes to all PMG employees in 1974/75, at a forecast cost of $65 million; furthermore, PMG pensions were automatically indexed to inflation, the legacy of an earlier Coalition government decision. Bishop advised that on current settings the PMG was forecasting a $67 million deficit for the coming year, reflecting a $50 million decline in the telecommunications surplus to a mere $4 million, and a $21 million increase in postal losses.

As already mooted by Whitlam at a premiers' conference in June, Bishop recommended increases in telecommunications and postal charges, a freeze in the PMG's Treasury funding—which, given the inflation rate, was a significant reduction in real terms—and stripping a further $30 million from the PMG's capital plan. Charges for complex telephone connections, which had already increased the previous October, were slated to rise another 33 per cent, with residential line rentals up 18 per cent and business line rentals up 36 per cent. Given the government's earlier move to equalise country and city line rentals, and the typically complex nature of rural connections, this meant price hikes for country subscribers of at least 75 per cent and up to 180 per cent within twelve months. On top of this, Labor would resurrect a pre-1964 Coalition policy in which businesses were charged more than consumers for the same service—on the grounds that they placed more demands on the network and derived 'greater value' from using it. On the other hand, Bishop proposed keeping simple telephone connection charges unchanged and significantly reducing long-distance call rates for the services most used by people in rural and outer-metropolitan areas.

As a package, these changes were forecast to boost telecommunications revenue by $133 million and bring the PMG's overall surplus to $106 million. This sat neatly with Bishop's objective for the new authorities to start life 'in the soundest possible operating condition'. But aware that such a large headline surplus would provoke a hostile political and community reaction, Bishop advised cabinet that if the accounting practices recommended by the Vernon commission were applied, the telecommunications trading surplus would be reduced to $60–$70 million—a level 'more comparable' with the PMG's financial results when Labor came to office.[8]

Bishop also advised that there was likely to be a welcome shortening of the waiting list for new telephones because higher charges would reduce 'artificially high demand'; more PMG staff were also being brought on board. He wanted to kill the queue as a political issue, not least because higher charges were going to trigger 'numerous public complaints'. At the wider economic level, raising telecommunications and postal charges and freezing the PMG's capital budget would help to temper inflation by slowing business activity; these moves would also free up more federal funds to 'ensure that high priority government programmes in education, welfare, health, etc. are not restricted because of competing demands on the Budget'. All recommendations were endorsed by cabinet when it met on 22 July.[9]

Bills were introduced to the House of Representatives, and the Vernon report was tabled in the Senate within 24 hours of cabinet's deliberations.[10] Representing Bishop in the lower house, Bowen framed the increased charges as funding 'growing demand' and covering the PMG's soaring costs. These costs were attributable to increasing wages and materials costs, which all Australian businesses were facing; costs associated with Labor's 'improvements in conditions of service, especially for recreation leave and superannuation'; and the long-run effects of the Coalition's 'hidden subsidies to selected areas of the community' that stimulated 'artificially high demand' for new telephone services and made 'inequitable inroads into the national resources available to meet total community needs'.[11]

On one level, the subsequent parliamentary debate followed a familiar pattern: the government attacked the Coalition for implementing policies that were 'based on political motivations rather than on sound commercial practice', while the Country Party and rural Liberals refused to acknowledge any merit in Labor's approach.[12] It was a 'bitter, deliberate vendetta' against country people, they said, accusing Labor of wanting to run telecommunications and post 'as a profitable business enterprise, not as a community service'.[13] With Whitlam in the vanguard, Labor's regular resort to sweeping user-pays rhetoric tended to obscure the fact that country people would remain heavily subsidised and that Labor's reduction of long-distance call rates was consistent with Country Party aspirations. When Whitlam was accused of anti-country bias during the debate, for example, he responded baldly that 'business enterprises run by governments should pay their way … it is seriously inflationary to subsidise people to receive a service such as the installation of telephones. They ought to pay for such installations on an economic basis.'[14] Rhetoric such as this inflamed the anger and anxiety already felt by rural politicians and communities in response to Labor's cuts to various bounties, subsidies and assistance schemes and its recent enactment of new laws that would reduce rural parliamentary representation.[15]

At another level, the debate became entangled in a broader and increasingly intense argument about the government's economic management. On 30 July, the Senate voted to defer consideration of Labor's proposed telecommunications and postal measures until after the treasurer, Frank Crean, had presented the 1974/75 budget in mid-September, on the grounds that higher charges were 'clearly inflationary' and should be examined as part of Labor's 'total financial program'.[16] The opposition was strongly criticised for this in the press. The *Australian Financial Review* described the move as 'almost totally inconsistent' with the Coalition's recent election campaigning for government spending cuts.[17] Melbourne's *Age* labelled it a 'tactical manoeuvre based on opportunism rather than a valid objection based on reason or principle'; the newspaper argued that Labor's proposals were 'not so much part of the government's anti-inflationary programme as a first step towards making the Post Office commercially viable, a proposition with which the opposition is basically in sympathy'.[18] Meanwhile, although Crean had expressed his 'sad conviction' that an expansionary budget would lead to 'the worst of all worlds … a vicious circle of spiralling inflation and depressed employment and activity', cabinet was gearing up for a budget in which government spending would leap by 46 per cent and the deficit would reach 4 per cent of GDP.[19]

Following Crean's budget speech, the Whitlam government reintroduced legislation to enact the measures, though they now included additional price rises to offset $30 million in revenue foregone by the two-month delay. Bowen said that Labor would not cover the shortfall with federal funds because it would come 'at the expense of our other high priority programmes in the fields of education, welfare and health'. Labor also rejected making deeper cuts to the PMG's capital budget, as this could add another 40,000 people to the 123,000 already on the waiting list for new telephones.

Business bore the brunt of the government's new charges. Line rentals for business customers would increase by 13 per cent on top of the 36 per cent increase already announced because, said Bowen, it was 'completely inequitable for the residential subscriber to pay more directly because of the opposition's action'.[20] A strident parliamentary debate ensued, but the opposition conceded up-front that it would not block the bills.[21]

Acting on Vernon

During August and September, the interdepartmental committee formed to deep dive into the Vernon commission's recommendations worked methodically through the report. Comprising officials from the PMG, the Department of the Special Minister of State, the Public Service Board, Treasury and the Prime Minister's Department, the committee generally supported the commissioners' recommendations and in most cases, though with some significant exceptions, was able to reach agreement. Bishop and Bowen received the committee's final report in early October, though it was another two months before the matter went before cabinet.

With respect to reconciling the social and commercial elements of Australia's telecommunications policy, committee members agreed that legislation should require both new statutory authorities to provide services 'which meet, within reasonable and responsible limits, the requirements of the whole community' and that they should operate 'in accordance with accepted principles of business management so that the efficiency and vitality of the organisation is constantly under review'. They also endorsed a pricing structure in which customers would cover 'reasonable costs' for their services and the commonwealth would receive 'a reasonable return'. The committee unanimously supported the commissioners' proposed system of financial, operational, policy and political checks and balances, but unanimously rejected their recommendation for two new arbitration bodies to deal exclusively with industrial matters.[22]

Consensus collapsed, however, over the financial treatment of the new authorities. Treasury saw a new telecommunications authority as an opportunity to 'start afresh' and wanted the PMG's past surpluses, which had been generated from telecommunications revenues and were worth around $400 million, capitalised and allocated to the authority as additional interest-bearing debt. Unsurprisingly, the PMG and Bowen's department had a different view. They wanted 'no discontinuity' and proposed that all assets and liabilities (including the PMG's pension liability, which Treasury wanted to remove from the new authority) simply pass on 'from old to new'.[23] Bishop and Bowen backed their officials and argued to cabinet that replacing the PMG with a new telecommunications authority 'should not be seen as imposing additional costs on the users of the telecommunications service'.[24]

Tax was also a tricky issue. Treasury and the Prime Minister's Department argued that the new authority be immediately liable for indirect tax because it would be profitable from the outset. The authority should, however, be exempted from direct tax 'at this stage' due to inconsistencies in the tax treatments of other commonwealth statutory authorities. But Bishop's and Bowen's departments, with support from their ministers, lined up with the Vernon commission's view. This was that neither new authority be subject to tax because each would provide 'essential community services in both economic and uneconomic areas' and would 'not be subsidised' for the latter.

The committee's toughest challenge was finding a position on OTC that satisfied Whitlam's repeated pledge to abolish it while also being 'mindful' of Vernon's strong advice to the contrary. Searching for options, the officials engaged consultants who had earlier worked on the commission's inquiry and invited OTC to put forward its thoughts. OTC responded with alacrity, claiming that 'business prudence and commonsense [and] the national interest' were all against Whitlam's plan. It proposed an 'incorporation' model that reflected, in all but name, a continuation of the status quo.

In its model, OTC would remain a separate legal entity that operated as a 'self-contained and largely autonomous division' within the new authority; its general manager would join the new authority's board, along with OTC's existing board members, and report directly to the board rather than to the new authority's chief executive; existing financial arrangements would continue, including the payment of dividends to the commonwealth; and there would be a separate career service for its staff. OTC executives were also pleased to advise, in follow-up discussions with the committee, that the 'vast majority' of their staff had formally confirmed their opposition to the government's policy.

The committee agreed that Labor's requirements would not be 'sufficiently met' if the new telecommunications authority's chief executive did not have direct remit over national and international services, but they disagreed over OTC's legal status. Treasury, the Public Service Board and Whitlam's own department sought to reconcile the irreconcilable positions of Whitlam, Vernon and OTC, and also to satisfy cabinet's desire not to lose OTC's dividend payments and tax revenues, by proposing a model based on the state-owned Commonwealth Bank and its subsidiaries. OTC would remain legally and financially distinct and become a subsidiary of the new authority, with OTC's general manager reporting to the authority's chief executive. But this was still a bridge too far for the PMG and Bowen's department: they simply reasserted that Whitlam's decree be implemented as announced.[25]

The campaign by OTC and its influential supporters played out prominently in public. This was helped by an advertising budget reputed to be $900,000 and by Harold White's personal collaboration with the opposition.[26] In parliament, shadow postmaster-general Peter Durack repeatedly flagged hostility to Labor's plan from the PREIA and the smaller Association of Professional Engineers. This extracted an admission from Bishop that 'somebody in OTC'—most likely he meant White—was 'resisting being absorbed into the new telecommunications commission' and fostering 'agitation among the staff who fear the future'. Bishop worked hard to build bridges with OTC staff and the opposition, meeting repeatedly with union officials to put the government's case and give assurances about employee rights and conditions. He also sought to arrange discussions between Durack, PMG officials and OTC board members.[27] Bishop's efforts, however, were for naught. OTC and the opposition remained resolute.

As these events were going on, cabinet also began the process of subordinating OTC's board to the interim board of the mooted new authority. It confirmed on 14 November that Bill Gibbs, the interim board chairman, would also become OTC chairman and be joined on OTC's board by his recently appointed interim board colleagues Peter Lawler, the secretary of the Department of the Special Minister of State, and Jack Curtis, a deputy director-general of the PMG who in 1975 would become inaugural managing director of the new telecommunications authority.[28]

When cabinet ministers met to consider Bishop and Bowen's joint submission on the Vernon commission in early December, they agreed to 'reaffirm' the plan to abolish OTC. Cabinet also cherry-picked from the conflicting financial advice offered by officials in such a way as to advantage federal coffers at the new telecommunications authority's expense. The authority was lumbered not only with the PMG's pension liabilities, but also with about $400 million worth of additional interest-bearing debt.[29]

Cabinet's decision was taken at the same time as Rex Connor, the minerals and energy minister, received an infamously unconventional authorisation to raise a $US4 billion offshore loan. Both decisions highlight the extent to which the government by then was searching for new revenue streams wherever it might find them. The telecommunications decision also marked a significant shift for Labor.

The party had loudly opposed the Coalition's policy of making the PMG liable for interest on Treasury advances ever since 1960. Indeed, just five months earlier, Whitlam had publicly referred to 'the spurious debt burdens imposed on the users of the Post Office through the former government's idea that the customers of the Post Office had to pay back the capital that had been notionally invested in postal facilities throughout the century'.[30]

Implementation

In February the government confirmed its intention to implement nearly all the Vernon commission's recommendations, and in April Bishop tabled bills in the Senate to effect the myriad changes required. Bishop described this as the 'final product' of Labor's eight-year commitment to reform Australia's telecommunications and postal arrangements.[31] The opposition, now led by Malcolm Fraser following Billy Snedden's ouster the previous month, was lukewarm in its response. Confronted by the clearly unviable status quo and lacking an alternative to the cogently developed framework before it, the Coalition decided not to oppose the PMG's replacement with two new statutory authorities, but it warned that it 'should never be assumed that the opposition has given general support to the Vernon commission report'.[32]

In practice, the Coalition adopted a broadly bipartisan approach to Labor's reform package, though the notable exception was its outright rejection of the government's plan for OTC. Labor and Coalition senators worked line-by-line through the complex and hurriedly drafted legislation, correcting various errors along the way, including at one point replacing the word 'debtor' with 'creditor', to the consternation of former South Australian premier Steele Hall.[33] This relative bipartisanship is noteworthy given the increasingly toxic political atmosphere in Australia at the time. The Coalition's posture reflected the wide respect accorded to Vernon in non-Labor circles, the scrupulously apolitical way in which the royal commission had been conducted, and Bishop's down-to-earth willingness to engage meaningfully with the opposition.

The Coalition voiced no in-principle objections to many of the significant proposed changes. These included providing the new authorities with discretion to amend prices, subject to ministerial approval for basic services but with provision for parliamentary appropriations if approval was declined; removing Public

Service Board jurisdiction over the authorities and establishing formal consultative councils to promote, in Bishop's words, 'the maximum use of negotiation and consultation between management and staff organisations'; and requiring the new telecommunications authority—to be called the Australian Telecommunications Commission (hereafter Telecom)—to self-finance half of its capital program and all of its operating expenditure.[34]

Opposition politicians did, however, carve out sufficient wiggle room to enable them to censure Labor if the government's reforms did not meet expectations, especially regarding the government's assurances, in the face of general scepticism, that the new model would yield both industrial harmony and financially disciplined agreements between the new authorities and unions. Worried especially about the flow-on impact of a wages blowout in the new authorities, Durack expressed the 'hope that the commissions will be able to evolve relations with their staff in such a way that ... we will see fewer industrial troubles ... I hope that the commissions will not believe that they can enter into sweetheart deals ... with their staff in the hope of buying industrial peace'.[35]

The Coalition was also unwavering in its distrust of the Whitlam government's general policy agenda for rural communities. While the bipartisan commitment to affordable universal service provision in telecommunications was as secure as ever, opposition members of parliament, especially those from the renamed National Country Party, remained deeply concerned that the more commercial orientation of Telecom and its relative freedom from direct political intervention posed a risk to the availability, cost and quality of rural services. This concern persisted even though the legislation required both new authorities to perform their functions 'in such a manner as will, in the opinion of the Commission, best meet the reasonable needs of the Australian people'. It also disregarded Bishop's reassurance that the presence of senior government officials on the authorities' boards would ensure that 'ministerial influence will be carried into the daily workings of the commissions'.[36]

The Coalition struggled to reconcile its wish for greater commercial efficiency with its commitment to Australia's traditional arrangements regarding rural services. The opposition doubted that the Whitlam government or the Vernon commission 'fully' appreciated that 'these services are a public utility'. Durack reasserted the Coalition parties' position that 'many aspects' of telecommunications services were 'akin to those of a social service' and that the framework for their delivery could not be 'purely commercial'. The Coalition believed that 'the operation must be run in such a way as to provide communications for all sections of the Australian community in all parts of Australia ... regardless of whether the provision of those services can be regarded as a commercial operation or not'. But at the same time the Coalition wanted Telecom and the new postal authority, Australia Post, to 'run on commercial lines [with] particular regard to the principles of efficiency, productivity [and] economy ... Hopefully they will be more market orientated and will have closer regard to increasing productivity so that the services will be able to be delivered in a more efficient manner.'[37]

The Coalition and Labor were each walking a fine line. The Coalition was advocating business management principles and improved productivity, by which it largely meant reducing fixed labour costs and employing more contractors, while not acknowledging the politically and financially unsustainable system its last period in government had bequeathed to Labor. And Labor, while also arguing for financial efficiency and greater operational autonomy, was wilfully shutting its eyes to the widely acknowledged risk that its policy could strengthen the telecommunications and postal unions and result in greater industrial disruption, featherbedding or both, with the costs borne by Australian households and businesses and, ultimately, the wider economy.

In parliament, the Coalition insisted on more prescriptive 'political obligations' for the new authorities and for stronger ministerial powers in order to keep responsibility for service delivery 'where it has been and where we believe it must continue to be ... squarely on the shoulders of the government of the day'. In a particularly convoluted legislative amendment proposed by the opposition, each authority was to have the duty 'to meet the social, industrial and commercial needs of Australia and, in particular, to provide throughout Australia such services ... as satisfy all reasonable demands for them'. Each authority should also have specific regard for 'improving and developing its operating systems', technological developments, 'efficiency and economy [and] the special needs of the non-metropolitan areas of Australia'. Regarding ministerial powers, the Coalition amendment stated that 'if it appears to the Minister that there is a defect in the general plans or arrangements of the Commission for exercising any of its powers [or] that the Commission is showing undue preference to, or is exercising undue discrimination against, any person or persons of any class or description in the charges or other terms or conditions applicable to services provided', then the minister could give the authority 'such directions of a general character as to the exercise by it of its powers as appear to the Minister to be requisite in the national interest'.[38]

Although Bishop believed the government's bills as drafted satisfied the substance of Coalition concerns, he was willing to accommodate an added element of prescription and ministerial authority to keep the opposition on side. He therefore had the amendment redrafted to 'tidy it up'. In simplifying the text, however, the revised amendment widened ministerial power even further, opening the way back to the kind of arbitrary political interference that Labor had long criticised. The responsible minister would now possess a general power to issue Telecom or Australia Post with a written notice, after first consulting the authority, regarding 'the performance of its functions and the exercise of its powers, as appear to the Minister to be necessary in the public interest'.[39] As the political journalist Alan Reid has observed, even politicians with 'integrity and high morality' tended to equate the national interest with 'the moves they make to secure electoral loyalty', and Durack, perhaps thinking along these lines, declared himself 'rather surprised' that Labor's proposal went 'much further' than the Coalition's earlier draft, particularly 'in view of its stated claims that it is seeking to set up this independent Commission'. Nonetheless, somewhat ironically given that the revisions had been made to satisfy opposition concerns, Durack indicated that the Coalition preferred ministerial direction powers to be 'of a general kind' but 'if the government wants to have a wider power of direction, we will not oppose that'.[40]

Steele Hall was a rare voice of dissent, dismissing the government and opposition as 'both wrong'. He declared it 'a great pity that, in this bright new age when we had an independent commission … we are allowing the independence of the commission to go by the board and instituting political control of the commission's functions'.[41] It is indeed notable that as Labor neared the finishing line of this eight-year project, it fumbled the key reform objective of reducing the capacity of governments to interfere politically in service delivery arrangements by needlessly overreaching to satisfy Coalition concerns.

Several contributing factors were at play. By late May 1975, cabinet was consumed by internal dysfunction and external crises. In pursuit of the telecommunications and postal reforms, Bishop and Bowen were racing against time to pass the government's bills so that the new authorities could begin operations in six weeks. The ministers knew that their most critical challenge was to resolve the impasse over OTC. It seems that, in this context, wider ministerial powers and added prescription were allowed to slip through.

The government's determination to merge OTC into Telecom was matched by the Coalition's determination to oppose it. The debate was intense and became increasingly emotional, though the arguments put by both sides for the most part revisited well-trodden ground. In essence, network and operational integration would either save costs and improve efficiency or wreck a 'highly productive and market orientated body [making] very handsome profits'.[42] One Labor senator declared himself 'giddy and tired from the tedious monotony of repeating the same old arguments for and against'.[43] Bishop was at pains to acknowledge OTC's 'fine record' and gave assurances that its staff would 'retain their identity as a working group' within Telecom, but this counted for little.[44] The Coalition controlled the Senate, so it won the contest.

When the government's telecommunications bill was sent to the lower house with all OTC incorporation-related clauses removed, Labor was not ready to concede defeat, but, with the 1 July deadline for Telecom's inauguration just five weeks away, it needed to advance where it could. As such, it passed the amended bill and then tabled another containing all its original OTC clauses; this was inevitably defeated in the Senate. Senior National Country Party figure Peter Nixon was bemused, describing Labor's legislative move as 'novel, if not unique'.[45] Durack was likely close to the mark when he suggested that the government's 'obstinacy' stemmed from Whitlam's determination to push on 'come hell or high water' because he was personally invested in the outcome.[46] Another factor may have been precipitous cabinet decision-making in the context of further economic deterioration, with inflation reaching 17 per cent, and following a messy reshuffle in which Lance Barnard left parliament and Jim Cairns departed Treasury. With Labor, the issue had become personal. Bowen railed against an OTC 'personality cult which … requires that one has to live at Point Piper and drive a Mercedes-Benz'.[47] Whitlam was still seething a decade later, dismissing OTC as a 'cosy bureaucracy' that 'remains an extravagant excrescence'.[48]

Telecom's first days

Following rapid royal assent, Telecom and Australia Post began operations on 1 July. The PMG's director-general, Eber Lane, who had been appointed by former Liberal postmaster-general Alan Hulme and shared his preference for keeping telecommunications and post together, retired, and one of his deputies, Jack Curtis, became Telecom's first managing director. Curtis was well respected but hardly new blood. He had joined the PMG in 1949 with dual degrees in engineering and arts after military service in the Second World War. Following cabinet's reshuffle in June, Bishop remained in situ, but with less to do on a day-to-day basis given the government's reforms. The PMG also, rather unexpectedly, continued to exist, primarily because abolishing it as planned would have left Whitlam with more ministers than departments following Social Security's merger with Repatriation. The rump PMG, which was renamed the Department of Post and Telecommunications by the new Fraser government in late 1975, soon became an influential player on the telecommunications policy stage. Fred Green, a former secretary of the Department of the Air who had worked for the PMG thirty years earlier, was appointed the PMG's new director-general and also took seats on the boards of Telecom and Australia Post.[49]

Telecom's senior executives looked forward to their new autonomy and Bishop was committed to letting the new authorities 'get off to a fair start and ... not to be too restricted in proving that they can operate efficiently'.[50] At their first board meeting, Telecom's directors agreed that chairman Bill Gibbs would write to the minister after each meeting to outline key issues discussed and decisions taken and, to the extent deemed necessary, provide 'a clear indication of the need for ministerial approval and the section of the [Telecommunications] Act under which the minister's agreement was sought'.[51] Within weeks, however, actions by Telecom demonstrated that the traditional political dynamics in telecommunications were likely to continue: a number of former PMG officials were promoted into more senior roles as a precursor to hundreds of senior role classifications being reviewed; and in an awkwardly timed statement, Gibbs also announced increases to telephone charges of up to 50 per cent and the cutting of some concessional rates so as to drive additional revenues of $150 million in order to meet Telecom's new financial obligations.

The reaction from within the bureaucracy and cabinet and from the media and opposition was swift—and aimed squarely at the government. (Telecom's announcement that new push-button telephones would be available by 1976 did not mollify its critics.) The Department of Labour was worried that the outbreak of high-profile promotions would undermine already besieged wage indexation policies. The chairman of the reduced Public Service Board, Alan Cooley, reportedly told Gibbs and his counterpart at Australia Post that their actions placed the board in an 'untenable position' and, in a meeting with Whitlam, described Telecom's senior managers as 'over-salaried and over-classified'. Labor senator Doug McClelland, who had replaced Bowen as special minister of state, pressed Bishop and Gibbs to intervene, but Bishop was unwilling to establish such an early precedent of ministerial intervention in operational matters. Regarding Cooley, he steered clear of what looked like a rear-guard action by the board to re-establish its control. Gibbs resigned soon afterwards, likely deterred by a working environment that was more intensely political that he had expected.[52]

Though media criticism of 'the new fat cat management structure' was probably predictable, it also reflected genuine concerns about whether the reforms underway would provide the promised cost efficiencies and delivery improvements. Respected commentators saw the same people doing the same jobs for more money. Brian Toohey of the *Australian Financial Review*, for example, asserted that Telecom already contained more top-level managers than 'the whole of the old PMG', and its leadership had made 'little attempt to get in new blood'. Peter Samuel in the *Bulletin* labelled Telecom and Australia Post's senior appointments 'provocative' because, he argued, a key justification for the new authorities' 'independence' from the Public Service Board was so that they could 'attract new talent', which clearly had not occurred. Toohey focused also on the nature of political accountability, warning presciently that a 'resurgent' PMG might lead to 'detailed ministerial involvement' that was contrary to Labor's policy intent. If this eventuated, and the new authorities failed to demonstrably improve performance, blame would be sheeted to Labor and the party would have 'little explanation of why it went to the trouble and expense of setting up supposedly independent commissions in the first place'. More immediately, Toohey said, Bishop's hands-off approach would not save the Whitlam government from the 'odium' of Telecom's price hikes, following as closely as they did on those of 1973 and 1974.[53]

Toohey was right. The Coalition demanded to know if Bishop had 'approved those sections of the large increases in postal and telecommunications charges recently announced which he is required to approve under the legislation' and whether the postmaster-general had 'considered the serious economic and social consequences of the charges'. The opposition also sought to tie Bishop to the senior appointments controversy, asking whether he had been consulted. Consistent with his determination to allow Telecom and Australia Post a long leash, Bishop reiterated that Labor's intent was to let the new authorities operate 'on a proper financial and management basis' and to leave strategic decision-making to 'the practical businessmen' and their colleagues on their boards. But Bishop also took a swipe at the Coalition's 'tradition of ... giant subsidies', which he said had driven the 'general inefficiencies' that the government had sought to resolve.[54]

In the end, though, it was not Bishop or Whitlam or anyone else in Labor who had the most significant influence over how Australia's new telecommunications arrangements worked in practice. The Fraser-led Coalition inherited this role when it swept to office following Labor's dismissal just four months later.

4

A Fast-changing Area

I was conscious that there were opportunities in telecommunications and that it was going to be a fast-changing area.

Malcolm Fraser[1]

Malcolm Fraser became prime minister determined to restore order to government and discipline to public expenditure. He wanted a profitable business sector to foster prosperity, create jobs and pay the taxes that funded social services. In his view, government was there to safeguard against a 'free-for-all, winner-take-all, tooth-and-claw approach to economic life'.[2] A top priority was slashing government spending, which had reached 30 per cent of GDP under Whitlam. A first round of cuts, $360 million deliverable within six months, was announced soon after the Coalition's landslide election win in December 1975.[3]

Old assumptions and new realities

To the extent that Fraser thought about telecommunications policy, it was from the conventional perspective that providing affordable basic telephone services was a core responsibility of government. He has claimed that he wanted Australia to have 'the best and most modern communications possible', but in practice was mostly hands-off, content to leave it 'to the minister whose job it was'.[4] Fraser's communications ministers confirm this. Tony Staley, who became the minister for post and telecommunications following the Coalition's re-election in December 1977, recalls 'no discussion whatsoever' with Fraser about his policy priorities or expectations; his successor, National Country Party deputy leader Ian Sinclair, also claims he had a free hand.[5] Neil Brown, the responsible minister from 1982 until the Coalition's electoral defeat in 1983, found Fraser to be a consultative leader who 'scarcely ever intruded' into his portfolio responsibilities.[6]

The Coalition parties' 1975 telecommunications policy revealed that they had done little fresh thinking during their three years in opposition and suggested that, notwithstanding Telecom's establishment five months earlier, the new government would likely approach this policy area in much the same way as the Coalition had the last time it was in office. The customary challenges associated with balancing the commercial and social aspects of telecommunications were readily evident in Coalition policy, as was the classic public administration dilemma about how best to reconcile the need for controls over government authorities with the need to delegate operational autonomy.

The Fraser government professed to want an 'entrepreneurial' Telecom, but it was also keen to ensure that Telecom's financial objectives did not interfere with its social responsibilities to country areas. Telecom could manage its day-to-day operations without interference, the Coalition said, subject to fulfilling policy directives; a principal priority was to improve rural services through 'a steady extension of the local call area and a relative reduction in the charges for [long distance] calls.' The government reiterated its support for 'expanding the role of private enterprise in the provision of communications services', but this was not foreshadowing later reforms: it was simply about backing Telecom to resume the use of contractors for various provisioning and maintenance jobs.[7]

Ann Moyal's account of Telecom's first year portrays an optimistic new enterprise keen to take advantage of the many opportunities offered by Australia's new telecommunications framework. Business plans were developed, corporate targets were set and the government's cuts to spending and staffing gave added impetus to the organisation's search for operational efficiencies. The push to slash spending also prompted the Coalition to accept Telecom's proposal that it seek to raise $200 million in capital by issuing government-guaranteed, tradable securities.

This sum was four times greater than any previously offered in Australia. The minister for post and telecommunications, Eric Robinson, doubted it was possible to raise such an amount, so he sought cabinet's agreement to make good any shortfall with an appropriation from Treasury. But his concerns were unwarranted: investor interest was strong and the target was met within a few weeks of going to market in September 1976. Telecom continued to raise capital in this way, reducing its reliance on Treasury and helping the government's savings agenda.[8] It enabled cabinet to cut Telecom's appropriation from $215 million to $100 million in April 1977 and then, a year later, to nothing at all.[9]

Telecommunications remained on the policy periphery for most of the Fraser government's first term. During the 1977 election campaign, there was little hint of the challenges just around the corner. To the extent that the topic came up, it was of an entirely conventional nature: Fraser and his deputy prime minister, National Country Party leader Doug Anthony, promised cuts to off-peak calling rates, with Anthony also announcing some more rural subsidies.[10] Opposition Leader Whitlam simply promised to 'correct an injustice suffered' by Sydney's outer-western residents by bringing them within the city's local call zone.[11]

New business interests

Australian businesses emerged from the 1974–75 recession with a pressing need to boost productivity and profits. From about the mid-1970s, advanced communications equipment and data services were emerging, offering businesses and other organisations the potential for productivity improvements, and also raising the prospect of new commercial opportunities for private-sector operators. This underpinned the emergence of new telecommunications-specific business interests, which would soon place fundamental strains on Australia's telecommunications system and present the Fraser government with serious political and policy challenges.

The new developments included improvements to office telephone switchboards, known as private automatic branch exchanges (PABXs), and data being increasingly transmitted between computers, word processors, faxes and answering machines, all of which were becoming more sophisticated. The business sector was eagerly anticipating the Australian launch of videotex, which enabled data to be carried over telephone lines and displayed on screens. Companies in Britain, France and Canada were already using videotex to access operational and financial data across sites and time zones, displaying stock exchange information and managing airline timetables and hotel booking systems.[12]

The basic telephone still accounted for most business and government communications, but there was a pronounced surge in data usage. The first three years of the Fraser government saw a doubling of demand for Telecom's data transmission service, known as Datel, which had been introduced in 1969 by the PMG.[13]

And as more businesses and organisations utilised more advanced communications systems, these systems became more integrated into standard operations and constituted an upward and increasingly visible expenditure item. By the late 1970s, spending by large Australian organisations on telecommunications services had become their second or third highest overhead after property and labour. By 1981, some Australian companies were paying over $5 million a year to Telecom. This increased expenditure was driven not by higher prices but a sustained growth in demand of around 15 per cent year-on-year during the government's tenure.[14]

With greater integration of advanced communications products and services into business operations also came greater dependence on Telecom. Businesses of all sizes were soon looking for a degree of customer care, service assurance, product choice and customisation from Telecom that sat uncomfortably with a government monopoly geared towards providing universal one-size-fits-all services.[15] Telecom also had regulatory discretion over which equipment was permitted to connect to the telecommunications network. This was to safeguard the network's technical integrity, but also protected domestic equipment manufacturers from imports and meant that Telecom controlled Australia's operating environment. With more advanced products available in the United States and elsewhere, local businesses became intensely frustrated at Telecom's unwillingness, or inability, to meet their needs.

Business concerns were validated by a 1980 report by McKinsey & Company. According to McKinsey, Telecom was performing reasonably well in delivering basic telephone services, which within five years would reach all but remote areas, but the organisation had dropped the ball in the 'new services' that would drive future growth. Telecom was 'not meeting demand from its business customers'. Provisioning lead-times for services such as leased lines and data modems were too slow, and Telecom's planning had fallen behind businesses' future needs. Businesses wanted Telecom to provide services that were 'differentiated in both the type of product or service ... and the speed of service provision', rather than the 'undifferentiated ... universal public service' on offer, and were willing to pay a premium to get it. Telecommunications costs, even if only representing a small portion of businesses' total expenses, made 'a great deal of difference' to the efficiency and effectiveness of their operations.[16]

Demand-side business frustration with Telecom was matched by escalating supply-side pressure from Australia's domestic telecommunications equipment suppliers. They wanted greater access to the growing and profitable domestic market for products such as PABXs, modems, faxes and answering machines. But Telecom, newly autonomous and with its own financial targets to meet, was also looking for fresh commercial opportunities. Since 1957, the PMG had permitted approved PABX suppliers to access its network to meet private-sector demand while it retained exclusive rights over the federal and state government sectors. But in 1979, Telecom announced plans to enter the increasingly lucrative private-sector markets for PABXs, faxes and answering machines. In return, it would allow approved PABX suppliers to compete for government business.[17]

This development triggered an immediate backlash from affected suppliers. Two industry groups, the Australian Telecommunications Development Association and the Office Equipment Industry Association, protested to the minister, Tony Staley. He agreed with their complaints, stating publicly that 'the private sector can operate perfectly well' and that Telecom's entry into these markets was 'not only unnecessary but ... would give them undue influence in the market-place'.[18] The government barred Telecom from competing with private-sector PABX suppliers in the major cities, although it was allowed to address otherwise unserved rural areas. Staley also blocked Telecom from entering the markets for fax and answering machines by declining to sign the relevant contracts.[19] Two years later, after fierce lobbying from media magnate Kerry Packer and the retail firm Myer, Staley's successor, Ian Sinclair, similarly prevented Telecom from entering the market for new videotex services.[20]

These supply-side dynamics revealed a fundamental but hitherto latent incompatibility between the Fraser government's ideological view about the appropriate role of the public sector in economic activity, which was that it should not crowd out business, and Telecom's ambition, as an autonomous government enterprise, to exploit the same commercial opportunities that were attracting private-sector interest. This tension did not exist in the Labor Party. For Labor, Telecom's objectives were entirely consistent with what a government enterprise should do, and with what Telecom had been set up to do in 1975.

Industrial disputes and their consequences

Business disaffection with the telecommunications system was exacerbated by a series of national industrial disputes, which impressed on businesses the extent to which key sector unions could disrupt, or even block, their access to critical communications services. The first dispute (which Bob Hawke, then president of the Australian Council of Trade Unions (ACTU), later described as Australia's 'first real fight' over labour-displacing technology) was provoked by Telecom's plan to upgrade its exchanges with computerised switching equipment.[21] Telecom claimed that total technical staff numbers would not decline, but it was clear that over time the 3000 technicians employed to diagnose and rectify faults would make way for fewer staff specially trained to maintain the new equipment.[22]

In April 1978, after ten months of industrial hearings by the Australian Conciliation and Arbitration Commission, Telecom's technicians, represented by the Australian Telecommunications Employees' Association (ATEA), began go-slows on telephone maintenance and installations, and instituted work bans on any activities related to the exchange upgrade program. Over the next four months, inter-city telephone, data and telex links—services used mostly by business and government—were severely disrupted. For a time, Adelaide was reduced to communicating with the outside world by telegram.

In the immediate wake of the dispute, an internal government review found that the ATEA's refusal to conduct maintenance on Telecom's trunk exchanges (which connected Australia's major towns and cities) had played havoc with inter-capital telephone links. In particular, the breakdown of Telecom's coaxial cable between Melbourne, Canberra and Sydney had resulted in the failure of a third of all inter-capital leased line services. The ATEA targeted Telecom's business customers by refusing to repair network faults on which their services depended; however, not wishing to alienate the public, it publicised the locations of public telephones from which free calls could be made.[23]

As Hawke put it, the business sector was 'going berserk' and 'screaming at the government to do something'.[24] After four months, the industrial action was settled; the industrial relations minister, Tony Street, made a direct approach to Hawke, and Mary Gaudron, the Conciliation and Arbitration Commission's cigar-smoking young deputy president, brokered an agreement during an all-day Sunday mediation in which she reportedly refused to allow the parties any breaks or refreshments after 5 p.m.[25] But in June and July 1979 and again between April and June 1981, businesses were severely disrupted by two more bitter and highly politicised disputes.[26] Business was left in no doubt about its vulnerability to telecommunications union power, and, more pointedly, about its inability to take any mitigating steps because of its dependence on the state monopoly, Telecom. These disputes led to the establishment of two pressure groups focused exclusively on the telecommunications-related interests of businesses and other institutional users.

The first of these groups was Business Telecommunications Services (BTS), established in September 1980. Set up as a private company, it had shareholders representing some of Telecom's largest institutional customers and suppliers as well as others that were positioning to compete with Telecom in a future liberalised sector. In an early speech about the new group, BTS's general manager, Peter Holmes à Court, emphasised the Australian business sector's 'acute sensitivity' to being 'almost totally dependent upon Telecom, as the sole source of supply for this most vital of commodities'. BTS was there to ensure 'business community input to the important government considerations on telecommunications policy and developments' and to seek 'private sector involvement in the provision of telecommunications services'.[27]

The second group established was the Australian Telecommunications Users Group (ATUG), which emerged in 1981. ATUG was chaired by Harold White, the former head of OTC, and encompassed about a hundred of Australia's largest private and public-sector organisations.[28] BTS and ATUG were both prominent in the contentious policy debates of the Fraser government's third term. BTS closed down shortly after Fraser lost power in 1983, but ATUG went on to become a respected contributor to telecommunications policy debates well into the 1990s.

The emergence of new telecommunications-focused business interests in the latter 1970s was driven by the new opportunities being enabled by technological advances, post-recession productivity imperatives, discontent with Telecom's iron grip on critical business inputs and deep concern about the unions' disruptive power over essential services. In pressing for more flexibility, openness and private-sector involvement in Australian telecommunications, the new business lobby inserted a fundamentally disruptive dynamic into what was essentially a closed system not configured to serve contemporary business needs but substantially sustained by subsidies funded by business. The objectives of business were broadly aligned with Coalition ideology and Fraser government policy, but they presented the government with a substantial challenge, because they pitted the interests of the Coalition's core business constituency against those of its traditional rural supporter base, which depended on the existing system for subsidised services.

This issue would become one of the Fraser government's key conundrums, and one it was ultimately unable to resolve.

The industrial disputes of 1978–81 also confronted the government with its dependence on telecommunications for its day-to-day operations and economic policy. An interdepartmental taskforce set up by cabinet as the first dispute escalated had raised 'serious questions' about how rapidly critical parts of the system had collapsed as a result of union action. The taskforce asked 'whether it is in the national interest that telecommunications services which are essential to maintain the community and commercial interest should be wholly dependent on the Telecom network'.[29]

Tony Staley, who already believed he was facing 'a huge task with the telecommunications unions', strongly backed this advice.[30] On Australia Day 1979, he signed off on a cabinet submission drawing attention to the 'increasing extent' to which 'government, business and social/community activities are dependent on reliable and efficient telecommunications services'. He argued that the 1978 dispute, by then resolved, had highlighted the fact that Telecom's network was vulnerable to 'industrial sabotage' and, with support from Telecom, he successfully sought cabinet's agreement to give 'high priority' to detailed contingency planning to protect the network from industrial disruption.[31]

This planning was still underway four months later when the nation became embroiled in another telecommunications dispute. Cabinet moved to identify emergency mechanisms to safeguard 'the flow of essential government communications', quickly forming a policy committee headed by the Prime Minister's Department and an 'operational and technical' group headed by Defence. Though the Department of Transport oversaw Australia's most extensive alternative telecommunications network, cabinet assumed that its staff would not break solidarity with the telecommunications unions, so it looked to Defence to 'provide alternative communications facilities at short notice for essential government business'.[32] But even Defence relied on Telecom for voice communications, so the government would need to subsist on its telex facilities in an emergency.[33] Nonetheless, by mid-1979 cabinet had the comfort of knowing that the machinery of government, unlike the business sector, could maintain basic inter-city communications come what may.

The 1981 dispute prompted further cabinet contingency planning. The Interdepartmental Committee on the Vulnerability of the Telecommunications

System advised, with cabinet's strong backing, that more private-sector involvement in providing telecommunications services 'would lead to a diversification of employers and unions and ultimately a reduction in the capacity of unions to maintain disruption'.[34] By then the Fraser government had also initiated a public inquiry into this issue. But ministers were less concerned to make fundamental changes to the telecommunications system than to find ways to let more non-union staff gain access to strategically vulnerable parts of Telecom's network.

In November 1981, communications minister Ian Sinclair and the industrial relations minister, Ian Viner, identified 'the nub of the current vulnerability problem' as being that switching capacity and transmission control in the network were now concentrated 'in a few key points maintained by a few key people'.[35] There was some irony in this, given that it was an outcome of Telecom's exchange upgrade program, which had aimed at boosting productivity and improving network performance. But what to do? Cabinet rejected the option of private contractors maintaining Telecom's network for fear of industrial opposition. It also rejected the idea of letting private-sector interests own and operate some trunk exchanges, because the unions would likely enforce 'bans ... on the construction of exchange buildings to be owned by contractors' and because it was unclear how network interconnection between Telecom and other operators could be regulated.

Cabinet ultimately supported two measures that were demonstrably practical, not least because Telecom was already implementing them. These were, first, to dilute ATEA power in key exchanges by employing a 'small cell' of private contractors alongside the union's technicians; and secondly, to allocate network maintenance responsibilities to some Telecom engineers. Cabinet also agreed to permit Telecom to use contractors to carry out maintenance and repairs on PABX equipment. Though in principle ministers favoured facilitating more telecommunications 'flexibility' for business by way of dedicated private networks leased from Telecom, they shied away from making any moves in this direction due to uncertainty about the possible negative implications it might have for social policy. Specifically, cabinet was concerned, on the basis of advice from Telecom, which had its own agenda on the issue, that private networks could take such a slice from the profits Telecom made from its inter-city links that the authority would no longer be able to subsidise rural services.[36]

Matters of scale

Another source of rolling cabinet consternation was Telecom's capital expenditure. The organisation's borrowings added to government debt and its spending was 'of such magnitude' (nearing $1 billion by the late 1970s) that it threatened the government's fiscal agenda.[37] Fraser refused to accept that any enterprise could need so much money, according to Staley, and in 1978 cabinet cut Telecom's budget and borrowing limit.[38] The following year, cabinet decided to investigate Telecom's operations. This flew in the face of advice from officials that such a review would probably impinge on Telecom's autonomy and also carried the risk of 'some embarrassment' to the government. The officials considered it plausible that an inquiry might find Telecom's capital expenditure reasonable and recommend that it be funded from higher debt, given that two-thirds of its spending was already being financed from internal sources.[39]

The review, by McKinsey & Company, did in fact suggest a 'moderate' increase in Telecom's capital spending, to remedy its underperformance in the 'new services' that were being demanded by business and would drive future growth. However, the review did not criticise Telecom's government-imposed capital constraints. Rather, it advised Telecom to become more disciplined and commercial in its operations. Potential projects should be assessed on the basis of their marginal cost of capital: when forecast return exceeded cost of capital, Telecom should seek government borrowing approval, while for loss-making public policy-driven projects it should seek direct funding from government. Like the Vernon and Coombs inquiries before it, the McKinsey review also wanted Telecom to get a better handle on its internal economics so as to more accurately reflect its underlying costs in pricing, specifically by giving more weight to provisioning costs and relying less on call rates.[40]

In mid-1981, cabinet agreed to increase Telecom's borrowing limit to nearly $1.3 billion as part of the authority's first capital expenditure increase for some years.[41] This further entrenched Telecom's position as the largest semi-government borrower on Australia's public loan market, accounting for about 5 per cent of total public-sector borrowing.[42] In making its decision, cabinet accepted Sinclair's view that 'growth in private sector demand' was a key factor in Telecom's demand for capital; it ignored advice from the Department of Finance that Telecom's 'significant … under-pricing' was distorting demand and that its prices, not borrowings, should increase. Sinclair has since conceded that the Fraser government was loath to challenge the 'political expectation [that] the taxpayer should meet the capital costs of connection while the subscriber paid for calls, with some contribution towards installation'. In any case, projects focused on traditional telecommunications priorities still dominated Telecom's 1981/82 capital works program: basic telephone connections, exchange automation and public telephone upgrades all came well ahead of business-orientated digital data network and packet switching data rollouts.[43]

The government also kept a tight rein on Telecom's industrial arrangements. Though Telecom was permitted to negotiate directly with its staff, via the unions, about wages and employment terms, it could not seal a deal without approval from an Industrial Relations Department-led committee that included the Public Service Board.[44] This was contrary to Labor's intent when establishing Telecom and gainsaid earlier union optimism, but the development was unsurprising given widely held concerns, not least within the Coalition, that implementing the Whitlam government's telecommunications reforms would risk wage and cost blowouts. The Fraser government's industrial coordination arrangements reflected its struggle to uphold Australia's centralised wage-fixing system in the face of rapid and contentious changes in the telecommunications sector—and a still-evolving power balance between the government and an increasingly assertive Telecom.

The industrial coordination system caused significant strains between Fraser's government and Telecom. In 1979, for example, cabinet censured Telecom over a wages agreement struck with the Australian Postal and Telecommunications Union (APTU) (successor to the APWU) that 'had not followed consultation with the Minister for Industrial Relations and which was contrary to government wages policy'.[45] And at the height of the national telecommunications dispute in 1981, a Telecom–ATEA–APTU pay deal sparked a cabinet whirlwind that both asserted the government's authority over Telecom and exposed the limits of its power. The pay deal fell outside the Coalition's wages policy and cabinet responded forcefully, worried about knock-on wage rises and also, by this stage, somewhat leery of Telecom's leadership, which had shown a marked lack of enthusiasm for the government's atypically audacious plan to establish a national satellite system.

Cabinet's view was that Telecom had been wilfully disobedient. At short notice, Telecom's managing director, Jack Curtis, and his senior colleague Jim Smith were summoned to Canberra where, according to a direct witness, they were subjected to 'cross-examination … by a Prime Minister with all the authority of the government'.[46] Though cabinet concluded that it had 'no alternative but to allow Telecom to honour its agreement', it resolved to take 'all necessary steps' to ensure that its industrial policies were 'strictly adhered to at all times in the future' and also to give Telecom a public whipping.[47] Sinclair and the acting industrial relations minister, Wal Fife, declared that the authority's actions were 'contrary to standing government instructions [and] cannot be condoned', and warned that any flow-on economic consequences would provide 'a further ground for government condemnation'.[48] In response, Curtis resigned. He was replaced by Bill Pollock, another member of the PMG old guard, who had joined the department as a teenager more than forty years before.

By late 1981, the Fraser government's increasingly frequent use of market liberal rhetoric, coupled with its public inquiry into private-sector involvement in telecommunications, was exciting both hopes and fears that significant liberalisation was on the horizon. Cabinet's focus, however, was on mitigating the risk of industrial disruption to Australia's telecommunications system rather than on changing the system itself. To the extent that ministers were considering greater flexibility and openness in telecommunications, they were motivated less by emerging market liberal ideas about competition than by the perceived need to reduce arbitrary union power without upsetting the cross-subsidy structure that underpinned the provision of loss-making services to mostly rural areas.

5

Blue Sky Dreaming

I was desperate that we have a satellite, our own system.

Tony Staley[1]

The Fraser government's uncharacteristically gung-ho decision to establish a national satellite system, and a new state enterprise to run it, introduced disruptive forces into Australia's telecommunications sector. It sparked immediate defensive responses from Telecom and had long-term ramifications. In particular, the decision later created political problems for the Hawke government, compromising both its initial decision-making on telecommunications policy and its subsequent telecommunications reform program. The Fraser government's atypical approach in part reflected the fact that its lengthy deliberations about satellite were not really about telecommunications at all. Telecommunications was always in the policy mix, but it consistently ranked below broadcasting policy and satellite's seemingly transformative potential to meet other intractable challenges important to the Coalition, such as how to provide city-quality health and education services to rural and remote communities.

Political momentum

Australia had long been integrated into global satellite arrangements for international telecommunications and broadcasting when Fraser became prime minister in 1975, but using satellite technology for domestic communications was new, at that point being done only in North America. First the PMG and then Telecom had considered the feasibility of a national satellite system since the early 1970s and a subsequent review into broadcasting by the Department of Post and Telecommunications was also looking into satellite's potential. Political momentum came, however, from a well-timed and self-interested personal approach to Fraser in August 1977 from Kerry Packer. For Packer, satellite was the key to unlock international cricket broadcasting beyond his metropolitan television network. He wanted Fraser on board before the release of Telecom's report, which was widely expected to be hostile to the idea.[2]

With his rural ties and, in his words, his general sense of Australia's proper place in 'the modern world', Fraser was receptive to Packer's upbeat account of Canada's national satellite system and its potential to close Australia's city–country gap.[3] Soon afterwards, Packer released a commissioned report advocating satellite for Australia.[4] He later claimed that the report was Fraser's idea, but more likely the wheels were in motion before he approached the Prime Minister. Either way, official interest was such that Fred Green, the Post and Telecommunications Department secretary, travelled to Sydney to collect a copy.[5] Within weeks, cabinet agreed that 'detailed investigation' was merited and established a taskforce of officials and experts, the Commonwealth Government Task Force on the National Communications Satellite System, to do the job.[6] OTC's redoubtable boss, Harold White, a long-term satellite proponent and proven campaigner, was put in charge.

From the outset, the government's deliberative process led inexorably towards an affirmative recommendation. White made no effort to hide his enthusiasm; he assured Packer during a public hearing that the question was not whether Australia would acquire a national satellite system but 'when, what design, who controls it, how much it's going to cost [and] who pays for it'.[7] In July 1978, the White taskforce, as it was known, recommended that the government proceed with planning for a satellite system and, significantly, that it establish a new state enterprise to run it.[8] The taskforce's key recommendations were ratified a year later by another committee of officials, the National Satellite System Working Group, set up by Staley.[9]

Deliberations and decisions

Cabinet's decision to investigate Packer's satellite report made no reference to telecommunications, despite its implications for the sector, but the White taskforce's terms of reference, reportedly prepared in consultation with Packer executives, required it to take account of the implications of a satellite system for Telecom, OTC and the telecommunications network. Broadcasting was the main focus, followed by the government's general excitement about satellite's transformative potential for rural and remote health and education services and the nation's science and defence capabilities.[10] While acknowledging satellite's potential to enable telephone (and television) services to isolated 'communities and homesteads', the taskforce explicitly excluded telecommunications as a determining factor in its advice to proceed with a national system.[11]

Telecom's satellite study was released in October 1977, a few months after Packer's, by which time the government was already in the process of establishing the White taskforce. As expected, Telecom concluded that a national satellite system was technically feasible, but its costs would outweigh its benefits. Much weight was given to this finding in later criticism of the government for favouring vested business interests over Telecom's expert analysis.[12] But Telecom's cost-benefit analysis was explicitly qualified. It took account only of its own services and specifically acknowledged that broader considerations, such as 'wider TV distribution, improved medical and educational services in the more remote areas, and improved defence and Foreign Affairs communications ... need to be considered'. According to Telecom, these considerations were beyond its 'capacity to evaluate'.[13]

The terms of reference given to the White taskforce were therefore not inconsistent with Telecom's position. The Fraser government did not set out to sideline Telecom or fundamentally remake Australia's telecommunications arrangements. Rather, it had before it a precedent in Canada, a country with comparable geography and demography to Australia, which seemed to be using satellite technology in ways that, if applied in Australia, might finally solve the perennial challenge of delivering equivalent services to all citizens no matter where they lived, while also obtaining other social and economic benefits.

The White taskforce recommended that a new state enterprise rather than Telecom be given responsibility for developing and operating the mooted system. OTC's influence was clear, with the taskforce report replaying several of the arguments Harold White had used in his campaign against the Whitlam government's plan for Telecom to absorb the organisation. Telecom's 'huge size and concern with a multitude of matters', for example, 'could not match the flexible, adaptable and dynamic character which a small organisation could have, able to act and react quickly to user requirements'.[14] OTC remained concerned about its future after the contentious events of 1974–75, and the taskforce's enthusiasm for a new stand-alone enterprise may have been partly a hedge against this. If a national satellite system was eventually incorporated into OTC (though OTC did not lobby for this within the taskforce) then OTC would be less vulnerable to a Telecom takeover. Another consideration was that OTC was Telecom's largest customer, spending $35 million in 1978, and a stand-alone satellite operator offered it the prospect of accessing an alternative network to carry inter-city communications traffic.[15]

As the responsible minister, however, Staley initially preferred Telecom to set up and operate the new system. He was 'desperate that we have a satellite' and considered that handing the project to Telecom would be the fastest and simplest way forward.[16] Contrary to some commentators at the time, who claimed that the Fraser government was 'actively siding with the competitors ... against the national network', the Coalition was driven more by a positive agenda toward satellite than by a negative view of Telecom.[17] Indeed, Staley considered that a key advantage of giving the satellite system to Telecom was to 'forestall a number of difficult questions' that would otherwise need to be addressed.[18] These included working out how to safeguard existing cross-subsidy arrangements and regulate inter-operator network interconnection. Staley has said that 'an important factor in the Fraser government's national satellite decision was encouraging a degree of competition in telecommunications services' and that, as minister, he wanted to 'encourage competition between structures'.[19] While these claims are reasonable in the context of the time, the Fraser government did not have an agenda to fundamentally reshape Australia's telecommunications system. The significance of Staley's comments should not be overstated in light of later events.

By October 1979, when cabinet decided in principle to proceed with a national satellite system and establish a state enterprise to develop and operate it, Telecom was well and truly on the outer. Addressing cabinet, Staley dismissed Telecom as 'a minor user' of satellite services and said he could see 'no compelling reasons' why it need have any responsibility for the project. The 'majority users' were Australia's commercial broadcasters and the Australian Broadcasting Commission (ABC). In giving the go-ahead for detailed implementation planning, cabinet was principally interested in ensuring that 'the implications of a domestic satellite system for broadcasting policy and practice' were fully evaluated. It was in this context that the instruction was given for private-sector interests to be consulted.

Telecommunications policy barely rated in cabinet's deliberations. To the extent that competition with Telecom was contemplated at all, it related only to high-growth niche data services such as private inter-city networks, which were used by large organisations with geographically dispersed operations. Staley specifically assured cabinet that there was no risk to Telecom's 'essential revenue areas', in particular the inter-city links from which it gained monopoly profits, which were used to fund subsidies. He pointed out that Telecom was already unable to keep up with business demand for data services and, in any case, its data revenues did not underpin the cross-subsidy system. In fact, cabinet saw satellite as a future resource for Telecom; it would be able to provide additional capacity and geographic coverage for the authority's data and remote telephone services. Staley's submission to cabinet, which was prepared in the wake of two crippling industrial disputes, also noted, in passing and without elaboration, that an independent satellite system could provide a degree of telecommunications network redundancy in 'critical/emergency situations'.[20]

An 'act of faith'

A combination of personal and structural factors, which played out in the broader context of the issues discussed in this and the previous chapter, contributed to the relative rapidity with which Telecom went from principal to peripheral along the path to a new satellite system. These factors related especially to Staley's relationship with Telecom's managing director, Jack Curtis, and to the influence of the Department of Post and Telecommunications (the rump PMG), which challenged Telecom, newly autonomous and with its own institutional interests, as principal policy adviser to the government. Even so, politicians and departmental officials remained dependent on Telecom for technical and operational advice about Australia's telecommunications system.

Staley was an activist minister who came to the telecommunications portfolio without any particular experience in the area. Having taught politics for a time at Melbourne University, he had, in his words, a 'strong intellectual interest' in community access to information and saw 'harnessing modern technology to assist people to have more power in their lives as enormously important'. But he found Telecom culturally 'arrogant' and unresponsive to him as minister. Its senior managers would 'politely listen [to him] but not necessarily take any notice' of what he had to say. Staley's office would receive 'huge' numbers of complaints about Telecom that his department would investigate, but it was dependent on advice from Telecom, and he was perpetually 'concerned about how we could know if we were being misled. And we never knew.' He was mindful that Telecom was intended to be 'independent of government', but 'railed against' being a hands-off minister and resolved to 'kick Telecom into shape' where he thought necessary, albeit at an informal level rather than by written direction tabled in parliament.

Staley's working relationship with Curtis (who was serving in the Pacific during the Second World War before Staley was even at school) was mutually respectful but not close; the young minister found Telecom's boss to be 'civil and decent … an almost fatherly old boy'. In the context of Australia's still evolving post-1975 telecommunications arrangements, there was a mismatch of perspectives and expectations between minister and official. Staley's enthusiasm for a national satellite system and his 'old-fashioned' presumption that, like the former PMG, Telecom would comply with his wishes, sat uncomfortably with Curtis's legitimate focus on the authority's own strategic priorities, as well as a fair degree of institutional hubris that led Telecom to mishandle the politics of satellite.[21]

According to Staley, Curtis rejected his push for Telecom to take on satellite because the project did not align with Telecom's operating plans and would significantly distort its capital program in the absence of compensatory funding of about $400 million. His confidence in Telecom was weakened during a study tour to see Canada's satellite system, when he concluded that Curtis had given him 'demonstrably wrong' technical advice on the technology's limitations during a personal briefing. Staley was unsure whether this reflected Curtis's 'economic conservatism, a power play or an interrelatedness of those two factors'.[22] It seems that minister and official were also talking past each other: Curtis's advice to Staley was correct as far as Telecom's own operations were concerned, but did not take account of the government's broader interests. Taken together, these dynamics saw Telecom lose its seat at the policy table. Staley decided that if he could not work with Telecom then he would go around it, in a move that shares strong similarities with the later Rudd government's decision to establish a new state-owned company to build the NBN.

Staley was confident that cabinet's decision to proceed with satellite in October 1979 would have 'wide community support', and the media coverage that followed the announcement broadly confirmed this.[23] Although the project's economic viability was highly questionable from the start, and the Department of Finance consistently opposed it for this reason, such concerns had little influence on the Fraser government because its commitment to satellite was based, in the words of Staley's department head Robert Lansdown, on an 'act of faith'.[24] In similar vein, the Finance official seconded to the White taskforce, John Coleman, later recalled Harold White dismissing his reservations about the project by contrasting 'men of vision' such as himself who backed satellite with 'small minded accountants' such as Coleman, who did not.[25] According to Staley, cabinet gave due consideration to Finance's views but 'thought that there was enough in the counter-argument to do it'.[26]

Even when Staley advised cabinet to issue a formal tender request for the satellite system, he acknowledged that financial clarity was 'constrained by [the] absence of firm cost estimates' because the 'precise final system configuration' remained unclear, and that this would remain so until the government decided on 'overall systems, ownership and financing'.[27] Cabinet moved forward based on aspiration, not hard numbers, and did not really pretend otherwise. Staley stated publicly in mid-1980, for example, that 'we have not made the decision to go satellite because the satellite is cost effective ... we are going for social policy reasons.'[28] By January 1981, the government was in talks with more than fifty companies about the planned system.[29]

The Fraser government was genuinely keen to foster greater private-sector involvement in Australia's telecommunications sector and sought business input on specifications for the satellite system, but its prime focus stayed firmly on broadcasting policy issues. Notwithstanding this, its economic officials and the business sector used the government's consultative process to urge a degree of liberalisation in telecommunications that went beyond the Coalition's comfort zone or policy ambition. In hindsight, this underlines the extent to which Fraser's government was caught between, on the one hand, the new telecommunications-related interests of its business constituency and the nascent rise of market liberalism, and on the other its strong commitment to the traditional universal service arrangements that continued to serve its core rural supporter base.

Finance and Treasury, the former still voicing opposition to satellite, both pushed for significant private-sector ownership and management of the satellite system. Treasury linked the private sector's investment appetite with 'the extent to which broadcasting and telecommunications policy is deregulated to permit the private sector to make use of the satellite services'.[30] The finance minister, Eric Robinson, similarly urged Staley to facilitate strong private-sector involvement in planning for the system to ensure that it did not ultimately serve only the public sector's needs.[31] The Trade Practices Commission had nailed its colours to the mast in the late 1970s, stating that 'public policy should not shield established firms or agencies from competition from new entrants who may have more efficient methods or new technology'. The commission wanted full competition between Telecom and a new satellite enterprise and argued that protecting Telecom's monopoly would 'exclude opportunities for competition in the provision of services which are important to business efficiency and costs and are important for social reasons as well'.[32]

At this point, in mid-1980, business was yet to organise collectively around its telecommunications interests. Nonetheless, during the consultation process on satellite, individual businesses made clear their strong wish to be freed from dependence on Telecom and their vulnerability to its unions. Staley was sensitive to these aspirations, advising cabinet that business 'would favour an alternative telecommunications system independent of the Telecom monopoly'.[33] And indeed, by late 1980 the new lobby group BTS was calling for telecommunications liberalisation in Australia along the lines of the United States, where inter-city services had long been open to competition.[34]

BTS was unimpressed with the Coalition's modest appetite for market liberalism. In early 1982, its head, Peter Holmes à Court, told Ian Sinclair, now the communications minister, that he was particularly concerned at the government's decision to establish Australia's new satellite operator, Aussat, as a wholly government-owned company, albeit with an aspiration to privatise up to 49 per cent of it at some point. Holmes à Court accurately observed that the Fraser government and BTS had 'totally different' concepts of private-sector involvement in telecommunications.[35]

After Australia's third national industrial dispute over telecommunications in three years, the government considered anew the mooted satellite system's potential to provide 'a degree of independence from the Telecom system, and trunk lines to diversify and strengthen the public switched network'.[36] These deliberations (from late 1981) reveal that the Fraser government's policy agenda fell well short of open competition in telecommunications services. They also show the extent to which uncertainty about the robustness of Australia's cross-subsidy model constrained meaningful consideration of deeper reform options. Cabinet could give an in-principle nod to liberalising private network arrangements, for example, only because it knew that this would not have any meaningful effect on Telecom's ability to fund its cross-subsidies.[37]

Beyond this, the Fraser government was focused more on reducing union power within the existing system than on changing the system itself. Officials noted, for example, that an additional benefit of the network redundancy provided by a national satellite system was the potential for greater 'diversity of union involvement'.[38] By this stage the government had already launched the Davidson inquiry into private-sector involvement in the telecommunications sector (discussed in the next chapter). In this context, cabinet endorsed further longer-term studies of 'the use of the domestic satellite for telecommunications purposes'.[39]

Telecom was essentially excluded from detailed planning for the satellite system, which was led by the Department of Post and Telecommunications, with close involvement from OTC.[40] Throughout 1980, Jack Curtis repeatedly but ineffectually contested the way the department presented technical information about Telecom's potential use of satellite to ministers. He also criticised the 'unduly optimistic scenarios' being promoted.[41] Telecom applied direct political pressure on the government too. In the lead-up to the 1980 election, it warned cabinet that a new satellite system might force 'sharp increases' in telephone call rates.[42] And after the Coalition's re-election, Curtis put his new minister, Ian Sinclair, on notice that 'unlimited competition' against Telecom would imperil existing universal service arrangements and 'inevitably lead to a radical change in the pricing, and availability of services'. This would be 'an unexpected outcome', Curtis observed, given that satellite was 'being portrayed as providing the solution to rural communication problems'.[43]

The Labor opposition did not play an especially consequential role in the satellite debate. Like the Coalition, it viewed satellite primarily through the prism of broadcasting policy. Labor's position was sceptically agnostic, focused on the project's lack of detail and its potential harm to Telecom. Following the party's second consecutive electoral thrashing in December 1977, and under new leadership for the first time in a decade, Labor worked to maintain an uneasy balance: to stay aligned with the telecommunications and media unions, which fiercely opposed the satellite project, while also avoiding being cast by the government as anti-progress stick-in-the-muds. Leading into the election, former Whitlam government minister Charlie Jones complained that for all anyone knew the proposed satellite system could cost anywhere from '$10 [million] to $100 million'.[44] In the Senate, shadow communications minister Susan Ryan repeatedly targeted the Coalition's inability to quantify the project's costs and benefits.[45] At the 1979 Labor national conference, the party's platform was updated to offer support for a national satellite system provided that, among other things, government funding for Telecom's facilities was maintained and the authority's remote area telephone and broadcasting services were expanded.[46]

An inherently disruptive force

It has long been a truism that the Fraser government talked more market liberalism than it walked. In telecommunications, those who wanted to retain the status quo, for whatever reason, were unsettled by claims such as Sinclair's declaration in 1982 that the new satellite system 'changes our ... notions of the organisational structure of the business of providing telecommunications services [and] makes it technically possible for private telecommunications firms to provide services alongside government telecommunications facilities'.[47] At the same time, these kinds of statements raised the hopes of those who wanted change. The Coalition was genuine in its conviction that the satellite project was in Australia's national interests (and also in its political interests), but its inherent conservatism and fidelity to traditional universal service objectives and cross-subsidy arrangements meant that, in practice, its decision-making consistently prioritised social policy considerations over private-sector interests.

An information paper released by the government in May 1982 stated that, once operational, the satellite system would enable 'remote and underserved' communities to receive television, radio and telephone services; provide 'distance education and telemedicine services' in Australia; make telephone and broadcasting services available in Papua New Guinea; fulfil the needs of the Transport Department; and be used by the ABC and, possibly, Australia's commercial broadcasters. Sinclair also told parliament that the system might one day facilitate 'private specialised communications networks [for] voice communications and the transfer of computer data' for large corporations and 'research bodies'.[48] BTS's unhappiness with where the Coalition's satellite deliberations had ended up has already been noted. For his part, Kerry Packer was scathing. Sinclair claims that, as minister, he saw Aussat as 'a compromise to embrace public policy and commercial purposes' and that the government's main focus was on ensuring that services were supplied to 'areas otherwise inadequately serviced' and to 'assist' Telecom with access to additional network capacity and reach.[49]

Regardless of the Fraser government's policy intent, its establishment of Aussat in 1981—amid tensions over the Davidson inquiry into the private sector's role in telecommunications—inserted an inherently disruptive force into Australia's telecommunications system. It meant that from the mid-1980s, when satellite came online, there would be a stand-alone government enterprise with the technical potential to replicate hitherto Telecom-only services. This had profound implications for the structure and assumptions that had previously underpinned Australian telecommunications provision. That the parameters of Aussat's operational activities would be set by government policy and regulation was irrelevant to its latent potential to break open Australia's closed telecommunications system, on which both sides of politics relied for the fulfilment of their social policy objectives.

As such, Aussat became another lightning rod for parties both for and against telecommunications liberalisation. It triggered immediate defensive responses from Telecom, which accelerated the rollout of its data networks and some rural programs and made adjustments to various service charges.[50] But its effects were most significant in the longer term, after the Fraser government's defeat. Aussat presented deep political challenges to the Hawke government that distorted its early decision-making and ultimately complicated and narrowed its policy options when it embarked on telecommunications reform in the latter 1980s.

6

Intractable Conundrums

*If we fail to provide the telecommunications services essential to
modern society we will not only create substantial hardships for
Australia but also miss the wave of technology which offers great
potential for social and economic benefits.*

Davidson report, 1982[1]

In April 1981, Malcolm Fraser announced the findings of the Review of
Commonwealth Functions, better known as the 'razor gang', which had
investigated ways to 'streamline and fine down' federal government activities,
including by shifting some to the states and leaving others to the private sector.
Not much escaped the gang's hunt for 'waste, duplication and unnecessary
costs', and Fraser had some justification for claiming it as 'the most significant
and far reaching ministerial undertaking of its kind ever undertaken by a federal
government'.

Fraser highlighted telecommunications, however, as a policy area that was
too 'complex' and with too many 'significant issues' for the review. Citing the
'technological explosion' underway and 'exciting opportunities for private activity
to introduce diversity and innovation' in telecommunications, Fraser suggested
that 'the traditional monopoly in this area can no longer be considered sacrosanct';
he committed the government to a separate 'major review' into Telecom 'to
determine the extent to which the services it offers might be more effectively
provided by the private sector', and he flagged transferring Telecom's technical
regulatory powers to 'an independent body'.[2]

Fraser was signalling that his government wanted to address the rising
commercial and economic pressures urging greater flexibility and openness in
Australia's telecommunications arrangements, while still ensuring that the system

continued to fulfil its traditional social policy role. There was also a political subtext that reflected the government's by then indifferent relationship with Telecom. But, as was frequently the case with Fraser, his words went further than his deeds. Though his rhetoric reflected the rising tide of market liberalism, Fraser remained a cautious traditionalist in telecommunications, with no agenda to overturn the Australian system.

Fraser viewed telecommunications policy through the prism of governmental responsibility to ensure the provision of essential services at affordable prices. Even at the peak of the national industrial disruption to services in 1979, he had dismissed any notion of the government 'divesting itself' of Telecom. He defended the existing cross-subsidy system, arguing that without it 'you just wouldn't have a service ... in many remote areas, in many rural areas, that could be afforded by the people'.[3] And though not then known publicly, the cabinet had specifically prevented the razor gang from considering reducing government ownership in Telecom or OTC (or Australia's airlines).[4] In fact, shortly after Fraser's statement in April, cabinet raised Telecom's capital borrowing limit for the first time in years, over objections from the Department of Finance.[5]

The Davidson inquiry

Five months later, the communications minister, Ian Sinclair, announced details of the government's Committee of Inquiry into Telecommunications Services in Australia. He foreshadowed changes to 'those areas in Telecom's activities now protected from competition'.[6] In the wake of the latest industrial dispute, he wondered whether Australia's telecommunications and postal monopolies had 'unwittingly spawned a union monster which can paralyse the whole country to serve its own short-term and sectional ends'.[7]

Sinclair recalls that as minister he had two overriding concerns: first, that the government wanted 'to attract significant investment from the private sector' into telecommunications because Telecom could not access sufficient capital in a tight public-sector environment; and second, that Telecom's productivity was not good enough, partly because the sector unions could 'determine whether or not there would be a service'. Sinclair says he was open to 'pursuing and experimenting with available options' to achieve greater flexibility and innovation, but Telecom's capacity to fulfil its traditional social role came first.[8]

Sinclair's retrospective comments are consistent with those he made at the time. In September 1981, he stated that the government did not want 'in any way to prejudice' Telecom's universal service activities, which were at the foundational core of national policy and, since 1975, had been set out in legislation. In exploring how the private sector might 'complement' the services provided by Telecom, the government's inquiry would consider the authority's revenues, costs and financial performance as well as 'the new technologies and equipment' that were animating the sector.[9] Later, Sinclair reiterated that regardless of the inquiry's findings, the Coalition would aim to marry its objective for 'the greatest efficiency of resources' with the commitment that 'all citizens, whether they live in the remote and isolated areas of Australia or the more rapidly growing centres of population' should have access to 'the services which are rightly expected of a communications authority'.[10] Even one of the Liberal Party's leading market liberals, Jim Carlton, stated that country people had nothing to fear from the government's inquiry. He said that the Coalition 'would come in and correct any failure of the market' if there was 'any suggestion' that Telecom's traditional universal service activities were being undermined.[11]

The inquiry's terms of reference were broadly drafted and highly contentious in light of Australia's inflamed industrial environment and concerns about the government's apparent market liberalism. Though the inquiry would take account of 'the continuing need to provide adequate telecommunications services throughout Australia', its mandate was to investigate 'the extent to which the private sector could be more widely involved in the provision of existing or proposed telecommunications services in Australia either alone, in competition with or in conjunction' with Telecom. It would also consider what 'consequential changes may be necessary in the statutory functions, duties, financial objectives and monopoly provisions' of Telecom and the effectiveness of Telecom's 'operational policies and organisational arrangements'.[12] As noted by journalist Deborah Snow, the Coalition was reviewing 'the whole basis of the relationship between Telecom and the private sector in providing telecommunications services'.[13]

Contemporary commentators were strongly critical of what they considered the Fraser government's radical agenda.[14] Yet it was reasonably clear even then that the Coalition's inquiry was underpinned by a traditional commitment to bipartisan social policy and universal service objectives. At the same time, it directly challenged the telecommunications establishment's institutional power, especially that of Telecom and the unions. The government appointed Jim Davidson, the long-term managing director of Commonwealth Industrial Gases, as inquiry chairman. He was joined by two other business figures: Malcolm King, who was already leading a related government inquiry into the telecommunications equipment sector, and William Dick, a former Victorian state cricketer now in the carpet textiles trade. The fourth member was Tony Karbowiak, a professor of electrical engineering at the University of New South Wales who had advised Telecom during its 1978 dispute with the ATEA.

The Davidson inquiry received more than 140 public and confidential submissions and conducted numerous hearings around the country. It provided an opportune advocacy platform for new lobby groups BTS and ATUG. Both called for more flexibility, innovation and choice from Australia's telecommunications sector, and more opportunities for the private sector, while acknowledging 'national interest requirements'.[15] But BTS and ATUG approached telecommunications policy differently: the former epitomised orthodox market liberalism, rooted particularly in the lived experience of the United States and Britain; whereas the latter, not unlike the Fraser government itself, represented a distinctly Australian outlook that somewhat awkwardly combined a strong practical imperative to free up the telecommunications system with a need to remain committed to traditional universal service objectives.

BTS's data-rich, sophisticated submission drew heavily on American precedents as 'the only available experience of competition in telecommunications services'. Since the advent of competition, it argued, local and long-distance call rates in the United States had dropped more than 40 per cent even as the long-distance call revenues of AT&T, the former monopolist, had grown by a quarter. BTS's central point was that a monopoly operator could no longer meet all market needs. In Australia's case, Telecom was failing to satisfy demand for modern business services: leased-line service provisioning took upwards of a year, and its planned data networks, which were not even configured for the latest applications, were significantly delayed. BTS wanted a form of structural separation for Telecom: the core network and basic services (telephone calls and line rentals) should remain in a cross-subsidising government monopoly responsible for universal service provision, while all 'enhanced' services should reside in a separate state enterprise that competed with private-sector operators in an open market governed by uniform network-access regulations.[16]

In contrast to BTS's ideological clarity, ATUG's submission synthesised the results of a survey of its members and therefore provides insight into the contemporary practical concerns and interests of Australia's largest private- and public-sector institutions. According to ATUG, these organisations wanted competition in the supply, installation and maintenance of modern telecommunications equipment, and were virtually unanimous in believing Telecom should operate more like a company, subject to tax and with its capital funded through standard business practices as determined by its board. But the great majority of them also wanted Telecom's monopoly service charges to be subject to public inquiry and appeal. About seven in ten agreed that Australia's traditional cross-subsidy model was the best means to ensure affordable universal services, with most also accepting an ongoing role for government and Telecom 'assistance ... to encourage local manufacturing of telecommunications products'.[17]

The long-established tensions within Australian telecommunications policy remained, but the nature of the debate was changing as Telecom's position in what was essentially a closed, self-sustaining service delivery and industry protection ecosystem was increasingly challenged by technological and commercial forces pushing for a more open, dynamic and multipolar model. Whereas political and policy attention had previously focused on the public provider's efficiency and effectiveness within the existing system, it was now broadening to consider the more complex and contentious question of how the system itself might need to change to accommodate new dynamics while still fulfilling traditional social policy objectives. Australia's cross-subsidy arrangements were a critical battleground in this highly charged debate. And in the context of the Davidson inquiry, a new term, 'cream-skimming', entered the popular lexicon.

The basic argument was that in a competitive market, private-sector operators would target the areas where Telecom enjoyed monopoly profits and, by winning this business from Telecom, would 'skim' the 'cream' that the organisation needed to subsidise the uneconomic services required if it was to fulfil social objectives. Telecom and its unions were, naturally, the fiercest proponents of this argument; Treasury and BTS were its most articulate opponents. Telecom mounted a thin-edge-of-the-wedge argument, asserting that liberalising access rules for the private networks used by large businesses and other organisations would open the floodgates to full competition along its lucrative inter-city routes. The Fraser government would pay a high political price if this happened, Telecom warned; it claimed its cross-subsidies were worth around $290 million and that any revenue leakage 'must result in an increase in average prices'.[18] The government faced several unsavoury choices, suggested Telecom: it could take the blame for higher telephone charges, or, if it decided to keep them as they were, it could expect flak for either raising Telecom's borrowing limit or tapping Treasury appropriations to cover the organisation's financial shortfall.

Treasury rightly pinpointed Telecom's cross-subsidies as the greatest barrier to reforming the telecommunications system. It dismissed claims that the monopoly profits Telecom received from its inter-city routes were justified because they funded uneconomic services. Treasury argued that this monopolistic 'cream' was a tax on all telecommunications users that 'would, in a generally competitive situation, be "skimmed"' not by competing telecommunications providers but 'by the consumers from whom it is currently extracted'. Treasury also reiterated its long-held position that, regardless of the political or practical difficulties, the economic costs of government directly financing telecommunications services provided in fulfilment of social policy would be less than that of persisting with the existing cross-subsidy framework.[19] The fundamental political problem was that successive governments had absolutely no idea what these cross-subsidies really cost, or the extent to which they could be reduced, nor any ready way to independently verify the financial and operational information provided by Telecom.

For its part, BTS asserted that even if Australia's private network arrangements were fully liberalised, with excess capacity on-sold to third parties, Telecom would retain the capacity to fund uneconomic services because only a small number of large organisations would operate such networks. According to BTS, the growth in private network usage would occur slowly enough for Telecom to adjust; and, citing American precedent, it argued that competition in 'enhanced' services would generate higher revenues for Telecom by driving greater traffic volumes over its network. Though significantly, BTS's bottom line was that government was ultimately responsible for ensuring the provision of basic essential services.[20] This meant that if for some reason Telecom could not fund the supply of these services, it was up to the government to pay. The crucial message for the Fraser government was that reforming the telecommunications system was not just an inherently uncertain business but that all key interests—including those advocating market liberalism—implicitly agreed that the political risk of any miscalculation would sit squarely with the government of the day.

The Davidson inquiry posed a clear and present danger to the telecommunications unions, but they inadvertently bolstered the case for reform by refusing to engage meaningfully with the forces pressing for greater openness and flexibility. The unions held to the line that 'there should be no extension of private sector involvement in telecommunications whatsoever ... Telecom should not be excluded from any telecommunications market and should retain its present monopoly in all markets.' They also argued for the government to remove all constraints on Telecom's borrowings and to keep its nose out of wage negotiations; Telecom should be free to 'determine its own staffing needs without interference'—except in the case of employing private contractors, who 'should not be used'.[21]

In denying any legitimacy to business and institutional requirements, the unions effectively confirmed that the status quo was untenable. Criticism that Telecom was not meeting organisations' needs was dismissed on the grounds that such customers represented only a fraction of Telecom's base. And when addressing the wave of industrial disputes in recent years, the unions ignored the impact on inter-city links, which were used mostly by businesses and other large organisations; they noted simply that 'in no case was the basic local community telephone network interrupted'. The unions also showed little awareness of the extent to which the recent disputes had prompted cabinet to look into structural vulnerabilities of Australia's telecommunications infrastructure, not least from the Telecom unions possessing exclusive coverage of essential-services workers. Indeed, the unions' inquiry submission threatened the government with further industrial action if it made 'any attempt to introduce contractors, open Telecom up to competition or privatise any of its functions'.[22]

The Davidson inquiry provoked ructions in Labor. Shadow communications minister John Button had made a measured submission that grappled with the conundrums confronting policy makers. He acknowledged the increasing importance of telecommunications for 'prosperity and jobs' and stated that Labor did 'not stand for regulation to obstruct business initiative[,] to create feather-bedded jobs or to preserve any existing arrangements'. In principle, the opposition saw 'no reason why there should not be private participation' in communications equipment such as telephone handsets, PABXs and modems, he said, though he maintained that Telecom should not face competition while responsible for providing universal services.

Button also argued that Australia's long-standing system of cross-subsidies was the only feasible mechanism to fund loss-making services: a true user-pays arrangement was 'politically unacceptable' and direct government funding was impractical. He wanted government policy to focus on applying targeted measures to drive productivity improvements in Telecom. Such measures might include 'strong private sector input into Telecom's planning processes' to keep it 'up-to-date and responsive', coupled with reductions in government controls over its borrowings and capital expenditure.[23]

The sector unions' response to Button's submission was immediate and harsh. APTU general secretary George Slater accused Button of supporting 'the dismantling of a vital and important asset owned by the Australian people' (despite Button's explicit statements to the contrary) and suggested he go 'sit on the other side of the Senate'.[24] The ATEA's Queensland branch wrote to each member of Labor's federal caucus calling for Button's sacking from the opposition front bench. With his place on Victoria's Labor Senate ticket soon looking shaky, Button surrendered. He sought to 'clarify' that Labor was in fact against telecommunications competition and any other measures that might weaken Telecom or the working conditions of union members.[25] At the party's national conference a few months later, Button dropped his proposed telecommunications policy in favour of the unions' version. This meant that Labor went to the 1983 election committed to Telecom's 'full participation in the provision of all terminal services' and to ensuring that the 'social and industrial costs' of technological change did not 'disadvantage those working in telecommunications, in terms of employment and working conditions'.[26]

Telecom accepted that the technological and commercial pressures for change were irreversible and so set out to shape its future operating environment in its own best interests. New managing director Bill Pollock led the charge, engaging extensively with MPs of all political shades, telecommunications equipment manufacturers and community groups, as well as with his minister, Ian Sinclair, and senior government officials.[27] Telecom proposed a model of 'controlled development'; it offered up some concessions in exchange for gaining specific freedoms. If the government granted it full access to all equipment markets, authority to enter into contracts without ministerial approval, and release from financial controls and industrial relations coordination rules, then Telecom would relax provisioning restrictions on private networks, provide more detailed financial reports, surrender some regulatory powers regarding equipment certification and offer network access for private-sector operators on the same terms as itself.[28]

Telecom's need for ministerial approval over contracts was particularly sensitive, as this had been how Staley and Sinclair had respectively blocked Telecom from markets for fax and answering machines and videotex. Sinclair's successor, Neil Brown, claims that when he became minister in May 1982, the only thing Pollock and Telecom's chairman, Robert Brack, wanted to talk about was 'the need to have the delegations increased to expand Telecom's power to enter into gigantic purchasing contracts without the minister's approval'. Brown says he refused to accede, because he considered this power to be central to the 'relative authority of the corporation and the minister'; the result was a spell of 'cool relations'.[29]

The Department of Communications (its new name since 1980) was uncertain about how to reconcile the conflicting forces pressing for change and continuity. It acknowledged the legitimacy of businesses' calls for greater attention to their needs and was open to Telecom being allowed to set up arms-length subsidiaries to compete with private-sector operators in equipment markets. But its overriding concern was safeguarding the provision of universal service. Like everyone else, the department depended on Telecom for the information on which to base its analysis. In this context, it accepted that any liberalisation-driven revenue leakage from Telecom would 'cut at the heart' of the cross-subsidy system; it therefore proposed that the cross-subsidies be enshrined in legislation.[30] The department's caution contributed to a risk-averse policy environment in which only the most marginal adjustments to the status quo could be contemplated for fear of the existing system unravelling.

A 'blueprint for revolution'

Neil Brown became communications minister while the Davidson inquiry was still deliberating and thus led the government's response to its report in October 1982. Davidson and his colleagues had done a good job of setting out the dynamics and pressure points of Australian telecommunications policy in the early 1980s, but they had fallen down when it came to providing a practical path forward. They warned that Australia would suffer 'substantial hardships [and] miss the wave of technology which offers great potential for social and economic benefits' if it failed to reconcile the right of 'every householder' to access a reasonably priced basic telephone with the business sector's need for 'a range and quality of telecommunications services' to maintain international competitiveness.[31] But how? They imagined a radically reworked telecommunications system and triggered a political storm.

As expected, the Davidson inquiry strongly favoured competition in Australian telecommunications. Competition was 'inevitable', it claimed, especially given the rapidly diversifying nature of technological developments and the expected national satellite system coming online in the mid-1980s. Any attempt to hold back this tide would be 'self-defeating'. The inquiry distinguished between Australia's telecommunications infrastructure and the equipment and services connected to it; it argued that Telecom's 'first priority' should be the former, that it had no legitimate role in the latter, provided an 'independent [technical] standards body' was in place. Telecom's recent expenditure of $224 million on equipment such as PABXs was sharply criticised for usurping the private-sector's role; according to the inquiry, its money should have been spent on its network.

The inquiry recommended full competition across all services over all networks, including alternative communications networks that interconnected with Telecom's infrastructure, the satellite network once operational and any future cable television networks. If private-sector operators could exploit commercial opportunities 'in any facet of telecommunications', the Australian public would ultimately benefit from lower prices, better service and greater choice. Telecom would only 'suffer from exposure to competition if it did not satisfy market demand'. To facilitate a competitive sector in equipment, where the immediate pressure was strongest, the inquiry favoured Telecom's structural separation. Telecom would become a government-owned company responsible for terrestrial network infrastructure. Another state entity would be established to take over all equipment-related activities, including customer premise wiring, installation and maintenance. It was envisaged that the new entity would compete in an open market with private-sector operators and all parties would access Telecom's infrastructure on equivalent terms.[32]

According to the Davidson inquiry, reconstituting Telecom as an incorporated company would ensure its 'full commercial orientation', freeing it from any obligations to provide unprofitable services or preference local industry. The report stated that Telecom's accounting practices also needed updating. With some irony, given the key part that Telecom's apparently bumper profits had played in the industrial disputes of 1978–81, the inquiry criticised Telecom's use of historical cost when valuing its fixed assets because this understated its depreciation costs and gave rise to 'misleading conclusions as to the profitability of the business'. Analysis commissioned by the inquiry found that, had Telecom valued its fixed assets more conventionally at current cost, its reported surplus in 1980/81 would have plunged by 98 per cent, from $228 million to just $4 million.[33]

Davidson and his colleagues accepted the policy objective of affordable universal service provision, but they did not see this as Telecom's responsibility. Their report stated that 'any social welfare or national development initiative which government wishes to implement through subsidised telecommunications should be funded from outside Telecom'—that is, directly funded by the government.[34]

At this point the inquiry's findings became essentially useless to the Fraser government. Davidson's model relied on transferring risk and responsibility for universal service provision from Telecom to government while simultaneously reducing the government's jurisdiction over Telecom's operations. The inquiry report argued that government already bore these responsibilities by way of the ministerial powers contained in the 1975 Telecommunications Act, but this interpretation relied on a selective and literal reading of the Act and ignored how the politics, policy and operation of telecommunications had evolved in Australia.[35]

Having transferred social responsibilities to the government, Davidson and his colleagues then took to its logical conclusion the well-established principle of cost-based pricing for telecommunications services: Telecom 'should provide subsidy only where it supports its business interests' and, in general, 'should not cross-subsidise services'. Government should provide subsidies for commercially unviable telephone services directly to end users.[36] This recommendation stood no chance under either Labor or the Coalition. A core priority of both Whitlam and Fraser had been to reduce government spending on telecommunications: for Whitlam it was to fund Labor's social programs, while for Fraser it was to cut public-sector fat. The recommendation would have been particularly unappealing for the Fraser government considering that it had divested itself of budgetary responsibility for Telecom just three years earlier.

The Davidson inquiry argued convincingly that reasonable price uniformity could be maintained under a cost-based pricing framework and that such a model would be less discriminatory, because it would reduce the extent to which some classes of customers subsidised others, regardless of need or capacity to pay. On this issue, the inquiry had found common cause with Whitlam, except that where Whitlam's concern had been for the urban poor subsidising the rural wealthy, the inquiry's concern was with struggling businesses. It called for ongoing increases to line rental charges and reductions to call rates and, in an economically rational but politically vexed recommendation, the introduction of timed local calls. Inquiry modelling found that if Telecom charged local calls in three-minute increments it could reduce the current rate by 40 per cent without losing any revenue; or, if it maintained the local call rate at the current level, revenues would increase by over 70 per cent without raising total calling costs for two-thirds of local calls made.[37]

Another reason that the inquiry wanted Telecom reconstituted as an incorporated company was to reduce government control over its operations. Telecom's board was to be 'the "source" of policy', though it would be appointed by government and Telecom's chairman would be expected to 'ensure that the views of government are taken into account'. Ministerial powers would be explicitly excluded from any matters related to 'revenues, management or resources', including price setting, borrowings and contractual arrangements, employment terms and procurement. Though under this plan Telecom would be obliged to ensure that its network had sufficient capacity to supply basic services to all Australians where 'reasonably practicable', the minister could only direct Telecom regarding supply or maintenance if Telecom and the commonwealth had already agreed financial terms that made it commercially rational for Telecom to do so.[38] This represented a fundamental power shift; it stripped the government of the means to ensure universal service provision without negotiating a commercial agreement with Telecom beforehand. No federal government would agree to this, not least the Fraser government, which considered that Telecom had too much power as it was. When the Hawke government turned its mind to telecommunications reform some five years later, it reached much the same conclusion.

Reality check

In the Davidson inquiry we see the Fraser government's attempt to reconcile the new dynamics in telecommunications with Australia's traditional social objectives and structural arrangements. The government also hoped to reduce union leverage over the telecommunications system and relieve pressure on public-sector borrowing and expenditure. A particular dilemma for Fraser's government was that its core business constituency was calling for more openness and flexibility in the telecommunications system and more opportunities for private-sector involvement, but these demands posed a direct threat to the Coalition's rural support base.

The Davidson inquiry envisaged overturning eighty years of Australian telecommunications policy norms and structural development. It radically reimagined telecommunications as a conventional business activity and, in doing so, sought to transfer all the risks and responsibilities associated with fulfilling bipartisan social policy objectives directly to the government. At its best, the inquiry underlined the key pressure points in Australia's telecommunications sector and provided a robust analytical framework to underpin further policy work. But the fundamental message that it gave the Fraser government (and other interested parties) was that addressing the business sector's telecommunications needs and capturing for Australia the economic upside of technological changes was, in practice, incompatible with the Australian telecommunications system's capacity to continue meeting social policy aims. And in revealing the complexity of embarking on even incremental changes, Davidson and his colleagues left policy makers overwhelmed.

It needs to be noted that as the 1980s dawned, no Australian government of any political persuasion could have decided to initiate significant telecommunications reform on the basis of hard evidence. The cases for and against liberalisation were credible, but Telecom had such a big advantage over all other parties, including government, in terms of technical and operational knowledge that its self-interested arguments against greater competition (for example) were insurmountably formidable. The Fraser government—and indeed the Whitlam government before it and the Hawke government after it—had little idea how sensitive Telecom's revenues really were in terms of its financial capacity to sustain the cross-subsidisation of uneconomic services. And critically, the political and financial risks of reform would clearly be borne by government. Even BTS, which argued compellingly that competition would not stop Telecom from being able to fund loss-making services internally, ultimately allocated the risk of any policy misjudgement to government.

With few international precedents to draw on, telecommunications liberalisation would have required the Fraser government to take a major leap of faith. Britain's new prime minister, Margaret Thatcher, had taken such a leap in 1980.

Although an inquiry commissioned by her government advised that the economic case for networks-based competition was 'poor', she went ahead anyway, establishing a new state-owned corporation, British Telecom, opening the equipment sector to full competition, and licensing a new carrier, Mercury Communications.[39] Taking such a step would have been uncharacteristic for the traditionalist Fraser but, in any case, the Coalition was caught between the conflicting interests of its subsidy-dependent rural base and its business constituency, which was now collectively organised and pushing for its own needs and vision for Australia's telecommunications sector.

When Neil Brown tabled the Davidson inquiry report in parliament, he proclaimed it 'a milestone in the history of telecommunications in Australia' and labelled its recommendations 'momentous'. Putting his best foot forward, Brown welcomed the 'vigorous' debate surely to come and invited 'community comments'.[40] The *Australian Financial Review* summed things up well: the report contained 'a blueprint for revolution' yet ignored 'the party political realities' not just between the Coalition and Labor but also within the Coalition itself.[41]

Labor immediately came out against the inquiry's recommendations, warning of a 'fragmented chaotic telephone service' and 'enormous' price rises.[42] The Australian Democrats, which since mid-1981 had held the Senate balance of power, were also opposed.[43] And behind the scenes, the National Country Party's deputy leader (and now defence minister) Ian Sinclair was reportedly encouraging Telecom's managing director, Bill Pollock, to uphold the authority's traditional social role.[44] Public petitions were soon circulating expressing concern about, among other things, the impact of timed local calls on the 'house bound frail aged and disabled; the lonely seeking help; the very many living on their own [and] people in rural areas'.[45]

Brown, his departmental officials and Telecom were soon negotiating a path forward. Telecom was accustomed to spotlighting its commercial functions when pushing for greater autonomy, but this time the telecommunications giant highlighted the core social responsibilities that were, at the end of the day, the political guarantor of its pre-eminence and power. Telecom reiterated to Brown that it 'must exercise a social responsibility and not only a commercial responsibility'. Cost-based pricing was fine in principle, said Telecom, but 'cannot be applied without regard to existing social circumstances'; going down the Davidson route risked 'profound social effects'.[46]

On 3–4 February 1983, Brown signed off on two cabinet submissions that gave his assessment of the political and policy state of play and his views on what the government should do next. His advice underlined the conundrums that cabinet faced, not just over telecommunications policy but also over the extent to which Australia's telecommunications system was intricately interconnected with various embedded industry-preference arrangements and economic policies. Cabinet was urged to 'make some early decisions [to] create scope for private sector involvement, provide stimulus for industrial and commercial development and employment growth' so as to 'loosen up the present monopoly arrangements'—but 'at the same time' it needed to take account of 'social and community factors' such as ensuring that Telecom continued providing services 'as a standard charge, supported by cross-subsidisation'.

Cabinet's challenge was to identify the 'perimeters' of Telecom's activities and determine the extent to which it should enjoy monopoly rights. A key problem, Brown noted, was that most of the Davidson inquiry's recommendations were, in the absence of more detailed evaluation, 'far too complex' to decide on. The cabinet was advised to rule out 'at this stage' a move towards independent telecommunications networks, whether based on Telecom leased lines or, when available, satellite, as they might 'disadvantage Telecom revenues'.[47] And so, regarding this top business priority, Brown was reduced to simply encouraging Telecom to 'adopt a more liberal attitude'—something that Telecom considered it was already doing—and also urging the authority to 'make special efforts' to improve its customer service.[48]

Brown proposed that cabinet postpone consideration of particularly contentious issues, such as 'cost-related pricing and the progressive reduction of cross-subsidisation', until after the next election, which was due by the end of the year, and that other difficult issues such as Telecom's financial objectives and obligations be put off until after Aussat's launch, potentially two elections away.[49] Any consideration of Telecom's structural separation was also 'premature', he submitted; instead, and consistent with Telecom's preferred position, he recommended obliging Telecom to institute a system of 'separate accounting' for its monopoly and competitive activities. The Davidson inquiry's politically poisonous preference for timed local calls was rejected out of hand. Brown noted that the idea had been 'vehemently opposed in representations I have received' and, ignoring the inquiry's compelling financial modelling, he stated that he could 'see no good reason' to proceed with it.

Cabinet's attention was instead directed to the low-hanging fruit—the relatively straightforward, non-contentious recommendations that could be 'implemented forthwith' because Telecom was agreeable or was already implementing them as part of its operational plans. The most significant change put forward by Brown was permitting private-sector operators to supply, install and maintain equipment such as small business systems, PABXs and teleprinters—a move Telecom concurred with provided that it was 'freely able to participate' and also retained its monopoly over the supply of the first telephone handset.[50] Telecom was also willing to surrender its technical standards-setting role to an independent body, the Standards Association of Australia, if the government wanted to go that way, but flagged the risk of 'delays and difficulties' and claimed that some equipment providers were already 'having second thoughts about the wisdom of disturbing the present arrangements'.[51]

In the lead-up to a cabinet meeting on 8 February, the Prime Minister's Department advised Fraser that the underlying 'conflict' between the economic and social aspects of Australia's telecommunications policy meant that ministers would ultimately have to make 'judgments … about the appropriate weight to be given to efficiency as opposed to social considerations'. As such, he was urged to avoid making any firm commitments one way or the other—even on Brown's cautiously phased approach—until all options had been more thoroughly evaluated, including by Telecom.[52] This is not to suggest that senior officials in Fraser's department opposed liberalising the telecommunications system. Indeed, they encouraged Fraser not to rule out timed local calls (even though this 'may be strongly resented by some domestic users') because there were strong equity-based arguments in favour, not least that businesses were currently able to 'tie up the network' transmitting data and faxes for the fixed price of a local call.[53]

Though it is hard to imagine Fraser ever being receptive to timed local calls, it is reasonable to presume that he would have supported Brown's carefully crafted plan. But by the time cabinet's coordination committee met to consider Brown's proposals, the Coalition was in the midst of an election campaign. On 3 February, Fraser called a snap poll in a misjudged bid to wrongfoot Labor over leadership jostling between Bill Hayden and Bob Hawke. In this context, the committee resolved, and cabinet agreed, that the government 'announce immediately' its continued commitment to Telecom's traditional roles and responsibilities;

that it rejected outright timed local calls and higher connection and line rental charges; and that, if re-elected, it would explore options for greater private-sector involvement 'in ancillary and new services'.[54]

Brown reassured the public that Telecom would 'remain, as it has been, the national terrestrial common carrier in telecommunications'. He characterised Telecom's cross-subsidy arrangements as 'essential ... in a country as large as Australia', repudiated the concept of timed local calls and, for good measure, promised that a re-elected Fraser government 'will not be implementing recommendations of the Davidson report which would change the traditional methods of paying for telecommunications services in Australia'.[55] Brown has since acknowledged that cabinet's intent was to avoid doing or saying anything that might 'frighten the horses'; telecommunications policy was placed in a 'holding pattern ... until after the election'.[56]

This was less the 'striking public policy reversal' perceived by the historian Ann Moyal than a reminder of the structural rigidity of Australia's telecommunications system and, more significantly, the mutual incompatibility at that time between the forces pressing for greater openness and flexibility of the system and its continued capacity to provide affordable universal services.[57] The Davidson inquiry ultimately failed to provide the Fraser government with any practical assistance in grappling with this conundrum. In fact, the inquiry proposed a reform model that could only address the new dynamics in Australian telecommunications by shifting direct risk and responsibility for uneconomic services onto the government. This not only ignored political reality but also announced, in effect, that the task of resolving this policy problem fell somewhere between perilously complicated and utterly insoluble.

For all the blood, sweat and tears shed on telecommunications policy during the Fraser government's third term, it failed to rate a single mention in the prime minister's campaign speech or that of the National Country leader, Doug Anthony.[58] The government's election policy did acknowledge that many changes had swept the sector since 1975, but in substance it was little more than a rehashing of traditional positions leavened with unsubtle attempts to ease concerns over liberalisation. The Coalition's overarching objective was 'to improve the access of all Australians to communications services [and] ensure all Australians get the best possible communications services at the lowest cost'. Aussat got a nod for bringing radio, television and telephones to 'areas which do not now have services'.

The Davidson inquiry's haunting presence could be heard in the Coalition's restated commitment to Telecom's traditional roles and responsibilities and its promise—printed in bold in its election manifesto—not to 'adopt timed local calls'. And in a statement that barely moved the dial from its 1975 telecommunications policy, the Coalition reiterated its support for 'encouraging private enterprise so that Australians will be able to take advantage of the major technological developments that are taking place in this area'.[59] But for all the conventional and rather timid aspects of the Coalition's policy, the Fraser government in its third term had genuinely sought to find ways to reconcile the new forces for change in telecommunications with long-standing bipartisan social objectives.

The Labor Party, in contrast, was still effectively in denial about the complex political and policy challenges in telecommunications. The unions had easily crushed Button's nascent attempt to chart a middle way forward and, in his 1983 election policy speech, new opposition leader Bob Hawke promised that under Labor, Telecom would be the 'base provider for all new information systems'; alternative telecommunications networks would be banned, and traditional cross-subsidy and 'Buy Australia' arrangements would be protected.[60] Internal polling by the Coalition and Labor reportedly picked up community angst about the potential impact of reform on telephone prices, and in marginal government seats, including Brown's, the ATEA campaigned alongside Labor on these concerns.[61] On 5 March, the Fraser government was swept aside by Labor. Australia's telecommunications establishment had good reason to be pleased with the result.

7

Turning Back the Tide

*Ministers will recall that when we first took office in 1983 we
confirmed that Telecom's traditional role would continue.*

Michael Duffy, 1985[1]

Immediately on winning office, Hawke and his economic ministers were consumed
by unexpectedly severe economic and budgetary challenges. A national economic
summit was scheduled for April, in fulfilment of a campaign promise, and a
major economic policy statement by new treasurer Paul Keating was set for May.
Treasury and Finance officials prepared a range of proposals to be considered by
cabinet's newly created Expenditure Review Committee (ERC), which comprised
Hawke, Keating, finance minister John Dawkins, employment and industrial
relations minister Ralph Willis and resources and energy minister Peter Walsh. To
the extent that the ministers turned their minds to telecommunications policy, it
was through the narrow prism of budgetary repair.

Budgetary repair

One lucrative proposal was to abolish Telecom's exemption from commonwealth
tax, which the ERC thought would be worth about $100 million for 1983/84
alone. But taxing Telecom raised contentious issues for Labor. Department of
Communications officials pointedly advised that the idea was 'clearly derived
from the Davidson report' and posed a threat to 'the whole basis' of Telecom's
ability to fund affordable universal services. The Prime Minister's Department
similarly warned that such a move could 'imply an endorsement of Davidson' and
would likely trigger a union backlash.[2] Given all this, the ministers opted for a
plan B approach suggested by Treasury and Finance: Telecom would get to keep

its tax exemption, but would have to pay into federal coffers an additional $100 million—an amount equivalent to its nominal tax liability. Cabinet endorsed the ERC's decision on 16 May, three days before Keating was to make his statement.[3]

Such was cabinet's focus on the forward estimates that it also agreed in principle to proceed with the Fraser government's plan to privatise up to 49 per cent of Aussat, so long as a 'wide spread' of shareholders could be secured and the 'public interest' was protected. This decision overrode strong opposition from the Communications Department, which saw 'an inherent risk of conflict of interest' between private-sector investment in Aussat and universal service delivery. More significantly, the decision was made despite the caucus and union unrest that would inevitably follow. It also sidestepped the fact that the government at this point had not even confirmed if it would go ahead with the satellite project. Treasury and Finance were pleased, making it clear that they would be happy to see most of Aussat sold off. They asserted, in what would become an oft-repeated argument, that state ownership was not necessary for policy control; this could be achieved through licensing powers and contractual arrangements governing Aussat's activities.[4]

Putting Davidson to bed

During Labor's first two terms in government, from 1983 until mid-1987, telecommunications policy was left to Michael Duffy, an ex-solicitor representing an outer-suburban Melbourne electorate. Duffy had come to the non-cabinet communications portfolio from the backbench without any relevant policy experience or apparent interest. A caucus colleague reportedly quipped unkindly that Duffy's understanding of his new portfolio was limited to 'how to turn the TV on'.[5] What Duffy did have, however, was a personal connection to Hawke (who later described him as an 'unspectacular but effective' minister) through their shared love of horse racing and his early backing of Hawke's leadership aspirations.[6]

Whatever Duffy's views on communications policy might have been when he was appointed minister, they soon mirrored those of Telecom and his department. After six months in office, Hawke's cabinet had made various uncoordinated tactical decisions affecting the communications portfolio but was yet to reach considered positions on the most urgent big-ticket issues. These were, specifically, responding to the Davidson inquiry's recommendations and deciding what to do about Aussat.

In September 1983, Duffy moved to lock the government into a policy position that unambiguously rejected the Fraser government's nascent liberalisation agenda, declaring to cabinet that it was time 'to put Davidson to bed'. Focusing on Telecom's 'social responsibilities', Duffy equated, without qualification, the 'preservation of cross-subsidisation arrangements' with universal service provision and argued that 'reaffirmation of the national monopoly' was needed to ensure price stability, employment opportunities and the viability of Australia's domestic telecommunications manufacturing sector.[7]

He acknowledged the pace and scale of technological change and the 'pressure from business and industry for improved and enhanced telecommunications', but his focus was on incumbent producer interests (which meant Telecom, the telecommunications unions and local equipment manufacturers) rather than on the complex issues associated with the dynamic drivers of innovation and growth. Regarding business and institutional telecommunications users, Duffy accepted Telecom's assurances that it would 'introduce new services expeditiously' so long as it had 'access to the necessary funds'. He supported ruling out competition to Telecom in the equipment sector in order to 'reassure' local manufacturers, which were vulnerable to imports, and 'encourage' Telecom's continued local investment.

Duffy's case was bolstered by a report from Telecom that was markedly more assertive in tone than the one the authority had prepared for Neil Brown eight months earlier. Regarding the quick-win initiatives that Brown had proposed to Fraser's cabinet in February that year, and which Telecom had supported, the authority made clear that they 'stood on their own merits' and, crucially, 'owed nothing' to Davidson. While reasserting traditional positions and prerogatives, Telecom also rescinded its earlier concessions about giving up regulatory powers and being amenable to open competition in the equipment sector. Telecom's revised position was that it was best placed to control the pace and scope of liberalisation while paying 'due regard' to 'the interests of customers, the local industry and employment within Telecom'. Regarding Aussat, Telecom stepped back from its earlier acceptance of an independent satellite operator and made a play to take over the system itself, on the grounds that it was 'clearly best placed both technically and operationally to integrate the satellite facilities into the national telecommunications and service delivery infrastructures efficiently and effectively' and, contingent on funding, 'stands ready to do so'.[8]

Duffy argued that if cabinet was to uphold Hawke's public statements during the 1983 election campaign, it had to reject Davidson's proposals. A 'painstaking consideration by ministers of each recommendation' was a waste of time, given that the result was 'not really in doubt'. He urged outright 'rejection ... based on our general policy and principles'. He believed such a move would ease public concerns about higher telephone charges and be welcomed by the sector unions 'as a predictable victory'. He even suggested, somewhat optimistically, that business would take heart from Telecom's 'assurances of a more liberal approach', pointedly dismissing the import of any criticism by 'specialised business interests' such as ATUG.

The government's economic policy officials were uneasy. Finance counselled against a blanket rejection of the Davidson inquiry because Australia's telecommunications sector was crucial to the nation's economic performance and its 'operations and future development have wide-ranging ramifications for most organisations and individuals in Australia—in their capacities as owners, users, suppliers and/or employers'. Treasury similarly warned that even if cabinet resolved to 'set aside' the inquiry's report, ministers would ultimately have to consider 'many of the issues' it had identified because technological developments would continue to disrupt the status quo. Furthermore, Australia's national satellite system would be operational in just two years. The Prime Minister's Department and the Industry and Commerce Department also pushed for competition in the equipment and videotex sectors because they did not interact with Telecom's core monopoly.[9] One senior official in Hawke's department noted privately that 'if there was one body which would benefit from new blood (and especially commercial competition) it is Telecom'.[10]

In the end, Duffy won the day. Cabinet agreed to reject 'the major thrust' of the Davidson inquiry. But it paid lip service to the importance of innovation and flexibility in Australia's telecommunications sector, formally noting Duffy's 'assurance' (which neither he nor any minister could really uphold) that Telecom would 'not be allowed' to leverage its network and regulatory powers to impede competition or unfairly advantage itself.[11]

Battles over Aussat

Having put Davidson to bed, Duffy turned his attention to tying up the loose ends around Aussat. As in the case of Davidson, the government's economic policy officials were deeply at odds with Duffy and his department. The feeling was mutual; in July 1983, officials from the Department of Communications accused the Finance Department of intentionally seeking to 'mislead' the government by circulating a projected cost for the satellite project of $650 million, nearly three times its own estimate.

Finance remained greatly concerned about the project's financial viability, notwithstanding Aussat's bullish assertions to the contrary. With prescience, it pointed out that the company's future depended 'very heavily' on government decisions about how far it was permitted to compete with Telecom, and under what terms; on whether private-sector investment would 'in fact eventuate'; and on the degree to which broadcasters were given access to the satellite system's capacity and facilities. Finance also reminded cabinet that, though Aussat itself might not require on-budget funding, the fact that between 59 and 80 per cent of its revenues would come from public-sector organisations meant that the satellite system would have a budgetary impact for the foreseeable future.[12] Countering this view was a coterie of satellite boosters, including the new Labor government in Western Australia, the Northern Territory's conservative government and the commonwealth's own Australian Science and Technology Council (ASTEC).

The Prime Minister's Department expressed concern to Hawke about the vehemence of Finance's opposition to the satellite project, though it did concur with the one matter on which Finance and Communications agreed. This was that, putting aside all other considerations, it was simply too expensive to terminate the project, given the costs already incurred and the contractual commitments already made. Cabinet agreed, and on 13 July it resolved to proceed as planned under Fraser.[13]

With satellite locked in, Duffy began pushing for cabinet to reverse its May decision in favour of Aussat's partial privatisation and to instead support Telecom's takeover of the company. He said that cabinet's earlier decision reflected a 'lack of wisdom', whereas allowing Telecom to absorb Aussat would be consistent with Labor's policy platform and its election commitment to ensuring a single telecommunications network. He also pointed out that, in practical terms, the government had no hope of realising any budgetary benefits from selling equity in Aussat in the 1983/84 financial year.[14] Duffy received unreserved support from Labor's left and the sector unions, which were also campaigning for a Telecom takeover, and qualified backing from Telecom, which argued that Aussat could become a subsidiary or operating division so long as funding was provided to offset the company's forecast short-term losses.[15] But just about everyone else was opposed.[16]

Having failed to have the satellite project cancelled, Telecom's unions were driving for Aussat's absorption into Telecom as a means of expanding their industrial coverage over the satellite system. Indeed, the Conciliation and Arbitration Commission was already considering a separate bid by the ATEA to gain coverage over Aussat's technical staff. In light of the ATEA's industrial muscle-flexing under Fraser, this development was deeply concerning for satellite's prospective commercial users; Duffy admitted to cabinet that some potential Aussat customers might boycott the system if the ATEA gained coverage.[17]

Media mogul Kerry Packer personally shirt-fronted Hawke, Keating and Duffy on the issue, and the major media company AAP lobbied hard against Telecom control.[18] In a clumsy attempt to counter fears about union control of an integrated terrestrial-satellite telecommunications network, APTU secretary-general Rob Arndt wrote to Lionel Bowen, the deputy prime minister (and former postmaster-general under Whitlam), warning that his union would 'resent' any hint of Labor giving credence to such views. He offered to give Bowen 'chapter and verse' on the issue. Bowen declined.[19]

All key government agencies opposed Duffy's plan. The Prime Minister's Department, Treasury, Finance and ASTEC wanted cabinet's 49 per cent privatisation decision to stand. Their fall-back, in the event of cabinet rescinding this position, was to keep Aussat as a separate company. Hawke's department advised him that a Telecom–Aussat merger would likely reduce the benefits of the satellite system by 'preventing healthy competition at the margin' of the terrestrial and satellite networks. ASTEC similarly worried that bringing satellite under Telecom would militate against 'the most innovative use of the technology'. The Department of Industrial Relations maintained its long-standing preference for an independent satellite network as a means to keep a section of Australia's communications infrastructure out of the sector unions' hands.[20] But the most vociferous opponent of Duffy's plan was Aussat, as the company's widely respected chairman, David Hoare, made very clear in a lengthy letter to Duffy in August.[21] Aussat's chief executive, Graham Gosewinckel, on the other hand, sought to soothe Labor sensitivities, publicly recanting his pre-election prediction that Aussat presaged the end of Telecom's monopoly and stating instead that the national satellite system would 'complement the terrestrial network [and] should not be seen as some sort of competitor to Telecom'.[22]

As with anything to do with telecommunications or privatisation, the Aussat issue was debated intensely in caucus. At some point between late October and early November, Duffy dropped his Telecom takeover proposal for a factional compromise backed by Hawke, Keating and Dawkins. Under this deal, cabinet would revoke its earlier part-privatisation decision in favour of Telecom taking a 25 per cent equity stake in Aussat. When caucus communications committee member John Saunderson, a member of Labor's left and a former ATEA official, sought to push ahead with a Telecom–Aussat merger, Duffy was among the slim majority who lined up to defeat the motion. The ERC agreed on 14 November to lift Telecom's borrowings ceiling to enable its part-acquisition of Aussat; cabinet rubber-stamped this view later that day, resolving also to enshrine the arrangement in legislation 'to prevent the sale of any shareholding in Aussat without the consent of … Parliament'.[23]

The Telecom–Aussat equity deal was the Hawke government's means of acceding to widespread opposition to Telecom's taking over the planned satellite system while still complying with Labor policy and, more to the point, obliging caucus and the unions. But the terms of the deal (and of Labor's 1984 Satellite Communications Act) jeopardised Aussat's commercial viability and, as a direct consequence, played a fundamental role in shaping Labor's later actions over telecommunications reform. With a 25 per cent stake in Aussat, Telecom gained two board positions, which, combined with new legislative restrictions on Aussat's activities, put it in the box seat to ensure that the satellite company served Telecom's own interests or, at the very least, did not act against them.

A few years later, when the government's telecommunications agenda had shifted towards liberalisation, Duffy's ministerial successor, the Victorian senator Gareth Evans, explicitly reminded his cabinet colleagues that the whole point of 'allowing' Telecom to take a stake in Aussat had been to give it a role in the 'strategic and policy decisions of the company'.[24] Under the 1984 Act, Aussat was prohibited from providing any public switched voice or data services (that is, not only basic telephone services but also the more complex and innovative services sought by business) in competition with Telecom or OTC. The legislative lock on Aussat's shareholdings also meant that the company could not raise capital by publicly issuing shares, a factor that became increasingly significant as its financial performance deteriorated.[25]

Though the Liberal and National parties welcomed a legislative framework that ensured satellite would proceed and accepted barring Aussat from providing public switched voice and data services on practicality grounds, they criticised other restrictions that 'unnecessarily protected and pandered' to Telecom. The opposition was especially critical of Telecom's 25 per cent share of Aussat, and the fact that Aussat was subject to constraints—such as a prohibition on forming subsidiaries or joint ventures and requiring ministerial approval to permit third parties to access leased or private lines—that did not apply to Telecom.[26]

Parties and policies at the 1984 election

On 8 October 1984, Hawke called an early election. After a long campaign, in which the Prime Minister was distracted by family problems and opposition leader Andrew Peacock's performance exceeded expectations, Labor was re-elected with a reduced majority in an enlarged House of Representatives. There was no hint of new government thinking on telecommunications. Hawke spoke of Australia becoming an exporter of advanced services and technology and promised cuts to business-inhibiting red tape, but telecommunications was not on his list of economic sectors in need of reform.[27] To the extent that Hawke's government was focused on the pressures bearing down on Australia's traditional telecommunications arrangements, its policy settings suggested that its priority remained defending the telecommunications establishment—Telecom, the sector unions and local equipment manufacturers—by building up Telecom's power. The government was content to accept Telecom's assurances that it could and would fulfil the increasingly diverse needs of its business and institutional customers.

The Coalition's formal adoption of market liberalism after its defeat in 1983 helped bring some clarity to its telecommunications policy framework, while also foreshadowing in broad terms the reform steps ultimately taken by Labor. The opposition's communications policy for the 1984 election declared that the 'only way' for Australia to reap the benefits of technological advances was through 'a more market-orientated, entrepreneurial, innovative and diverse framework with a minimum of government regulation and control'. In an explicit nod to the Davidson inquiry, the policy committed a Coalition government to reconstituting Telecom as a government-owned public company; privatising up to 49 per cent of Aussat; reviewing OTC's ownership structure; and, as Fraser had flagged in 1981, establishing an independent regulator to set 'Telecom charges and telecommunications standards'. On competition, the Coalition's policy drew from Neil Brown's recommendations to Fraser's cabinet in February 1983, promising that private-sector providers of new equipment-based services would be able to compete with Telecom.

Notwithstanding this, the Coalition remained committed to Telecom's common carrier monopoly, to ensure 'a modern telephone system at reasonable cost including the right to a local call on an untimed basis', and to accelerating the authority's long-running rural and remote area connection and upgrade program. It also supported retention of OTC's monopoly over international services, though Aussat's 'structure, role and restrictions' were slated for review. The Coalition further foreshadowed subjecting Telecom, OTC and Aussat to external (albeit unspecified) efficiency and accountability measures.[28]

The role of economic policy officials

Soon after its re-election, the Hawke government faced severe economic headwinds. Australia's deteriorating terms of trade and widening current account deficit were pushing net foreign debt up and the dollar down. In his cabinet diary, Gareth Evans recorded Treasurer Keating's 'scatological' warnings that the dollar was falling faster and harder than expected and that the top economic priority was budget deficit-busting (a process Evans characterised as 'sacrificial agony').[29] This was the perfect storm that prompted Keating's famous warning in May 1986 that if Australia continued along this path, it was 'basically done for. We will end up being a third rate economy ... a banana republic'.[30] It was also the policy prism through which the government's economic ministers continued to view telecommunications. Telecom consequently became a key ERC target during the painful budget preparations for 1985/86 and 1986/87.

An early decision was to require Telecom to repay $35 million (from internal sources, not borrowing) of the federal debt it had inherited from the PMG in

1975, thus reducing the budget deficit by the same amount.[31] The view was that Telecom could raise most of this sum by increasing local call rates by a cent.[32] Somewhat ironically, this quick fix was almost immediately offset when Aussat unexpectedly needed to increase its borrowings by $40 million. The company had signed new agreements, approved by Duffy without cabinet sanction, that necessitated accelerating the launch of its third satellite. New finance minister Peter Walsh looked dimly on Duffy for saddling cabinet with 'what amounts to a fait accompli'. He hit the junior minister with the prospect of increasing Aussat's dividend from 8.5 per cent to 'say, 10 per cent' and bringing forward its first payment by a year to 1987/88.[33]

From this point on, annual debt repayments from Telecom became standard practice. Another $81 million was extracted for the 1986/87 budget and $95 million for 1987/88 (an amount that, on ERC instructions, Telecom borrowed from Qantas, Australia's state-owned airline, so as to avoid increasing either total public-sector debt or telephone charges).[34] This arrangement was resented within Telecom and triggered a blistering protest from Telecom's chairman, Robert Brack, about 'yet another arbitrary amount ripped out of Telecom solely because it is big and is viewed as a cash cow'. Duffy also complained directly to Keating, who cited the 'difficult budgetary situation' as justification.[35]

None of this should suggest that the Hawke government's senior economic ministers, in particular Keating, Dawkins and Walsh, were resistant to liberalisation in telecommunications. It was simply that at this stage they were not paying attention. Keating had higher economic priorities; he later recalled that telecommunications policy 'wasn't on my radar in those early years'.[36] And Dawkins and Walsh, as successive finance ministers, focused on telecommunications only as a corollary of a long-running efficiency and accountability program targeted at all federal government enterprises and statutory authorities.

Throughout this period, Treasury and Finance officials, with broad support from the Prime Minister's Department, consistently encouraged ministers to take steps towards liberalising Australia's telecommunications arrangements or, failing that, at least not to make decisions that would close off options for future changes. Leading into the 1986/87 and 1987/88 budgets, officials put forward an array of Aussat equity sale scenarios with the dual objectives of raising short-term funds and providing a path to greater efficiency and innovation in Australian telecommunications. In early 1986, Walsh and Treasury backed a Finance

Department proposal to privatise 24 per cent of Aussat. It was considered that such a sale would generate about $24 million in revenue and, crucially, 'strengthen [Aussat's] commercial orientation' by increasing private-sector involvement and, with amendments to the Satellite Communications Act, 'enhance competition between Aussat and Telecom without prejudicing the government's broader objective of integrating Australia's satellite and terrestrial telecommunications systems'.[37]

Prime Minister's Department officials encouraged Hawke to support the Aussat equity sale so long as 'the impact in the privatisation debate is considered acceptable'.[38] But the impact was far from acceptable. Just months earlier, the government had banded together with South Australia's then election-fighting state Labor government, the ACTU, the ATEA and the South Australian union movement to wage what journalist Paul Kelly has described as a 'brutal and effective anti-privatisation campaign' against new federal Liberal leader John Howard and his state-based allies.[39] To Hawke's later regret, he publicly condemned privatisation as 'a recipe for disaster [and] the height of economic irrationality [that] is based on a blind and mindless commitment to a narrow, dogmatic and discredited ideology'.[40]

During meetings in May and July 1986, the ERC shied away from reopening the Aussat privatisation issue. It also declined to progress Finance's other fund-raising suggestion: to simply sell another 24 per cent of Aussat to Telecom.[41] The Department of Communications and Telecom jointly slammed this proposal as having 'no policy logic' and being 'tantamount to publicly stating that the policy of an independent Aussat has been abandoned in favour of Telecom control'.[42] More likely their real objection was the cost of acquisition to Telecom, especially as the authority's equity stake and board seats on Aussat meant it already had effective control.

The following year, Finance, Treasury and the Prime Minister's Department pushed again for an Aussat sell-off. They encouraged the government to privatise up to 49 per cent of the company, reducing the commonwealth's direct stake to as little as 26 per cent. Government revenues would be boosted, they argued, and competition could be kick-started from Aussat against Telecom and OTC. ERC ministers were once more assured that public policy control could be maintained via licensing and regulation. Hawke was urged to 'relax' the restrictions on Aussat, such as those preventing the company from carrying 'third party traffic and/or international traffic' in competition with Telecom and OTC, and also to review current regulatory arrangements with an eye to ensuring that Telecom could not 'exploit' its stake in Aussat 'to the cost of Aussat's competitiveness' (as it was indeed doing). With Aussat's accumulated losses now surpassing $61 million, the Finance Department was especially concerned that regulatory restrictions were killing Aussat's commercial viability and its potential sale value.[43]

By March 1987, Telecom's monopoly power and its conduct were coming under greater scrutiny from a variety of influential quarters. At the same time, Keating was gearing up for another major economic statement in which he would announce the need for $4 billion of public-sector savings, to be realised by spending cuts, asset sales, welfare tightening and tax adjustments. This would make sustained demands on ministers and officials. The government was also facing the complexities and sensitivities associated with telecommunications privatisation and competition, issues that were particularly acute for Labor. And an election deadline loomed. All of this was more than enough reason for ERC ministers to call a halt ('at this stage') to any more talk of Aussat or any other potential telecommunications shake-up.[44]

8

Imperatives for Change

We were internationalising the place, but we had this rigid
telecommunications structure and it had to be opened up.

Paul Keating[1]

Yet another significant debate, which joined a genuine policy contest with a political and bureaucratic turf battle, was playing out in the Hawke government between 1983 and 1987. Soon after Labor's election, the Department of Finance, backed by Treasury and the Prime Minister's Department, launched an initiative to develop a set of efficiency- and accountability-related metrics and measures applicable to all federal statutory authorities and government business enterprises. The immediate impetus came from Labor policy work led by Gareth Evans in opposition, though as was often the case its origins tracked back to Whitlam and Coombs.[2] Fraser's government had also sought to progress the issue via various government and parliamentary committees during its tenure and, in one of its final cabinet meetings, resolved to finalise a set of guidelines 'as soon as possible'.[3] The proposal, however, was still unresolved when Labor romped into office in March 1983.

Within months of the Hawke government's election, the Senate Standing Committee on Statutory Authority Financing released a report into the commonwealth's nine largest authorities, which included Telecom and OTC.[4] It contained some highly contentious conclusions for Labor. The report observed that government enterprises were underperforming their private-sector equivalents and argued for the imposition of rate-of-return financial targets, with any specific 'community service obligations' costed and disclosed where they impacted negatively on a specific enterprise's financial results.[5] New finance minister

John Dawkins took the matter in hand, aiming for a set of cabinet-approved performance measures by late 1983.[6] This proved hugely optimistic. In April 1984 Dawkins told Hawke that mid-1985 would be more realistic, but it was not until mid-1986 (under his successor Peter Walsh) that draft guidelines were released for public discussion, and not until November 1987 that a final version was tabled in the Senate.[7]

Although competition policy was not part of the Finance-led project, the guidelines it produced were important to the telecommunications competition reforms advanced later by Gareth Evans as transport and communications minister following Labor's re-election in July 1987. The outcomes of this fraught, drawn-out process also served to spotlight the capacity of the telecommunications establishment, represented in this case by Duffy, the Communications Department and Telecom, to dilute and delay policy objectives that it did not like and to shape policy outcomes in its own interests. And, finally, the project also revealed the extent of the preparatory policy work carried out by economic officials from Finance, Treasury, the Prime Minister's Department and other agencies well before the Hawke government began to pursue structural reform in its third term.

The broad parameters of the debate were fairly clear fairly early. They revolved around the perennial tension between political and administrative controls over a government enterprise and its level of operational autonomy.[8] On one side stood the finance minister and the economic policy departments, which wanted to implement accountability measures. On the other were ministers with responsibility for government enterprises, their departments, the enterprises themselves and parties dependent on them, including the unions (though within this broad group, perspectives were not always aligned). Finance and Treasury initially envisaged, for example, that enterprises would submit strategic corporate plans to their ministers 'for consideration and approval' and that the ministers in turn would consult with the treasurer and finance minister on matters requiring government approval. Duffy, his department and Telecom were united against this, but Telecom, OTC and Aussat were also pushing back on any moves that would grant their minister new powers over their operations.[9]

Each side had legitimate concerns about the other. The economic portfolios were convinced, with good reason, that Telecom and other government enterprises could readily operate more efficiently and utilise their capital more effectively, but they lacked independently verifiable data to test their assumptions or claims.

They were working in the dark and determined to do something about it. On the portfolio side, Duffy was unsympathetic to the market liberal trends in telecommunications policy and uninterested in engaging with the intensifying pressures for change. He was also unwilling to cede any ministerial authority to what he considered to be unwarranted bureaucratic meddling by Finance or Treasury.

The intense antagonism aroused by Dawkins' call for Finance to have 'a basic level of prudential control and oversight' over government enterprises came despite consistent assurances by him and Walsh that costs associated with enterprises' social responsibilities would be taken into account when establishing financial targets.[10] This was also Treasury's long-held position.[11] Dawkins was simply proposing 'a check list ... not hard and fast rules', he said, and warned ministers with government enterprise responsibilities (including Duffy) that by fighting to stay in the operational dark they were taking 'enormous risks' and ultimately would be 'the ones who will be caught when something comes unstuck'.[12] But at the same time, Dawkins was also counselling officials in his own department that, under Labor, state enterprises were not considered 'a "necessary evil" but rather a positive vehicle for implementing, with a bit of imagination, Labor government policies'. Successful government enterprises, Dawkins said, required 'skill, innovation, risk-judgment, imagination and animal spirits' (to which one bemused official speculated the minister meant 'profit motive') and these were the attributes he wanted to foster.[13]

Duffy, his departmental officials and Telecom, with support from transport minister Peter Morris, toiled consistently to shut down, or at least water down, the Finance-led guidelines initiative, to the extent that the Prime Minister's Department specifically highlighted the strength of Duffy's resistance when urging Hawke to back his finance minister.[14] Supported by caucus's infrastructure committee, Duffy harnessed Labor's party room to stonewall until after the December 1984 election; the following year, he and Morris lobbied caucus to oppose this 'unwarranted and unnecessary interference' in their portfolios. The ministers' claim that the initiative was 'inconsistent with the Westminster system of portfolio ministerial accountability' prompted one Treasury official to observe acidly that they were 'somewhat ignorant' of how cabinet processes had 'evolved in the last century'.[15]

The Communications Department battled Finance, Treasury and the Prime Minister's Department, warning of a union backlash and drawing tenuous comparisons with the Davidson inquiry, 'which incidentally this government soundly criticised and comprehensively rejected not 12 months ago'.[16] Duffy's departmental secretary, Charles Halton, took the fight directly to Michael Keating, his opposite number at Finance.[17] Telecom chairman Robert Brack publicly accused Finance and Treasury of mounting 'a classic power play'.[18] The ATEA agreed.[19]

The parties resisting the project took care to give in-principle praise to the objective of improving government enterprise efficiency and accountability while maintaining that in-practice it was impossible to develop metrics that could be applied at a whole-of-government level. The Department of Communications labelled Finance's plan 'heroic but doomed' and branded its officials 'hopelessly immature' for seeking a more direct role in enterprises' operations.[20] A common claim against external metrics was that they would actually reduce efficiency by diverting resources and distorting activities. In correspondence with finance minister Peter Walsh, for example, Robert Brack accused the Finance Department of having 'a lamentable lack of understanding' about commercial management and said it was 'quite extraordinary' that Walsh's 'wish to improve efficiency and reduce costs', and his support for new obligations on Telecom, would actually mean 'more controls, more public servants, more uncertainty and more delay'.[21]

OTC and Aussat also expressed their forthright displeasure, with OTC's managing director, George Maltby, taking exception to the very notion of his organisation being subject to external guidelines. He declared that OTC's profitability made it 'very different' from Australia's other government enterprises and challenged 'anyone' to find evidence that its performance had been 'in some way inadequate' over its 40-year history.[22] In mid-1986, Duffy sent a handwritten note to Walsh assuring him that 'this issue still has a long way to go'.[23]

The vexed politics of cross-subsidies

The goal of applying minimum rate-of-return targets to government enterprises brought with it the vexed issue of how community service obligations should be accounted for and costed. Telecom's universal service and cross-subsidy arrangements were a particular challenge. The central economic agencies accepted, as they had always done, that the costs associated with enterprises' social obligations had to be factored into their financial targets, and that the Finance-led external guidelines under development need 'not preclude the continued cross-subsidisation of those costs … if the government considers this to be appropriate'.[24]

The central problem—which became a critical issue for the Hawke government once it embarked upon telecommunications reform—was that neither Finance nor anyone else, including consecutive communications ministers, could objectively quantify Telecom's universal service costs. The Communications Department argued that the government faced a stark binary choice: it could have affordable universal services via existing cross-subsidy arrangements, or 'threaten [this] long standing and socially accepted policy' by placing a financial target on Telecom and suffer the consequences. In the absence of any reliable data, this proposition could not be substantiated one way or the other. Duffy's departmental officials were willing to concede that costing community service obligations had merit in principle, but they were quick to assert that any costing exercise would need to be 'very broad indeed' and that in practice it would be 'of little use' in ministerial decision-making.[25]

Duffy accepted, seemingly without reservation, the well-honed arguments of Telecom and sector unions that cross-subsidisation equated to a 'policy for equity' and that anything else, such as edging towards cost-based pricing, would be 'a discriminatory policy'.[26] He was an unwaveringly strong advocate for the status quo. In mid-1984, he lost no time putting his case to Hylda Rolfe, a founding member of the Industries Assistance Commission who had just been appointed as Prices Surveillance Authority chair. Duffy said she could have 'no room for doubt' that the government's support for 'uniform services at uniform prices' was rock solid and that existing cross-subsidies were 'entirely in harmony with Labor's broad policy objectives'.[27] He also pushed for cabinet agreement (consistent with his department's long-held preference) to enshrine Telecom's cross-subsidy arrangements in law. Duffy's stated goal was to 'constrain future governments of a different persuasion' from readily unwinding the cross-subsidies, but it is likely that he also had his internal opponents in Finance and Treasury in mind. And indeed, they gave his proposal short shrift.

Treasury considered that Duffy was presenting a 'distorted view' by equating Telecom's cross-subsidy system with equity; it pointed out that even on Telecom's own figures the authority was making a surplus of more than $1 billion annually on its inter-city routes, with prices set at more than three times costs. Treasury observed that this 'severe overcharging, which falls primarily on the business sector, represents a significant impediment to the efficiency of Australian industry' because it discouraged 'the use of more modern business practices involving communications services'. The Department of Industry, Technology and Commerce similarly noted that Telecom's system 'raises the costs of the majority of industry and commerce users of services which are essential to their efficient development'. Finance agreed, also accusing Duffy's department of pursuing a legislated subsidies policy to 'cut across' its guidelines initiative, which aimed to 'provide a suitable framework' for government to assess 'the level of resources devoted by public enterprises to achieving public policy objectives'. The Prime Minister's Department steered a middle path, counselling against legislating the status quo but advising that present arrangements be maintained 'for the time being'.[28] And this is what cabinet did.[29]

But telecommunications cross-subsidies remained a live issue. As seen in the previous chapter, the Hawke government had played a prominent anti-privatisation role in the lead-up to South Australia's election in December 1985. During the campaign, Duffy and others insisted that affordable telephone services depended on current cross-subsidies being maintained. But the following year, this longstanding system was coming under fire from several fronts. The Business Council of Australia and the Committee for Economic Development of Australia both urged the government to at least explore the potential for competition and private investment in telecommunications. At the same time, media reporting had the government's own Economic Planning Advisory Council calling for uneconomic telecommunications services to be funded directly and transparently by government.[30] Though this had been Whitlam's view in the 1960s, by the 1980s it was opposition leader John Howard's position and was being ridiculed by Labor: '$500 million from Mr Small Government, pigs might fly,' scoffed Duffy.[31] Behind the scenes, Telecom's chairman, Robert Brack, also promoted the privatisation bogey, warning Finance Minister Walsh that the guidelines initiative, if implemented, would 'give a boost to the privatisation cause' by causing 'delays and inefficiencies'.[32]

An uneasy accommodation

In late 1985, two years after Dawkins had kicked off the guidelines initiative in cabinet, but two years before Walsh would finally table the end product in the Senate, Hawke was coming under internal pressure to lend more support to the efficiency project. His senior economic adviser, Stephen Sedgwick (a future Finance Department secretary), told the Prime Minister that he 'strongly' supported Finance's position 'in each of the contentious areas' and argued that introducing external guidelines would 'complement' Hawke's public calls for the private sector to improve productivity 'by forcing public authorities to act more like private enterprise'. This would strengthen Labor's hand, he said, in countering the 'frequent claim' that government enterprise was inherently inefficient.

Sedgwick also urged Hawke to support efforts to quantify enterprises' community service obligations and make these costs more explicit, 'which, if nothing else, will encourage enterprises to adopt methods which minimise these costs'.[33] But beyond foreshadowing the imminent release of a discussion paper on the draft guidelines, Hawke did not offer his economic ministers any discernible support until draft guidelines were finally circulated in mid-1986. This was when Hawke began paying attention to public-sector productivity—in the context of Australia's deteriorating trade performance and cabinet concerns that the ongoing delay was embarrassing the government.[34]

By late 1986, some in Treasury were worried that the proposed guidelines were so 'watered down' that there was 'a danger of losing the basic rationale for financial targets'—which was to determine whether enterprises were earning a satisfactory return on funds employed taking account of any non-commercial obligations.[35] In response to the continuing 'serious resistance' to the guidelines in caucus, as well as from the enterprises themselves and 'their sponsoring departments and other apologists', some Finance officials considered encouraging their minister, Walsh, to make the argument that the only alternative to a robust set of efficiency metrics and accountability measures was privatisation.[36] But this idea was quickly quashed by Finance Department secretary Michael Keating, who said he would rather abandon the guidelines project entirely than go down that path.[37]

By April 1987, amid a renewed focus by Hawke on public-sector efficiency and rising pressures on Duffy to acknowledge that Australia's telecommunications system was unsustainable, Duffy and Walsh reached an uneasy accommodation. In essence, the economic policy departments ceded more ground, with Walsh now more modestly seeking government enterprise productivity improvements 'over time' and accepting that specific efficiency and accountability measures would need to be negotiated 'on an authority by authority and enterprise by enterprise basis'. The Communications Department welcomed this 'recognition of the primary role of the responsible portfolio minister and the boards of government business enterprises'.[38] But by this stage of the electoral cycle, Labor's immediate focus was on Paul Keating's next major economic statement and then, from late May, on getting re-elected.[39] The vexed guidelines project was again put on hold.

New pressures for change

During the final year of Labor's second term, Australia's troubled trading position and a new round of multilateral trade negotiations pushed senior Hawke government figures to focus for the first time on the nation's telecommunications system in the context of its economic enabling function and as an export opportunity. At the same time, there were mounting doubts about Telecom's compliance with Australian trade practices law dealing with anti-competitive conduct, and questions over the way the authority was exercising its regulatory powers. These combined to force an acknowledgment from Duffy that the government might need to consider at least some changes to the status quo.

International economic policy developments and Australia's increasing exposure to global financial and capital markets, following on from the macroeconomic reforms pursued by the government since 1983, provided the impetus for Labor's pivot to domestic structural (microeconomic) reform from 1987. Within months of Keating's 'banana republic' warning, Hawke, along with Walsh and industrial relations minister Ralph Willis, began calling for improved public-sector productivity. As Hawke later explained, the government would have been poorly placed 'to challenge the private sector to restructure and make itself more efficient if, as the largest employer in the country, we hadn't started to put our own house in order'.[40] In September 1986, Hawke announced a range of measures, including annual 'efficiency dividend' obligations on government departments and agencies, and, modelled on a Thatcher government initiative, the establishment of an Efficiency Scrutiny Unit, to be headed by a former South African banker, David Block, and to report directly to the Prime Minister. Hawke also put government officials on notice, declaring publicly that just as he had often exhorted the private sector to improve productivity, the government expected 'its own managers ... to take a tough, hard-nosed look at performance at all levels'.[41]

As early as October 1986, some nine months before any public announcement,

Hawke and his senior ministers were also discussing plans to consolidate the public service into a smaller number of so-called mega-departments more closely aligned with Labor's new priority policy areas. Keating and the resources and energy minister, Gareth Evans, were both consulted, and both were ambivalent. Keating preferred the power dynamic of dealing with 'a multiplicity of ministers rather than one minister representing a gigantic portfolio'. He was also sceptical that such huge departments could be 'effectively or efficiently run'.[42] For his part, Evans urged Hawke not to signal any changes until after the next election to avoid inducing anxiety and disruption within the public service. According to Evans, Hawke's response was 'Fuck the public service', but in the event no announcement was made until Labor had won a third term.[43]

By this time, several countries were pursuing their own versions of domestic structural reform, often well in advance of Australia and in many cases involving telecommunications. The United States, United Kingdom and Japan had each introduced various forms of competition in telecommunications networks and equipment, while New Zealand's Labour government was moving in the same direction. But the specific trigger for Hawke's cabinet to turn its attention to tele-communications was an impending round of multilateral trade talks in Uruguay, which would focus on services including telecommunications. Cabinet had high hopes for Australia's potential as an exporter 'in the field of high technology'. Cabinet made an early step along this path by giving Telecom's newly created international subsidiary the green light to begin operations by providing consul-tancy services in Indonesia.[44]

International developments had no discernible impact on the government's approach to telecommunications until after its re-election in July 1987. But on the domestic front, a political storm erupted in May when the Trade Practices Commission and then ATUG publicly questioned Telecom's compliance with Australian trade practices law. Duffy was worried that the issue could prompt a legal challenge to Telecom's monopoly and wanted to retain at least a semblance of policy initiative. He conceded that some adjustments to Australia's telecommunications arrangements were probably necessary and that Labor might need to accept gradually rolling back Telecom's exclusive rights over customers' first telephone.[45] Media reporting of Duffy's comments triggered immediate responses by those for and against change—but by this time Duffy had already been aware of the issue and its implications for at least five months.

The previous December, former Fraser government communications minister Tony Staley, speaking in his new capacity as ATUG chairman, informed Duffy that ATUG had solid legal advice that the by-law powers granted Telecom in the 1975 Telecommunications Act were insufficient to exempt the authority from the Trade Practices Act of 1974. Telecom's monopoly over first telephone handsets therefore breached Australian law. This advice was contrary to Telecom's stated position but confirmed the view held by ATUG since at least 1985. Staley also told Duffy, with whom he had a good personal relationship, that the Trade Practices Commission had recently received two legal opinions consistent with ATUG's advice.[46] Duffy probably already knew this; according to a later account by the commission, it had urgently referred this advice to Duffy (and attorney general Lionel Bowen).[47]

Staley made clear to Duffy that ATUG accepted Telecom's common carrier role and its use of cross-subsidies, but he urged the minister to resist Telecom pressure to secure exemption from the relevant trade practices laws through new legislation. Staley asserted that Telecom consistently exercised its regulatory powers in its own commercial self-interest, well beyond what could be justified to protect its network monopoly or ensure its capacity to fund uneconomic services. It was blocking businesses and institutional users from setting up private networks by applying 'punitive' charges and preventing interconnection with the public switched network. Duffy was also told that even though Telecom could not meet demand for the ever-expanding range of advanced PABX systems, it consistently denied applications from private-sector operators, which were its potential competitors, to supply alternative products.[48]

As intimated by Staley, Telecom was indeed pressing Duffy for legislation to protect its first telephone monopoly. The authority's chairman, Robert Brack, sought Duffy's specific agreement on this point; failing that, he urged Duffy to commit to a three-year transition to competition in first handsets, during which Telecom was to be relieved of existing public-sector constraints.[49] In the wake of Duffy's public comments in May, Telecom's managing director, Mel Ward, called for the government to ensure a 'graceful transition period' while asserting both privately and in public that Telecom should retain its network monopoly and, most importantly, its regulatory powers.[50]

The backlash from the telecommunications establishment (sector unions, equipment manufacturers and their caucus supporters) was swift. Chairman of the caucus communications committee John Saunderson railed against any weakening of Telecom's monopoly and threatened a high-profile fight.[51] With some hyperbole, the ATEA claimed that 26,000 Telecom jobs were at stake.[52] APTU's general secretary, Rob Arndt, fired off telexes to Hawke, Willis and Duffy calling on them 'to immediately ensure that Telecom gives an undertaking that the jobs of Telecom workers are not under threat and that all staff numbers will be maintained'.[53] Meanwhile, the director of the Australian Electronics Industry Association, Richard Brett, warned that 'unbridled deregulation' would swamp local manufacturers under a torrent of cheap imports.[54]

Duffy's apparent willingness to take at least an in-principle step along the path towards liberalisation, even if only to mitigate a legal threat rather than in response to any of the technological, commercial and economic pressures bearing on Australia's telecommunications system, was observed with some satisfaction in parts of the federal bureaucracy. A mid-May meeting between Duffy and Keating prompted one senior Treasury official to note that, though the communications minister's continued resistance to Finance's guidelines initiative was 'more emotional than rational' and his defence of Telecom's monopoly 'too sweeping', it was nonetheless pleasing that 'even Mr Duffy recognises that there is greater scope for competition in this area than at present'.[55]

Parties and policies at the 1987 election

Whatever Duffy's personal ambivalence about the pressures on telecommunications policy settings, from late 1986 through to July 1987 policy tensions were playing out both within and between Australia's main political parties. For Labor, the priority was still to protect Telecom, the sector unions and local equipment manufacturers from competition, but the party was also beginning to acknowledge the technological and commercial pressures that had been bearing down on the telecommunications system since the 1970s. For the first time, Labor's platform in 1986 differentiated Telecom's 'basic charter obligations' from the concurrent increase in 'demand for new communication and information services'.[56] The policy Labor took to the election the following year highlighted the telecommunications sector's 'critical role … in Australia's future' and, in a significant shift, the importance of 'state-of-the-art specialised services to business'.[57] The internal policy tensions now confronting Labor echoed to some extent the earlier strains that had afflicted Fraser's government when it struggled, unsuccessfully, to reconcile the conflicting concerns of its business and rural supporter groups.

Telecommunications policy also became caught in the battle between the Liberal 'dries', who wanted public spending cuts and free markets, and the more socially liberal 'wets'. When Ian Macphee, the shadow minister for communications (and a prominent wet), took his draft policy to shadow cabinet in late 1986, he was slammed by his dry factional opponents and sacked. According to Neil Brown, now deputy party leader, he and opposition leader John Howard were 'appalled' to learn that Macphee had consulted with sector unions without approval.[58] Even if this was the case, Macphee's plan contained little to delight the unions; it was in fact not very different from the revised policy crafted by the new shadow minister, Julian Beale, a Howard ally. Both policies called for competition in the telecommunications equipment sector and more competitive freedom for Aussat, which would be part-privatised. Telecom would remain government owned and its cross-subsidy arrangements would be retained. Beale's additions were a commitment to privatising OTC and ending Telecom's first telephone monopoly (an aspiration that belonged in 'cloud cuckoo land', Duffy exclaimed), and his criticism of the Hawke government's 'excessive government intervention and undue caution'.[59]

In April 1987, the federal Coalition collapsed after Queensland premier Joh Bjelke-Petersen launched his infamous 'Joh for PM' campaign. As a result, the National Party (so called since 1982) took its own telecommunications policy to the election. Like the policies of Labor and Liberal, the Nationals' policy underlined its commitment to existing universal service and cross-subsidy arrangements, to untimed local calls and to Telecom's government ownership; along with the Liberals, it supported competition in the equipment sector and Aussat's partial sale. OTC, however, would stay in government hands. Reflecting the long-held views of former Fraser communications minister and current party leader Ian Sinclair, the Nationals also called for Telecom to outsource its line construction and maintenance, wiring premises and equipment installation to private-sector 'teletricians'.[60]

Though the Coalition parties' policies were not tested in government during the 1980s, they were clearly ahead of Labor, and had been since the Fraser government's third term, in that they were at least seeking to address the complex issues confronting Australia's telecommunications system. Their policy prescriptions foreshadowed many of the steps ultimately taken by Hawke's government. For his part, and perhaps to his relief, Duffy never had to act on the unavoidable challenges arising in his portfolio. In late May, Hawke called a double-dissolution election for July, which Labor won with an increased parliamentary majority. Telecommunications immediately moved to the centre of the political stage.

9

A New Agenda

The idea was to hit the ground running with a major reform agenda. We knew we had to do it in a staged way ... That was the brief.

Gareth Evans[1]

Structural reform was central to the Hawke government's third-term agenda, and central to this was telecommunications. The new approach was triggered by an imperative for greater efficiency and international competitiveness in Australia's increasingly open economy at a time when the nation's trading position was deteriorating and international trade talks were on the horizon.

Machinery-of-government changes to facilitate the new agenda were quickly effected. Sixteen mega-departments, including a new Department of Transport and Communications, were created under a hierarchy of cabinet and supporting ministers, and the Industries Assistance Commission was moved to Treasury. Paul Keating claims this move as his idea, intended to advance his role 'shaping, managing and pushing microeconomic change across many sectors'; others credit Treasury secretary Bernie Fraser.[2] A Structural Adjustment Committee of cabinet was established and charged with leading and coordinating Labor's reform program at a whole-of-government level. Hawke was soon lauding it as one of the core 'engine rooms' of government decision-making.[3]

New policy, new structures and new people

Gareth Evans was given responsibility for the pivotal transport and communications portfolio. Hawke considered Evans 'the most acute mind' in the ministry and valued his capacity for hard work. His uneven early period as attorney general had been redeemed in Hawke's eyes by his performance as resources and energy minister in Labor's second term.[4] Evans believes that Hawke saw him as 'a bit of an engine' and recalls his prime ministerial riding instructions as 'broad brush'— to produce 'as big a bang reform package as you can as fast as you can'. He says he approached his task through the prism of the government's Accord with the unions, which was all about balancing 'dry' economics with 'moist' social policies. According to Evans, he operated in a 'very non-ideological' manner.[5] His economic philosophy was 'what works'.[6]

When Evans became transport and communications minister in mid-1987, he was already conscious that 'pressures were mounting in a number of different ways' in the telecommunications sector. An immediate issue was the legal uncertainty about Telecom's compliance with trade practices law and doubts about whether its dual roles as regulator and service provider were 'really defensible'. Also focusing the government's mind, Evans says, were the rising international pressures already cited and new technological developments that were 'pushing' for greater responsiveness and innovation from Australia's 'tightly constrained' telecommunications system.[7]

The Hawke government's new approach to telecommunications was not due to any ideological conversion to market liberalism in response to the long-standing advice from economic policy officials or advocacy by groups such as ATUG. Rather, it was reacting to a set of specific, tangible issues both at a whole-of-government level and in areas particular to telecommunications policy. Senior Labor figures made a pragmatic political commitment to act and, having done so, were open to co-opting market liberal ideas and mechanisms where they offered a practical set of tools to resolve policy challenges and advance their policy objectives.

The point should be made that the domestic pressures Evans perceived as 'mounting' in 1987 had been doing so since at least the late 1970s, about when the Fraser government had sought to grapple with them in its final term. It was not that the issues were new; it was that Hawke and the economic pragmatists in cabinet were now paying attention and committed to addressing them.

If the government's new orientation in telecommunications meant personnel changes at the ministerial level, it also entailed changes in the bureaucracy. At the top, Peter Wilenski, previously Whitlam's principal private secretary and the incumbent chairman of the Public Service Board, was appointed secretary of the new Transport and Communications mega-department. Evans recalls Wilenski as 'a very important player'.[8] His immediate priorities included integrating three departments (Communications, Transport and Aviation) into one and repairing relations with the Finance and Treasury departments over the seemingly endless back-and-forth about government enterprise performance metrics. A fresh new pro-reform team was built up, substantially comprising officials from the former Department of Transport, the Bureau of Transport Economics and Treasury. Most of the public servants who had worked on telecommunications under Duffy and during the Fraser period were moved elsewhere.[9]

Developing a work program

Evans characterises the Hawke government's third-term plan as 'hitting the ground running with a major reform agenda'.[10] And this is what it did, though its alacrity is perhaps unremarkable given that Australia's economic problems were already well known and the remedies reasonably clear, at least to the government's economic advisers. With respect to telecommunications, the new element was a political commitment to reform. Within a month of the election, officials from Treasury, the Industry, Technology and Commerce Department and the Prime Minister's Department submitted a proposed work program to the Structural Adjustment Committee, which comprised, along with Hawke, Keating and Evans, the ministers for finance (Peter Walsh), industry, technology and commerce (John Button), employment, education and training (John Dawkins), industrial relations (Ralph Willis), and primary industries and energy (John Kerin). The case for structural reform was presented in terms aligned with Labor objectives: to foster economic growth and efficiency in order to provide 'employment opportunities, support welfare goals, and prosper in an increasingly competitive external environment'. The key challenges identified were Australia's inefficient use of capital ('including human capital') and the need for 'attitudinal change' to drive workplace productivity and 'entrepreneurial endeavour'.

At a whole-of-government level, the reform priorities included developing an education and training system that 'produces citizens attuned to a "productive culture"'; reducing labour market inflexibility; removing government 'succour' to inefficient and inward-looking industries in favour of 'export orientated ones'; and exposing government enterprises to greater competition through regulatory changes or privatisation. Each of these priorities had resonances for telecommunications.

The telecommunications and transport sectors were 'amongst the most important' areas for structural reform, the proposed work program stated, because they were so closely interconnected with other parts of the economy. Both sectors affected 'the cost structure of the rest of Australian industry, and rigidities and inefficiencies here may more significantly restrict Australia's efforts to become internationally competitive than policies elsewhere in the economy'.

An observation of central importance to the complexities inherent in executing telecommunications reform was that structural changes 'may be more palatable in one area if [they] also occur in others'. Specifically, 'lower industry protection may be more readily accepted if business costs associated with economic regulations in transport, communications and defence exports can be lessened'.[11]

Until the Hawke government embarked on its whole-of-government reform program in 1987, successive reviews of Australia's telecommunications arrangements had always occurred in political and policy silos. Even modest proposals for change quickly became caught in an impenetrable web of countervailing technical, financial and social considerations and powerful vested interests. As we saw in chapter 6, this dynamic was especially apparent under the Fraser government. That the Hawke government's new telecommunications agenda was a subset of a larger reform program was crucial in ameliorating this factor, although stakeholders with an interest in maintaining the status quo still found the new policy environment far from 'palatable' and had considerable success in delaying and diluting the outcomes that Evans ultimately produced in 1988.

The proposed work program made three key points about Telecom: that its dual roles as regulator and service provider were a 'substantial conflict of interest'; that by acquiescing to Telecom's 'broad interpretation' of its regulatory powers since the enterprise's establishment in 1975, the Fraser and Hawke governments had effectively ceded policy control over the 'development and cost of telecommunications in Australia' and enabled Telecom to 'stifle competition … in the supply of telephones'; and that the Labor government's rigid commitment to Telecom's cross-subsidy arrangements since 1983 had been 'a strong influence on restricting competition'. Moreover, the already 'uneasy' arrangements preventing Telecom, OTC and Aussat from competing against each other were becoming more problematic 'in the face of advancing technology'. In and of themselves, none of these points were new. What was new was the politics within Hawke's government. While Transport and Communications officials were willing to concede these points, they formally recorded their understandable disquiet that cabinet might get 'a misleading impression of the ease with which radical change might be secured'.[12]

The Structural Adjustment Committee considered the proposed program at a meeting on 19 August, during which it was agreed that the government's immediate priorities were preparing for the looming Uruguay trade talks and addressing Australia's collapsing two-airlines framework. Evans was given three months to prepare a detailed paper outlining the 'main issues and problems and broad approaches' for telecommunications reform.[13]

Reviewing telecommunications arrangements

In early September, Hawke and Evans announced that Australia's telecommunications arrangements would be reviewed. It might mean 'competition in some areas', Hawke suggested. Evans was blunter; in comments reminiscent of Fraser's foreshadowing of the Davidson inquiry six years earlier, he asserted that 'the time has obviously come when we should ask whether at least some of the traditional monopoly areas should be wound back, and the role of the private sector should be expanded in order to meet the increasing range and diversity of users' needs'.[14]

The statements by Hawke and Evans brought into sharp relief the realignment of interests being triggered by the government's new agenda and gave an early sign that its toughest fight would be on its own side of the political fence. In immediate responses, NSW Labor Council secretary John MacBean vowed resistance to any move towards government utility sales and the ATEA rejected out of hand the notion that any aspect of Telecom's monopoly might be reduced. ATUG chairman Tony Staley, however, praised Hawke's and Evans's public comments as 'the way to go'. Shadow communications minister Tony Messner offered the Coalition's in-principle support but challenged Labor to back its words with actions.[15]

The government's telecommunications review became immediately conflated with Labor's ongoing debate about privatisation, not least because Evans had emerged as a reluctantly high-profile advocate of selling Australia's state-owned airlines to free up funds for the party's social policy priorities. There was 'one heck of a difference', Evans said in a media interview, 'between spending $400 million on an equity injection for Qantas ... and spending $400 million on increases in pensions'.[16] Yet Hawke had already publicly ruled out privatising Telecom, and Evans soon did the same with caucus.[17]

Evans acknowledges that privatisation was the logical end point of liberalising Australia's telecommunications system, once Telecom had been corporatised and full competition embedded. But as minister his focus was on corporatisation and the initial competitive steps; selling Telecom was too far into the future to receive any serious thought.[18] Opinion polling at the time underlined the government's challenge: whereas about half of the public claimed to be supportive of Telecom's partial or full privatisation, the great bulk of Labor voters were solidly opposed.[19]

Earlier reviews of Australia's telecommunications system had acted independently of government and in an advisory capacity, but the Hawke government's review was different. It was carried out by Evans's departmental officials operating as a taskforce under his personal direction, and worked to generate realistic, actionable options in pursuit of specific policy objectives. The taskforce reported to an interdepartmental committee known as the Officials' Working Group on Communications Regulation, which was chaired by the Department of Transport and Communications and comprised representatives from the Prime Minister's Department, Treasury, Attorney General's, Finance, Industrial Relations, and Industry, Technology and Commerce. This meant that whatever proposals went to cabinet's Structural Adjustment Committee already had sufficient buy-in (albeit with varying degrees of enthusiasm) from those portfolios responsible for implementing them.[20]

The review taskforce was directed to investigate four core issues: the nature and extent of Telecom's, OTC's and Aussat's monopoly powers and what scope there was to reduce them; how private-sector involvement in the telecommunications sector could and should be increased; how the sector should be regulated, with particular focus on establishing an independent regulator; and the extent to which Telecom, OTC and Aussat should be restructured or released from public-sector constraints to foster greater efficiency and competitiveness (in essence: should there be mergers between them; should they compete with each other; and could private equity be utilised?).[21]

Highlighting how far the dial had shifted on telecommunications, the taskforce's terms of reference were strikingly similar to those that the Fraser government had set the Davidson inquiry. On this point, Evans distinguishes between Labor's 'steady as you go' approach under Duffy and his own view as minister from 1987 that 'whatever caution we demonstrated in the past, that was the past, and now was the time to open this book and look again'. Evans says he was indifferent to the Hawke government's earlier position ('it wasn't a matter of being spooked by that or being stimulated by that, it was just a matter of moving on') and assumed that his officials had the Davidson inquiry's report 'on their desks as a blueprint'.[22] According to Tony Shaw, an economist from the Bureau of Transport Economics who was recruited into Evans's taskforce (and later became chairman and chief executive of Australia's telecommunications regulator, the Australian Telecommunications Authority, and an expert adviser to successive governments on the NBN), the Davidson report did serve as a point of reference for officials, but nonetheless they conducted their review from 'a clean sheet of paper'.[23] It is clear that the approach of this review was materially different from Davidson's. Whereas Davidson dealt with core political and policy conundrums by essentially assuming them away, the Hawke government's review was grounded in the world as it existed.

The telecommunications establishment, specifically Telecom and the unions, with strong support from sections of caucus, engaged fiercely with Evans and the taskforce. Within days of Evans's appointment as minister, senior officials from the ACTU and sector unions were in his office pushing to limit the government's reform agenda.[24] As the nature of the proposals likely to go before the Structural Adjustment Committee became clearer, tensions escalated both publicly and behind closed doors. One well-sourced front-page newspaper article reported that Telecom had complained about insufficient consultation, the unions had threatened industrial action and there was increasingly heated agitation in caucus.[25]

Telecom's strategic response to the government's liberalisation agenda combined facilitation and obstruction; it facilitated measures that furthered its interests and obstructed those that didn't. The authority's newish managing director, Mel Ward, a PMG veteran in his mid-forties who had been appointed under Duffy, maintained a warm working relationship with Evans, who considered him 'sympathetic' to the government's agenda and 'crucial' to its implementation— but former officials from Evans's taskforce recall Ward pushing back hard against change, leading to consistently tense meetings with Telecom staff.[26]

On issues such as Telecom's first telephone monopoly, which was an over-staffed, inefficient and likely unprofitable part of the authority's operations, Ward looked to meet the government's needs while advancing Telecom's interests. In this case, he proposed (discreetly, due to strong union opposition) a three-year transition to competition in exchange for a freer operational hand.[27] But when its central interests—its core monopoly revenues—were at stake, Telecom could play an aggressive game.

In a Telecom discussion paper that circulated widely in government circles during 1987, the authority tied the introduction of competition to its lucrative inter-city routes to the end of universal service. To protect universal service, the paper claimed that the government would either have to pay Telecom upwards of $2 billion in subsidies or accept it increasing network access charges by 'a minimum' of 20 per cent a year for five years. This would particularly harm Labor's lower-income support base, Telecom pointed out; Evans 'might just be remembered as the "minister for few telephones"'.[28] Paul Keating similarly recalls Ward seeking to 'cajole' ministers into reversing planned spending cuts by linking them to the viability of Telecom projects in Labor-held electorates. Keating says he considered such conduct by a government enterprise to be 'a very bad ploy' and claims that 'at one stage I insisted that he be removed from the cabinet room'.[29]

It is well established that Hawke's government faced particular political challenges implementing structural economic reform because these changes severely tested Labor orthodoxy and the interests of what political economist Rolf Gerritsen has called the party's 'partisan coalition' (especially the union movement).[30] In *The End of Certainty*, Paul Kelly contrasts the Hawke government's cautious approach to structural reform, its 'pace of change largely dictated by the union movement', with its 'more audacious … almost heroic' dealings with business in pursuit of financial deregulation and tariff cuts.[31] Yet with respect to telecommunications reform, the formidable institutional power of key groups with vested interests in maintaining the status quo, including the sector unions, rural communities and Telecom itself, meant that any Coalition government would also have faced significant challenges. The Fraser government certainly did so in its final term.

As secretary of the Transport and Communications Department, Peter Wilenski had publicly stated that 'the responsibility of policy makers [is] to work out who are the winners and losers from any change, and to try to determine where the public interest lies'. In his view, technological change posed a particular challenge to reform because it tended to 'undermine longstanding institutional arrangements or the solutions to previous policy problems, solutions which were reached only after hard-fought battles among the interests involved, and which no-one is now anxious to see disturbed'.[32] Wilenski's successor, Graham Evans (Transport and Communications secretary from 1988 to 1993), similarly notes that a core characteristic of structural reform is that 'the losers know who they are and fight like hell, whereas the winners don't know who they are'. He identifies the Hawke government's willingness to engage consistently and meaningfully with the potential losers from telecommunications reform as crucial to advancing its agenda.[33] As we will see, this was the approach taken by Gareth Evans and his ministerial successors, Ralph Willis and Kim Beazley.

In late October 1987, to avoid a looming confrontation with the party room so early in the review process, Evans acceded to caucus's establishment of a telecommunications liaison committee. Its members were Neil O'Keefe (who chaired the House of Representatives standing committee on community affairs) and two former ATEA officials, John Saunderson from Labor's left and Roger Price from the right. In effect, the committee's mission was to administer a strong dose of traditional Laborism to Evans's 'non-ideological' review. The caucus trio engaged extensively with the sector unions and the protected local communications equipment manufacturers, along with Evans's taskforce officials and Evans himself. Ensuring that the equipment manufacturing sector remained viable during its transition from Telecom-dependence to export-orientation was a top priority; O'Keefe considered it a breakthrough when the taskforce received instructions to take specific account of industry transition and assistance measures.[34]

Media reports and the opposition portrayed Evans's accommodation of caucus as an 'abject cave-in'; indeed, taskforce members did initially wish to prosecute liberalisation faster and further than the government was comfortable with.[35] But the overarching approach by Evans and his officials was closely aligned; they accepted that key interest groups would need at least to acquiesce in any telecommunications reform measures. The government's program would therefore be inherently incremental. Looking back, Evans emphasises that his personal approach as minister, and that of cabinet, was to push ahead 'a step at a time … in a very consultative way [and] to try to take the unions with us'.[36]

Issues, problems and 'broad approaches'

In mid-December, after three intense and often contentious months for Evans's taskforce and the officials' working group on communications regulation, the Structural Adjustment Committee met to consider what 'main issues and problems and broad approaches' had been identified. It was not a pretty picture. The ministers were told that they faced an entrenched web of self-reinforcing policy and institutional arrangements, built around the vexed and interrelated matters of statutory monopoly, cross-subsidisation, universal service and competition, that were working directly against the government's stated economic reform objectives while also counting Labor orthodoxy and the party's partisan coalition as their strongest defenders. Having made that clear, the working group's report then spent the best part of fifty pages seeking to untangle these 'issues and problems' and propose some politically acceptable paths forward.

In officials' frank judgment, the nub of the problem was that Australia's system of telecommunications monopolies was irreconcilable with the government's objective of 'improving economic efficiency'. Technological advances were blurring the lines between telecommunications networks and services, and between telecommunications and information technology. Moreover, these developments were casting doubt on the conventional 'natural monopoly' justification for a single telecommunications network operator, which was that this was the most economically efficient way to provide affordable universal services throughout the sparsely populated Australian continent.

The answer was competition, the working group's report asserted. This would provide the most effective means of improving the sector's efficiency and responsiveness to customer needs, and, crucially, advancing the government's wider economic objectives. The high quality of Australia's network infrastructure meant that barriers to entry and exit for 'providers of innovative and entrepreneurial services' were low; indeed, officials said, it was 'technically possible now' to introduce full competition across all services and for alternative networks to interconnect with existing infrastructure. The key obstacle (even greater than the scarifying political and regulatory challenges) was Australia's ostensibly monopoly-dependent universal service cross-subsidy system.

Hawke and his ministers were told that they, and before them Fraser and his ministers, had in effect ceded significant social policy control to Telecom by deferring to its interpretation of how to fulfil its national-interest obligations, most materially over cross-subsidy arrangements, and by neglecting to provide Telecom with any 'specific social or geographic objectives'. Telecom, not the government, since 1975 had been the 'arbiter of telecommunications provision for welfare and rural support'. Consequently, the Hawke government found itself knowing 'little about the size of the subsidies and who benefits from them'.[37] The government's commitment to structural reform was seriously impeded, not just by resistance from the forces already discussed, but by the unacceptably high risk that uninformed decisions would trigger unintended and possibly dire consequences.

The problem was not that telecommunications cross-subsidies existed. The problem was their scale and scope and the fact that politicians and officials were dependent on Telecom, which was strongly vested in the issue, for information and explanation about the operations of the cross-subsidy system. Even Telecom's own numbers varied enormously. In the course of the review process, its estimates ranged from $670 million (later adjusted up to $1 billion) to $2.5 billion.[38] The working group observed that the lowest subsidy figure cited by Telecom was still well above its latest profit figure of $443 million. If these numbers were accurate, then opening parts of Telecom's core monopoly to competition could 'drive [its] finances into a serious loss-making position'.

But for 'various methodological reasons', the working group dismissed Telecom's claimed costs as 'significant over-estimates'.[39] During the report's preparation, Treasury had criticised the $2.5 billion figure as 'over-stated, probably grossly so'.[40] Finance wanted it excluded from the report entirely because it 'unnecessarily dramatises the financial magnitude of the [community-service obligation] problem'.[41] Hawke's own department advised him that even the lower-range $1 billion figure seemed 'unduly large relative to other social welfare programs' and encouraged him to consider the potential 'net community benefits [of] redirecting these subsidies to other purposes'.[42] But at the end of the day, no-one outside Telecom could come up with any credible alternative figures. This meant it was imperative, the working group's report stated, that 'the size, scope and method of delivery of community service obligations' be subjected to 'immediate review'.[43] This was easier said than done, but it would have to be done if the Hawke government was to advance meaningful change.

The potentially astronomical scale of Telecom's cross-subsidies underpinned officials' advice to ministers that its community service activities be restricted to basic telephony only. Behind the scenes, the Finance Department was particularly keen for the government to issue a 'more explicit statement' to Telecom regarding its obligations.[44] Codifying the scope and scale of Telecom's social obligations would permit a 'closer alignment' between service charges and underlying provisioning costs, the working group asserted, even if cross-subsidies were maintained. In particular, it was hoped that a reduced obligation and lower subsidy costs might open the way for transparent on-budget funding options such as means testing. Other options in the mix included configuring Telecom's community-service activities on a designated 'remote area' or cost-per-service basis, or even removing them from Telecom and establishing a new agency with responsibility for 'rural and remote services'.[45]

Uncertainty about Telecom's cross-subsidy costs left officials focusing on the sector's innovative margins: on equipment such as advanced handsets, PABXs, modems and fax machines, and on 'value-added services' such as online databases, electronic funds transfer and brokerage services, and answering and paging services, where 'clear gains' could be achieved from competition without affecting Telecom's core monopoly profits.[46] Consistent with calls since the 1970s, equipment suppliers identified the liberalisation of installation and maintenance arrangements as especially important. This was by now Coalition policy. Suppliers complained that Telecom's installation 'work practices' were slow and costly and that its control over maintenance operations impeded the release of new products, since Telecom staff had to first be trained in how to service them. The working group advised ministers that Australia was 'virtually alone among OECD countries in enforcing centralised maintenance'.

But the Structural Adjustment Committee was also warned that liberalising the equipment sector would entail a 'major immediate industrial relations problem' because it was one of Telecom's 'very heavily staffed' areas. About 24,000 people were employed in relevant roles; three-quarters of them were ATEA or APTU members and, on Telecom's numbers, 8800 were vulnerable to redundancy.[47] The issue was primarily about union coverage; total employment in the sector was expected to grow in a competitive environment.[48] But the rolling industrial turmoil of the Fraser years was well remembered, and the implications of Telecom job losses had long weighed heavily on Labor minds.[49]

Ministers were further warned that the local equipment manufacturing sector would face serious import pressure in a liberalised environment.[50] It was calculated that Telecom's local content obligations, untenable in a competitive environment, were providing manufacturers with a level of protection equivalent to import duties of between 50 and 250 per cent.[51] Unsurprisingly, the sector was decidedly cool about liberalisation. Its industry group, the Australian Electronic Industry Association, noted sharply to working group officials that 'a comprehensive growth strategy based on increasing exports and local R&D' had already been developed at industry minister John Button's request. As such, 'any proposed restructuring of communications policy must have regard to those industry policy objectives which have already been endorsed by the government and accepted by the communications equipment industry'. The association also took exception to any notion that the sector was sheltering beneath Telecom's wings—though its claim to a relationship based on 'mutual benefits, not dependence' sat awkwardly with Telecom's own stated objective to 'limit ... the number of competitors to keep the telecommunications manufacturing industry viable'.[52]

Working group officials accepted that more substantial competition reform would remain on the political back burner until 'the size, scope and method of delivery' of Telecom's subsidised services were clarified. Consistent with advice to Hawke's government since 1983, they urged the Structural Adjustment Committee to avoid decisions that closed off options for 'further liberalisation in the future'; this included postponing decisions on merging any or all of the three telecommunications enterprises (despite deep concerns about Aussat's viability, but much to OTC's relief) as this would 'limit the scope for future domestic and/or international competition between the facilities, closing off future policy options'. But adjustments at the margin could only be a first step, ministers were told, because competitive pressure and the cost of delay would continue to rise. This would not just undermine Australia's economic efficiency and increase the price to be paid for missing out on the 'benefits of new technology', but also magnify the practical challenges of regulating a partially competitive sector.[53] In 'about 5 or so years', the task would become impossibly complex, even with an independent regulator.[54]

Whatever else the Structural Adjustment Committee decided, officials considered that establishing an independent telecommunications regulator was vital (and already overdue). Telecom's dominant position (which ATUG's chief executive characterised as it being 'the player, the referee, the judge and the jury') represented a clear and growing conflict of interest. Equipment suppliers were 'reluctant to disclose new products or services to Telecom for regulatory purposes', officials said, because Telecom competed in the same space. According to the Australian Information Industry Association, which represented more than a hundred equipment and software suppliers and manufacturers, Telecom was actively thwarting the nascent value-added service sector by refusing regulatory approvals in areas where it operated or planned to do so, such as mobile and packet switching data services. Officials stated that the Trade Practices Act had only 'theoretical' power against Telecom 'misusing its market power' because none of its potential competitors would initiate action 'for fear of reprisal'.[55]

Ministers were presented with three options. The first, which constituted the 'minimum' action required and had been specifically crafted by officials as a 'reasonably self-contained package that would meet most of Telecom's users', suppliers' and competitors' immediate concerns',[56] envisaged full competition in the supply, installation and maintenance of equipment and value-added services, including the contentious first telephone, and in the maintenance of PABX and small business systems. Telecom, OTC and Aussat's competitive operations were to be housed in subsidiaries to reduce the chance that their monopoly profits could be used to suppress competition. Aussat would be permitted to compete with OTC 'within the region of its current capability' and Telecom's regulatory functions would go to 'an independent regulator'. The second option was to allow competition in 'all services other than Telecom's monopoly on basic network facilities'. The third option was competition 'without limit'.[57]

Hawke went into the committee's pre-Christmas December meeting with advice that while most departments on the working group, including his own, favoured reform measures that were 'closest to full competition', the Transport and Communications Department was seeking to guide its minister to the 'least change option'. Given Evans's transactional approach to his portfolio and the not insignificant fact that he and his department were going to be on the hook to deliver any changes, this advice was hardly revelatory. It also exuded a whiff of sanctimony, not least because Hawke's officials themselves readily acknowledged that the 'minimum desirable change' option would 'generate substantial efficiency gains' and meet the 'major concerns' of many of Telecom's suppliers and large customers. Presuming that this was the option the ministers would probably choose, officials pushed Hawke to publicly commit to further rounds of reform— to lock in at least the prospect of 'additional gains' to come while also arming the government with 'useful negotiating coin' in its dealings with the unions.[58]

As it was, the Structural Adjustment Committee directed Evans's department, Treasury, John Button's Industry, Technology and Commerce Department and the Prime Minister's Department to do 'further detailed work' on all the competition scenarios presented short of open slather. At the same time—and of greater strategic significance in the longer term—they were also told to conduct 'detailed' investigations into the financial black hole that was Telecom's community service apparatus. The option of limiting these activities 'only to basic voice telephony' was explicitly flagged.[59] The Hawke government's move to break up Telecom's knowledge monopoly on the inner-workings of Australia's telecommunications cross-subsidy system was vital to enabling the government to consider more extensive reforms. It was intended, Evans says, to 'give us the ammunition ... to conclusively deal' with the battle that was most surely to come.[60]

10

Creating Momentum

The telecommunications reforms that we flagged and then implemented really did create the momentum for all that subsequently followed.

Gareth Evans[1]

Gareth Evans and his taskforce had just four months to pull together two telecommunications reform packages, one to kickstart competition and the other to deal with corporatisation. To say this was an intense period, made even more so by significant changes also underway in the aviation and transport parts of Evans's portfolio, is risking understatement. Minister and officials were consumed by complex policy and technical challenges and exhaustive, often trying, consultations with key individuals and groups in the telecommunications sector, the caucus and other government departments.

Competition baby steps

The competition workstream hit a major roadblock almost immediately. By about mid-January 1988, Evans had conceded that Telecom's community service obligations could not be credibly quantified in the time available.[2] Telecom's claimed costs were presumed to be substantially inflated, because it was in Telecom's interest to inflate them, and because nearly 95 per cent of Australian premises already had at least one telephone. But independently testing Telecom's figure and coming up with a tenable alternative would be a complicated technical and economic modelling exercise. The fallout from this was that all the network-based competition scenarios recently green-lighted for 'further detailed work' by the Structural Adjustment Committee were ruled out of scope—for now.

The scope of Evans's competition review was narrowed further when he took Telecom's first telephone monopoly, that bastion of union featherbedding, off the table. This was done in direct response to the political backlash Labor suffered from a union-led campaign against timed local calls, which gave the government a sharp foretaste of what to expect if it pushed ahead on too many fronts simultaneously. Evans says he was seeking to 'create the momentum' for sustainable, ongoing change, and in this light, he, and Hawke, were unwilling to openly confront the unions, the equipment manufacturers or the caucus. According to Evans, cabinet was also committed to proceeding 'in a very consultative way' because ministers were 'very conscious, not just rhetorically but substantively, about what all this meant for the ordinary Joe and the average household'.[3]

The conflict over timed local calls was triggered when Telecom publicly announced a comprehensive pricing review, just as the ministers on cabinet's Structural Adjustment Committee were considering their next steps on telecommunications. This was awkward for the government, given community sensitivity to the issue, but in this instance Telecom was not playing politics. It faced increasing network cost pressures from institutional customers tying up flat-rate local call lines by using them for always-on data and computer links. There were strong equity arguments for timed local calls, as the Davidson inquiry had established years earlier, and Evans and Hawke initially came out in support of Telecom. But the reaction from unions and within Labor was immediate and vituperative. The ATEA threatened work bans to block the change. In New South Wales, the Labor premier, Barrie Unsworth, who was three months out from a difficult election (which he lost), declared that his government would fight on an anti-timed local calls platform. And within federal caucus, the left and right publicly united in opposition.[4]

A by-election for the federal seat of Adelaide in February also proved fertile ground for a union-led scare campaign on telephone charges. The Coalition made hay with this intra-Labor fight, spurring ATUG's chairman, Tony Staley, a future Liberal Party president, to publicly criticise his party for its cynical opportunism. The result was brutal for the government. An anti-Labor swing of more than 8 per cent turned the seat Liberal for the first time since the 1960s. On election night, Hawke identified community concerns about timed local calls as 'demonstrably the motive behind the vote'—and killed it off as an option.[5]

With community service costs and the first telephone monopoly out of scope, Evans's taskforce spent the first three months of 1988 focusing on measures to liberalise the relatively uncontentious parts of the equipment and value-added services sectors. This was still seriously challenging, much of it involving complicated, contentious technical debates about how and where network boundaries between monopoly and non-monopoly areas could be set, and complex rolling negotiations about various transitional arrangements with Telecom and equipment manufacturers, who were largely dependent on Telecom for survival. Evans says that he did not want anyone able to credibly complain 'for a second that their positions were not understood or hadn't been listened to'; as such, he and his review team consulted to 'within an inch of our life'. Evans worked to 'take the backbenchers with us, particularly those who had manufacturing operations in their electorates'. He enjoyed collaborative discussions at 'the commanding heights' of the ACTU but recalls 'a lot of difficulty' with the sector unions.[6]

The work schedule was punishing. Priorities and weekly deliverables were often set at meetings between Evans and senior officials on Sunday nights, after the minister's arrival in Canberra. Evans would then be provided with updated reports at the end of the week to review at home in Melbourne over the weekend. As the May deadline neared, officials worked in shifts from 6 a.m. to 2 a.m. There was a strong esprit de corps between Evans and his team. Evans says that he wanted to know 'what was doable' and, once convinced, his view was 'just get on with it, guys'. He believes that the officials who worked on the competition reform package 'just loved it, getting into a big policy debate, rolling up their sleeves and getting stuck into it'. For the most part, Evans's former officials support this view, recalling the period as a career highlight, though some were offended by his irascible style.[7]

Evans's pitch to his colleagues on the Structural Adjustment Committee was for the government to pursue as much competition in telecommunications 'as possible without jeopardising industrial and manufacturing industry stability'. This meant that Telecom's first telephone monopoly was safe, for now, at a cost in foregone savings to consumers of up to $120 million. This was a 'threshold issue' for the sector unions, Evans said, and, as with their recent anti-timed local calls action, they would 'defend the monopoly with a campaign suggesting that liberal-isation would increase costs, reduce quality, and cause customer confusion'. Evans proposed, consistent with Telecom's preference, a three-year transition to first handset competition, with second handset competition permitted from January 1989. This also took account of local manufacturers' need to adjust to losing their 'exceptional industry protection' from Telecom's local preference obligations. Evans wanted new industry development arrangements established by late 1988.

Also ring-fenced from competition, to mollify Telecom and caucus, were Telecom's newer, innovative 'non-network based and advanced data services' (mobile services and data services such as packet switching) despite being independent of Telecom's cross-subsidies. Evans further proposed 'no changes now' to the existing arrangements between Telecom, OTC and Aussat; a review 'down the track' would be appropriate, though ministers were counselled against making 'unnecessarily provocative' statements along those lines.

In seeking a path forward that accommodated the concerns of unions, manufacturers, Telecom and caucus but still provided meaningful change for business and like telecommunications users, Evans pointed to the equipment sector as the 'logical' place to start. There was a trifecta of reasons: it 'neither contributes to, nor benefits from, cross-subsidy or community service obligations'; Telecom's performance 'appears to be relatively inefficient'; and prospective suppliers and customers were crying out for liberalisation.

Overshadowing these competition baby-steps was the continuing need to ensure supply of affordable, universal basic telephone services. The 'present impossibility' of independently quantifying Telecom's cross-subsidy costs meant that the government could not 'allow competition with Telecom for basic network facilities or services', Evans argued; to do so would risk 'undermining the capacity for it to continue to provide cross subsidies'. While Evans presumed Telecom's figures to be overstated, he was unwilling to instigate battle on this front, where fighting would be fiercest, until he was better armed. He conceded that progress in this area would remain stalled pending 'progressive resolution of this problem over the next few years'.[8]

Like his ministerial predecessors, both Labor and non-Labor, Evans was exasperated that he did not know 'the cost of this bloody cross-subsidy [because it] was all buried away in a black box'. He says that the Hawke government was determined to 'burrow into it and find out'.[9] In May 1988, the Bureau of Transport and Communications Economics was given twelve months to quantify 'the costs and cross-subsidies associated with meeting the identifiable community service obligations now met by Telecom'. This timeframe was set with Telecom's 1989/90 corporate plan in mind. [10] In the interim, Telecom was required to get ministerial sign-off on its community service plans and detail them in its annual corporate plan.[11]

The government was intent on reasserting strategic control over telecommunications policy decision-making; in Evans's words, it wanted to take 'control over the outputs' rather than rely on 'public service control over the inputs'.[12] This was a significant shift in thinking from the Whitlam government's plan for Telecom to have substantial autonomy in determining what Australia's telecommunications needs were and how they should be met; it reflected how much more dynamic, complex and prevalent telecommunications had become within a few short years. In advocating to his Structural Adjustment Committee colleagues for the establishment of an independent telecommunications regulator, Evans argued that the limited level of competition in the sector to that point, such as for PABX systems and second telephone handsets, had been determined 'at Telecom's discretion'; moreover, Telecom continued to 'exercise its regulatory authority ... to safeguard its central monopoly, control the scope of any competition it allows, and protect the communications equipment industry'. Evans recommended a new regulator be set up 'along the lines of Britain's "Oftel"' and affiliated with the Trade Practices Commission 'to ensure appropriate application of competition policy legislation'.

Though Evans's competition reform package was the product of collaborative public service processes and received cabinet endorsement, the inevitable compromises involved in pulling it together remained a source of frustration for the government's central economic agencies. Indeed, it fell well short of the 'minimum desirable change' flagged the previous December. The Department of Finance considered the proposed package to be 'excessively weighted towards the status quo and the interests of telecommunications producers'. Treasury said it did 'not go far enough in freeing-up current regulation of telecommunications'. The Business Regulation Review Unit was 'concerned' to note how much emphasis was placed on social policy rather than economic objectives.[13] Evans and his taskforce may well have agreed with the tenor of these criticisms, but at the end of the day they had been tasked by Hawke to advance along the liberalisation path without sparking all-out political or industrial war.

The Hawke government publicly anchored its May 1988 reforms (covering competition and corporatisation) in Whitlam's 'pioneering step' of 1975 to establish Telecom as an 'independent' government enterprise. But these 1975 arrangements had been 'overtaken by events', it asserted. Though the provision of affordable, universal services remained the government's 'principal' policy objective, it was 'no longer sufficient, by itself, to meet Australia's future needs'. It claimed that three factors were driving the need for structural reform: technological change, business requirements, and a liberalising world economy. As we have already seen, though, the first two of these factors were not new at all; they had been relentlessly applying pressure to telecommunications policy settings and then to institutional arrangements since the 1960s. What had changed was that Labor was no longer either ignoring or actively resisting the legitimate interests of business.

In a first for an Australian government of any political persuasion, the Hawke government publicly articulated a detailed set of policy objectives in telecommunications, and some 'fundamental constraints'. Together they represented a valiant effort to construct a recognisable Labor program that sought to balance the inherent social and commercial tensions in telecommunications policy, while also seeking to reconcile the contemporary forces pressing for liberalisation with traditional Labor sensibilities and the varied concerns of the party's support base.

The first policy objective was uninterrupted fidelity to Australia's universal service objective, 'in recognition of its social importance'—though now explicitly limited to 'standard telephone services'. Next was a commitment to retaining Telecom, OTC and Aussat in government hands, but with measures to ensure that they delivered 'the highest possible levels of accountability and responsiveness to customer and community needs' and 'appropriate returns on investment'. The government also acknowledged the need for the telecommunications sector to have 'capacity [to provide] a full range of modern ... services at the lowest possible prices'; this was paired uncomfortably with a requirement that all sectoral elements, notably domestic equipment manufacturers, could 'participate effectively in the rapidly growing Australian and world telecommunications markets'.

Cutting across these objectives were three 'fundamental constraints', each of which had long been a feature of Australia's telecommunications system. They were the need to reconcile the system's immense demand for capital with continuous technological developments and related investment risks; the need to reconcile adjusting prices to be closer to costs with the 'far-reaching social concerns regarding these changes'; and the need to reconcile accountability controls over government enterprises with their ever-growing need for greater operational autonomy.[14]

At Labor's national conference in 1988, its policy platform was amended to reflect these new positions. This also shone a light on the party's ambivalence about this shift. Labor's commitment to state ownership and monopoly remained, but was now confined to 'key elements' of the telecommunications system. Thus Telecom's 'exclusive rights' would stay, but only 'to the extent necessary to guarantee universal service'. What 'the extent necessary' actually meant would have to wait until Telecom's community service obligations were independently costed. In the meantime, the continued political sanctity of existing cross-subsidy arrangements provided cover for the sector unions to hang on to their territory, including the first telephone monopoly, which was explicitly highlighted.[15]

Corporatisation and control

As we saw in chapter 8, former communications minister Michael Duffy and finance minister Peter Walsh had by April 1987 reached an uneasy accommodation over the fraught guidelines project. Shortly after Labor's re-election in July, Walsh sought cabinet support for a revised plan that had been, to his mind, watered down 'as far as we should go' to meet the objections of government enterprises and 'dispel most concerns expressed during the consultative process'. He conceded that granting portfolio ministers approval powers over enterprises' operational plans and targets had proved to be unworkably contentious and instead proposed that their role be limited to signing-off, 'where appropriate', on high-level operational and financial 'intentions' and major targets. A logical outcome of this, which was welcomed by portfolio ministers, was abandoning the mooted and much resisted obligation for them to consult with the treasurer and finance minister on enterprises' corporate plans. As such, portfolio ministers who were 'troubled' by a particular enterprise's plan would do well, Walsh recommended, to encourage the relevant board to 'think again'.

But with $12 billion in federal equity and debt tied up in statutory authorities and state enterprises, accounting for nearly 80 per cent of federal government expenditure and about half its civilian workforce, the fundamental point of the guidelines project was unchanged. This was, Walsh advised, to 'provide incentive, enhance efficiency and improve public accountability' of enterprises by replacing 'unnecessary central controls' with alternative measures to ensure a 'greater emphasis on bottom-line performance'. Though direct Treasury and Finance involvement in strategic planning and target-setting was now off the table, the two departments would remain the arbiters of whether the commonwealth was receiving 'an adequate return' from its enterprises; they would retain the right to access 'relevant information' to assess this.[16]

After cabinet endorsed Walsh's diluted plan in September 1987, officials began the daunting task of developing detailed corporatisation plans tailored to individual enterprises. In terms of identifying 'unnecessary central controls' for removal or relaxation, a distinction was made between those that were 'specific to an enterprise', which Walsh suggested would be best determined by the enterprises themselves, and those that were applicable across the board—such as Loan Council borrowing limits, industrial relations coordination, remuneration structures, public works procedures and procurement and offsets rules—that required 'detailed consideration of the implications beyond the interests' of any one enterprise. For Telecom, by far the largest enterprise, these controls represented a list of bugbears that it and its predecessor, the PMG, had railed against for decades.

The public servants advising cabinet's Structural Adjustment Committee considered competition to be the 'most direct method' to improve the efficiency of government enterprises.[17] Officials in Hawke's department also made this point to him directly. They told him that competition would 'achieve sustainable efficiency gains with less continued government intervention' while mitigating the risk of enterprises simply raising prices to meet financial targets.[18] Hawke was advised to tie any withdrawal of external controls with increased exposure to competition, using the former as a 'carrot' to achieve the latter.

Telecom was particularly in the Prime Minister's Department's sights, underlining its king-of-the-castle status and the close relationship between the government's telecommunications review and the long-running corporatisation project. Hawke was told that most of the departments with ministers on the Structural Adjustment Committee 'strongly' considered that Telecom did not face significant competition; he was urged to hold the line on accountability controls and competition against resolute lobbying from Telecom, the sector unions and their allies in caucus.[19]

In October, the Structural Adjustment Committee endorsed a proposal by officials to prepare a series of papers dealing with government controls applicable to all enterprises.[20] In parallel, Evans and his department began negotiating tailored corporatisation reform packages for Telecom, OTC and Aussat (and its other portfolio enterprises and agencies). Walsh tabled the guidelines in the Senate in early November, characterising them as a 'major step' in the government's 'overhaul' of the public service. His parliamentary statement ranged in detail over Labor's policy objectives, acknowledging the areas of contention and outlining next steps. But there was no disguising the extent to which the final product, after more than four years of deliberation, reflected a series of lowest-common-denominator compromises.[21] Rising in reply, former Treasury secretary John Stone, now newly (and incongruously) elected as a National Party senator from Queensland, made hay on this point, exclaiming 'Is that it? Is that really it?'[22]

The six months to May 1988 involved intense, gruelling engagement between Evans, his department, the enterprises and agencies in his portfolio, and Finance, to agree a set of specific corporate and financial targets. Looking back, Evans recalls it as a 'huge, huge, huge task'. Whereas his predecessor, Duffy, had championed Telecom's traditional powers and prerogatives and worked to delay and dilute the Finance Department's guidelines project, Evans considered Telecom ill-suited for Australia's contemporary needs; it was, he says, a 'staid, flaccid public service' institution operating 'in the guise' of a business enterprise. Evans worked intensely to translate the guidelines' 'general aspirations … into some really serious programs' that would do away with 'the old approach of government focusing on the inputs and letting the outputs take care of themselves'. He wanted 'properly structured corporate entities with proper accountability'.[23]

It was critically important that the Hawke government's development of tailored corporatisation measures was carried out within a centrally coordinated across-the-board program. Regarding Telecom, this meant that perennially vexed issues such as industrial relations coordination arrangements and capital borrowing controls, which had previously proved irresolvable because of their direct impact on other areas of the public sector and economy, could be dealt with as part of the government's concurrent focus on measures and controls applicable to other federal enterprises. It also meant that Telecom (or other government enterprises) could not credibly reject the introduction of new corporate objectives and financial targets because they were being enacted under a framework applicable to all enterprises after four-plus years of exhaustive consultations. Telecom had been co-opted into the process. But, on the other hand, the specific measures flowing from these enterprise-by-enterprise negotiations would be, by their nature, incremental, and could only be implemented with the relevant enterprise's agreement and cooperation.

Cabinet's Structural Adjustment Committee formally considered Evans's proposed corporatisation measures in late April and early May 1988 and substantially accepted his recommendations, which he then announced in the Senate. While this project was driven principally by the need to improve Australia's productivity, the core policy challenge underlying it was a familiar one: how best to balance accountability controls over government enterprises with the operational autonomy they needed to function efficiently.[24] Indeed, Evans's explicit claim that his plan for Telecom would 'simultaneously offer greater operating autonomy and enhanced accountability' echoed almost precisely the same claims by former Liberal postmaster-general Alan Hulme some twenty years earlier (as discussed in chapter 1).[25]

Evans argued that government enterprises with a 'well-developed commercial culture' that competed with the private sector or fulfilled 'no explicit social objectives' should become government-owned companies. Those not satisfying these criteria should remain as statutory authorities.[26] On this basis, cabinet agreed that Aussat would remain a state-owned company (though ministerial powers would be expanded to enable the dismissal of board members for 'ongoing underperformance'), OTC would become one, and Telecom would stay as it was albeit with more commercially oriented financial settings for debt, dividends and tax, clearer leadership accountabilities, and the more businesslike moniker of 'Corporation'.[27] OTC gained its new status in the face of departmental advice to Hawke that Australia's company director obligations would sit 'badly' with OTC's 'social objectives'; senior officials flagged the prospect of a profit-maximising OTC exploiting its market monopoly to raise charges for calling 'the US, UK, Greece and Italy'.[28] This appears not to have unduly concerned the prime minister.

The new obligations regarding government enterprises and their strategic planning outlined in Evans's statement were in line with Walsh's proposals to cabinet shortly after the 1987 election, though Evans paid special attention to the politically sensitive issue of basic telephone pricing. Ministerial approval would make way for a transparent 'pricing formula for monopoly prices' and be subject to 'oversight and monitoring' by an independent telecommunications regulator. A more contentious issue, unsurprisingly, related to setting financial targets for state enterprises. Reflecting this, Evans publicly released a lengthy list of mandatory matters to be considered for each enterprise in determining a reasonable figure. This included assessing an enterprise's degree of market power and the impact of ministerial directions and residual government controls on its profitability and, specifically for Telecom and Australia Post, their costs to deliver community service obligations.[29]

Consistent with the thrust of regulatory changes for telephone price-setting, Evans also foreshadowed further reducing the scope for government intervention in the operations of commonwealth enterprises. This was underpinned by the principle that government enterprises should not be subject to regulations not applicable to the private sector; it would, said former senior official Alex Arena, put an end to bureaucratic 'second guessing' of enterprises' operational activities. They would no longer require ministerial approval to enter into contracts, invest surplus funds, establish subsidiaries, buy and sell property, or negotiate terms and conditions related to borrowings and leases. They could freely enter joint ventures and take minor shareholdings in other companies, so long as these moves were flagged beforehand in their strategic corporate plans. Enterprises' capital works programs would be removed from parliamentary scrutiny. The government also planned to relax Loan Council restrictions on the enterprises operating within the Transport and Communications portfolio. Telecom would be permitted to maintain a rolling three-year borrowings schedule in recognition of the longer-term nature of its capital expenditure program.[30]

The Hawke government planned to retain ultimate control over common-wealth enterprises by way of reserve-style powers in the form of ministerial directions for statutory authorities like Telecom and shareholder rights for government-owned companies like OTC and Aussat. It had other levers too, such as setting total public-sector borrowing levels and extracting dividend payments.[31]

An early test case of the government's shareholder rights was provided by OTC, when an unsanctioned pay deal, struck in breach of Labor's national wage guidelines, resulted in the swift resignations of its managing director and chairman. Evans also exercised his ministerial powers to issue Telecom with its first formal direction: to restrict its 'regulatory policies and practices' now that an independent telecommunications regulator was in the process of being established. This was a response to private-sector concerns that Telecom would exploit its regulatory powers, while it still could, to bolster its market position in preparation for the more challenging operating environment ahead.[32]

Where the Structural Adjustment Committee made material adjustments to Evans's proposals, in relation to dividends and the perpetually problematic issue of industrial relations coordination, it was to tip the scales in favour of greater government control. Evans had backed the position on coordination arrangements traditionally advanced by Telecom (and before it by the PMG), that they unreasonably restricted operational autonomy.[33] It was a 'clumsy' framework, said his department, and against the spirit of Labor's policy objectives for government enterprises. But the Industrial Relations Department, having inherited responsibility for coordination from the Public Service Board, argued that the system was sufficiently flexible for Telecom's needs and, more to the point, that exempting Telecom (and other like enterprises with 'near monopoly' market power) risked opening the floodgates to 'feather-bedding and sweetheart deals' that could imperil the government's national wage case principles.[34] The Prime Minister's Department strongly agreed.[35]

Cabinet's Structural Adjustment Committee sought to balance these concerns with its commitment to fostering greater flexibility and efficiency by state enterprises. Ministers agreed that once 'standard guidelines' for the government's wages and industrial relations policies were prepared, Industrial Relations officials were only to involve themselves in such matters when the new processes failed; however, as insurance, the minister for industrial relations was provided with an explicit mandate to seek cabinet agreement to revert to the arrangements 'as they existed before these changes', and for 'appropriate action to be taken against managers or directors' if Telecom or another enterprise substantially breached the new settlement.[36]

Evans's Structural Adjustment Committee colleagues resolved 'specifically not to endorse' his recommendations to limit cabinet's prerogatives on state enterprise dividends. Regarding Telecom, they explicitly rejected an obligation for cabinet to 'take into consideration the interdependent effects which the level of dividends would have on capital structure, cash flow, capital expenditure requirements, tariff increases, borrowing levels and profit growth as well as the ensuing financial ratios upon which Telecom's financial performance is judged'. Ministers also rejected Evans's proposal that Telecom's board of directors be granted 'a significant degree of flexibility in recommending the level of dividend to the government and must not be constrained by the government's annual budgetary considerations'.[37] In sum, the Hawke government would decide the level of dividends coming to its coffers and the circumstances in which they came.

Legislating for change

In mid-1988, former Labor leader Bill Hayden vacated the foreign affairs and trade portfolio as a precursor to becoming governor-general. Evans moved into Hayden's old job, realising a long-held ambition. Ralph Willis replaced Evans and took charge of implementing the government's telecommunications reform program announced a few months earlier. Senior public servant Graham Evans, who had been secretary of the new Primary Industries and Energy mega-department since 1987, succeeded Peter Wilenski (who was off to New York as ambassador to the United Nations).

Gareth Evans describes Labor's incipient reforms to Australia's telecommunications system as 'very cautious [and] rather conservative', yet he also asserts that these first steps added up to 'a big mouthful [that] really did create the momentum for all that subsequently followed'.[38] There is certainly merit to this assessment, and it is not to underplay the unquestionably substantial challenges and complexities associated with the Hawke government's initial moves to also recognise that Evans clearly enjoyed a first-mover advantage as a reforming communications minister in 1987–88. Politically pragmatic and ideologically uninvested in telecommunications policy, he took charge of developing a set of tightly targeted, exhaustively negotiated changes to an outdated and cumbersome system. These reforms were sufficiently incremental to keep faith with caucus, unions and local manufacturers, but consequential enough to meet at least baseline business requirements. As he said at the time, 'everyone got roughly 50 per cent of what they asked for'.[39]

Graham Evans describes Willis as a 'key player' in progressing the government's program. It was he who oversaw implementation of the 1988 reforms and who made the critical decisions, most notably about costing Telecom's community service obligations, which set the stage for the subsequent reforms that Hawke tasked to Kim Beazley following Labor's re-election in March 1990.[40] Senior officials in the Transport and Communications Department respected Willis's intellect and commitment to structural reform; they found him more understated and somewhat slower at decision-making than his frenetic predecessor.[41] In Willis's own words, the reform process while he was minister from 1988 to 1990 did not reflect 'some ideological, bureaucratic blueprint'; it was 'pragmatic and flexible'.[42]

The task of translating the May 1988 statements into legislation that could pass the parliament quickly enough to allow a new regulator to be operational by

1 July 1989 was, in the words of senior Transport and Communications official Vanessa Fanning, a 'technically, legally and philosophically complex' process. The complicated and contested nature of the government's reform measures, and its wish to avoid provoking unintended sectoral consequences, prompted Willis and his department to adopt the then unusual practice of releasing exposure drafts of its telecommunications bill to key parties in order to gain their feedback and to test the substance of competing claims. According to Fanning, important amendments to the draft bill were made 'up to and including the final day of consultation'. Most of these related to refining the legislation's pro-competition objectives and strengthening the measures to constrain Telecom and OTC from taking 'undue advantage of their dominance'.[43]

A particular challenge was determining the boundaries between the networks and services to be 'reserved' for Telecom, OTC and Aussat, and those to be opened to competition. The technical nature of telecommunications meant this was an inherently complex process; the pace of technological change made it more so. The option of defining reserved services was rejected to avert what would surely become a perpetual lawyers' picnic. Also rejected was the option of giving greater discretionary power to the new regulator to resolve such issues. The government wanted to keep this regulatory prerogative for itself, and the uncertainty that such a model entailed caused concern within the state enterprises as well as their prospective private-sector competitors.

It was ultimately decided to permit the three government enterprises to retain monopolies over their physical networks and the services carried over them, while opening to the market everything attached to or operating outside the networks. This provided for competition in cabling, value-added services, private networks and customer equipment installation and maintenance. A price cap mechanism would operate for reserved services. The government's bill also contained various sunset clauses, including those to allow the temporary preservation of Telecom's first telephone monopoly. According to Fanning, these clauses were key to ensuring that it was clear to all and sundry that the government's 1989 reform measures represented only the initial steps along a clearly marked path to further changes.

Shortly after the Telecommunications Act 1989 was enacted, the telecommunications scholar Mark Armstrong noted the considerable ambiguity that still remained: practical arrangements for Telecom's community service obligations were 'far from settled'; the demarcation between telecommunications and trade practices laws was unresolved; and both parliament and the new regulator, the Australian Telecommunications Authority (Austel), had powers to amend the boundary between reserved and competitive services. As it was, the boundary was already somewhat unclear; there were concerns that Telecom (in particular), OTC and Aussat might exploit future technological developments to leverage their monopoly advantages into new competitive areas, such as by integrating value-added functionality into reserved networks.[44]

Opposition and business perspectives

The Hawke government's third-term telecommunications agenda was, with the notable exception of privatisation, effectively a move toward Coalition policy positions, albeit for Labor's own reasons. This meant that the focal point of political and policy friction between government and opposition was associated not with the underlying need for change or its general direction but with its pace and scope. Indeed, from early in the government's policy review process, at around the time Evans was acquiescing to the formation of caucus's telecommunications liaison committee, but especially after his May announcements about competition and corporatisation, the opposition was sharply critical of Labor incrementalism under pressure from incumbent vested interests and internal party dissent.

From the late 1980s, the Victorian Liberal senator Richard Alston was a thoughtful and articulate contributor to telecommunications policy debates, serving twice as shadow communications minister and then in John Howard's cabinet for seven years, during which he led Australia's shift to full telecommunications competition and the privatisation of Telstra. Alston initially made common cause with the Hawke government about maintaining Telecom's common carrier monopoly, which he considered 'sensible', but he railed against the government's pretence that it had baulked at allowing competition in data, text, video or mobile services or ending the first telephone monopoly out of concern about the viability of Telecom's community-service obligations. He dismissed government attempts to deflect attention onto the opposition's privatisation policies, declaring that 'not for a moment' was the Coalition considering selling Telecom's basic network infrastructure.[45]

During parliamentary debate about the telecommunications bill in June 1989, the opposition targeted Labor's internal divisions and the limited nature of its reform program. Happily pointing out that the government's senior economic ministers, including Transport and Communications Minister Willis, understood and accepted the 'imperative for competition to drive government business enterprises', Alston criticised the extent to which government decision-making was being distorted by 'the left wing of the Australian Labor Party, the anti-privateers, those members of caucus who live in rural areas and a whole range of nervous nellies'. Labor's bill should be called the 'Telecom monopoly preservation package', Alston proclaimed, characterising Telecom as a 'lion locked in a cage of the government's own making'; if allowed to 'roam the competitive jungles', he argued, it would undoubtedly 'thrive'.[46]

Regarding traditional social policy objectives, Alston accepted the legitimacy of government making 'an explicit political decision' to subsidise uneconomic services, but he attacked the opaque and unaccountable nature of Australia's telecommunications cross-subsidy system (as Labor had in opposition twenty years earlier). He argued that 'the cost should be transparent and a sensible, political judgment should be made about whether that is the most effective use of a government subsidy'.[47] During the 1989 debate, Alston accused the government of hiding behind the Bureau of Transport and Communications Economics' review into the costs of Telecom's community-service obligation in order to justify its inaction on telecommunications competition policy. He accepted that 'we simply do not know' what the total cost was (citing estimates of $200–250 million) but argued that whatever figure was ultimately calculated, it would certainly be well below Telecom's $1 billion annual profit. As such, there was no valid justification for delay.[48]

The views of Australia's businesses and larger telecommunications users, as represented by ATUG, were broadly consistent with those of senior officials in the economic policy departments and agencies, the opposition and, indeed, those also being considered by government ministers. ATUG accepted Telecom's ongoing role as the common carrier monopoly and was prepared to accommodate some form of cross-subsidisation to pay for uneconomic services. It also recognised that Labor's reforms would be inherently incremental; they would occur in 'fits and starts', Tony Staley remarked immediately after the government's third term re-election.

ATUG's immediate policy priority, Staley stated, was to achieve 'full and fair' competition in the customer equipment and value-added services sectors, and the establishment of an independent regulator with responsibility for technical standards and network access arrangements. He explicitly distanced ATUG from ideologically driven market liberal policy prescriptions such as those being espoused by business figure Hugh Morgan, who was calling for the abolition of Telecom's monopoly and the carrier's full privatisation. According to Staley, 'at this stage, subject to decent policy development', Australia's institutional telecommunications users were not interested in going 'the whole hog ... they believe there is a role for Telecom, down into the future'. But ATUG was soon frustrated by the degree to which the government was bowing to incumbent vested interests, particularly by delaying competition in first telephones and data and mobile services.[49]

There was consensus about the broad direction of telecommunications policy between the economic pragmatists in Hawke's government and the officials advising them, the Coalition, the business sector, groups such as ATUG, the top people in Telecom and, to some extent, even within the ACTU. The central debate among this diverse circle of interests was less about the need for change than about how fast it went and how far. Among the Liberal and Labor parties, the issue was much more straightforward for the former than the latter, since the forces for liberalisation were consistent with the interests of the Liberals' core business base and their underlying policy instincts, especially since embracing market liberalism after losing the 1983 election. It was also more straightforward for them because complex structural economic reform is much easier to advocate in opposition than to achieve in government.

Gareth Evans's pragmatic policy agnosticism about telecommunications and his unwillingness to risk industrial conflict, consistent with Hawke's commitment to keeping the unions and caucus on side, were important factors in the government's ability to progress meaningful reform in 1987, but this also led an already incremental process to become even more incremental than initially planned. However, taking account of Labor's poor result in the February 1988 Adelaide by-election and the fillip this gave the telecommunications unions, it remains an open question whether a more economically activist Labor minister could have advanced much further than Evans during this period—or, indeed, how far a Coalition government could have gone.

Austel's balancing act

The most immediately noticeable change to come from the Hawke government's 1989 reforms was the establishment of Austel as independent regulator. Its remit was wide, encompassing technical and economic regulation; granting and revising class licences for value-added services and permits for equipment network connections; promoting efficiency in state enterprises; implementing Labor's industry development policies for local equipment manufacturers; undertaking investigations and reviews as directed by government; and, in the words of junior telecommunications minister Ros Kelly, being a 'consumer watchdog'.[50]

Austel's inaugural chairman, Robin Davey, was a lawyer and previously with the Trade Practices Commission. He saw the regulator's top priorities as protecting carrier monopolies; protecting competition; protecting consumers; promoting carrier efficiency; and ensuring the safety and technical quality of products and services.[51] It would be like walking 'a tightrope', Davey said; he was at pains to urge all parties to 'talk to us direct rather than take the strictly legalistic approach that has plagued other regulatory bodies'.[52] Almost immediately there were doubts about whether all this was possible, not least due to the number of former Telecom staff now working for the new agency.[53] Richard Alston worried that Austel's obligation to safeguard Telecom's monopoly rights when considering licensing of customer equipment and value-added services would provide the incumbent with critical intelligence on its competitors' plans.[54] And it was not long before value-added services providers were accusing Telecom of undermining competition and Telecom was proclaiming its unhappiness with regulatory decisions.[55]

Davey's view was that if both sides were complaining then he was probably doing something right.[56] He took Austel's policy administration role seriously, saying that he 'deliberately distanced' himself and Austel from ongoing political and policy debates to insulate the regulator's decisions from 'challenge for perceived bias'.[57] He also kept clear of Willis and, after him, Kim Beazley, delegating what he considered 'the political side of things' to Alex Arena, a former Transport and Communications Department official who had been appointed as one of Austel's inaugural members.[58]

The new regulator started life with a full plate. In addition to its day-to-day activities, Austel was charged with reviewing various contentious matters that had been left hanging in the reform package announced back in May 1988.

This included advising the government on arrangements for private networks and, more significantly, the implications of licensing another mobile services operator to compete with Telecom. The mobile review prompted submissions from prospective providers keen to enter the Australian market and vigorous lobbying from Telecom against such a move, notwithstanding complaints that the incumbent was already failing to meet demand and, behind closed doors, debate within Telecom's top echelons about whether its interests would be better served by accepting the inevitability of mobile competition and focusing instead on shaping Australia's future regulatory environment to its advantage.[59]

There was something of a stir within the government when Austel recommended that it not only issue two new mobile licences, but also that it structurally separate Telecom's mobile group, MobileNet, from the rest of its operations, require Telecom to provide non-discriminatory mobile network access to the new competitors, and have everything in place by December 1990.[60] Looking back, Davey likens the impact of these recommendations to 'throwing a dead cat on the table', though having made them, he kept himself and Austel aloof from the ensuing debate so that the regulator could implement whatever course of action was ultimately decided on.[61]

Austel's report into mobile services competition triggered a whirlwind of controversy when it was publicly released. In full expectation of this, the government held back the report until after the March 1990 election and Beazley's appointment as the new transport and communications minister. In Davey's opinion, the mobile services review was the 'tipping point' that announced Austel's arrival as a player in Australia's telecommunications scene.[62]

Costing Telecom's community service obligations

Of the matters held over by the Hawke government in 1989 for later resolution, the most critical was the need to independently quantify the cost of Telecom's community service obligations. To that end, Tony Shaw returned to the Bureau of Transport and Communications Economics to lead this complex and politically sensitive project. The bureau and Telecom each employed the global management consulting firm LEK to acquire the data needed for the review and then assist their respective analyses.

Telecom engaged LEK to build an economic model using a fully distributed cost methodology, in which it allocated all costs between Telecom's commercial and community service-related operations regardless of whether or not they would be incurred if Telecom fulfilled only commercial activities. In contrast, Shaw used the LEK-derived data to populate the bureau's own in-house economic model, which was based on avoidable costs and sought to quantify only those additional costs that Telecom incurred in fulfilling its obligations.[63] This approach identified three categories of community service obligations: loss-making basic infrastructure and services, loss-incurring public telephones, and concessions provided to pensioners, people with disabilities and public institutions.

Shaw's avoidable cost method calculated Telecom's costs at between $120 million and $240 million, depending on assumptions about its opportunity cost of capital. Telecom's model generated total costs of between $508 million and $800 million.[64] Shaw considered Telecom's approach to be 'plainly wrong' because it included costs that would be incurred regardless of whether service obligations applied or not. Willis, who was himself an economist, shared this view. At a lengthy meeting that included Graham Evans and Shaw and continued into the early hours, Willis confirmed his support for the bureau's analysis over Telecom's.[65]

This decision by Willis is arguably the most critical that he made during his eighteen months as Australia's minister for transport and communications. In making it, he opened the door that enabled the Hawke government to embark on its last great political and policy battle over telecommunications.

11

Competitive Influences

In the important growth area of telecommunications, we must significantly increase competitive influences.

Bob Hawke[1]

Gareth Evans had foreshadowed in May 1988 that the structural arrangements governing Telecom, OTC and Aussat would be reviewed, though no timeframe was set. Officials in the Department of Transport and Communications started preparing for such a review in the latter half of 1989, after the government's first-wave reforms had been legislated, but Aussat's increasingly calamitous finances decidedly pushed things along.[2] The satellite company's debt-to-equity ratio by then had hit 22:1 and accumulated losses were over $118 million.[3] It looked as if Aussat would struggle to fund its first generation of satellites, let alone the second.[4] As its once bullish managing director, Graham Gosewinckel, conceded, 'Blind Freddy can see we need a capital injection'.[5]

Transport and Communications Department secretary Graham Evans and Tony Shaw, recently returned from the Bureau of Transport and Communications Economics, put it to Ralph Willis that Aussat's perilous position needed to be addressed as a matter of urgency, and that this should be part of a wider review into the three government telecommunications enterprises. Even with a capital injection, and putting aside management missteps, Aussat could never be viable while it was lumbered with the operating restrictions imposed on it during Labor's first term. Willis concurred and gave his senior officers an unfettered mandate to consider remedies for Aussat as part of a comprehensive review, contingent on open engagement with key stakeholders and interest groups.[6]

Willis announced a Review of Structural Arrangements (known as 'ROSA') in early December 1989. It was to explore options to sort out the Aussat mess and investigate 'the scope for and costs and benefits of merging one or more of the carriers into a single organisation', and to report by 30 June 1990. Given that ROSA sparked a wide-ranging debate about telecommunications competition and ultimately formed the basis of the Hawke government's competition reforms, it is striking that this issue featured only cursorily in the review's terms of reference; its final clause prescribed an evaluation of the 'the boundaries of the respective carriers' monopolies to allow greater competition between the carriers'.[7] But grappling with these challenges was not to be Willis's burden. This responsibility would instead fall to Hawke acolyte Kim Beazley.

Baptism of fire

Labor was re-elected to a fourth term in March 1990. In the post-election cabinet reshuffle, Willis moved to the finance portfolio and Beazley replaced him in transport and communications. Beazley had been the minister for defence for more than five years. He had no economic policy experience and had played no significant role in the government's economic reform debates. He was reluctant to change jobs and recalls Hawke jesting with him that during his time in defence, 'I had been working for myself, but now I had to work for the country'.[8] According to his senior policy adviser Paddy Costanzo, Beazley also knew that if he was to advance further in politics, perhaps even to national leadership, he needed solid experience in a big, economically important domestic portfolio.[9]

Telecommunications reform was absolutely central to Labor's fourth-term economic agenda and Hawke's appointment of Beazley to run it blended Labor politics with policy pragmatism. Hawke viewed Beazley as 'future prime ministerial material' and wanted to blood him in a critical economic policy area to round out his experience while also building him up as a foil to Paul Keating, with whom leadership tensions were escalating.[10] In Beazley, Hawke saw a trusted ally who was amenable to liberalising Australia's telecommunications system but was also deeply imbued with traditional Labor values; he was someone able to construct a reform package that was both economically credible and acceptable to caucus, the unions and the party.[11]

It was to be a baptism of fire. On Beazley's first full day as 'the minister for microeconomic reform' (his term), his department confronted him with the looming financial and political catastrophe of Aussat.[12] The company's 'severe financial problems' included a forecast increase in accumulated losses of almost 60 per cent for 1989/90, to $123.2 million, and a $45 million collapse in shareholders' funds to minus $23.2 million. With only $100 million of paid-up capital and weak market demand (Costanzo observed to Beazley's senior private secretary Patrick Walters that Aussat's customers were 'either broke or rely on government handouts'), Aussat was heavily reliant on debt. Beazley was advised that, as of February 1990, Aussat's debt-to-equity ratio had ballooned to 46:1.[13] Just two days earlier, the Commonwealth Bank had given Gosewinckel formal notice that Aussat's underwriting banks, led by the Commonwealth, feared the company was on the precipice of being unable to service its debt and foreshadowed the bank's withdrawal of support. In this case, 'an event of default would be triggered'. It was 'essential', said the bank's head of lending, that Aussat's shareholders (that is, the federal government and/or Telecom) inject at least $100 million into the company by 30 June at the latest, less than three months away, to save Aussat from the financial abyss.[14]

A key problem, Beazley was advised, was the limited addressable market that was available to Aussat. While the Fraser government's intention when establishing the company had been for it to have an 'open competitive charter', Hawke's government had shackled it to a narrow range of permitted activities (the provision of private network facilities and services) which covered only 10 per cent of Australia's telecommunications sector.[15] Senior official Vanessa Fanning told Beazley that it was not only beyond question that Aussat required a government bailout (though there was a question about the amount), but that this bailout must be linked to broader structural changes, not just related to Aussat's operating environment but also to the arrangements governing Telecom, OTC and the wider telecommunications sector.[16] Solving the Aussat problem was a 'critical factor' in the government's review, Fanning said; there was 'an urgent requirement to decide on the desired direction of future changes to carrier ownership and structural relationships in the long term … so a decision can be taken now in relation to Aussat's current financial position'.[17]

The impending crisis at Aussat was not just driving the timing of ROSA, but also setting the parameters and timing of the government's decision-making process. A particular sensitivity for the government was that its own decisions were substantially responsible for Aussat's predicament. It was 'somewhat embarrassed' by its culpability, says Costanzo, and this prevented the consideration of options such as simply writing off Aussat's debt.[18] Both Gareth Evans and Beazley acknowledged this at the time.[19] Beazley's department stated the issue plainly: allowing Telecom to take a 25 per cent stake in Aussat and two positions on its board had created 'immediate ... anomalies' since Telecom considered Aussat to be a 'threat'. Telecom's 'commercially inspired disinclination' to utilise Aussat's network over its own, even when this would have been more cost-effective, had undermined the satellite company's 'overall viability'. It was 'reasonable to suspect' that Telecom's decisions were motivated by a 'desire ... to minimise its competitor's viability and credibility and/or pave the way for Aussat's absorption into Telecom'. It was further noted that Telecom's investment in Aussat was not achieving a commercial return, suggesting that it must be seen as 'a strategic investment to protect Telecom's interests and hence almost by definition is not conducive to Aussat's interests'.[20]

In retrospect, Beazley considers that Aussat was 'a sinkhole of government money' and that Telecom 'killed' the company by a 'quite deliberate' strategy.[21] Perhaps his awareness of Labor's complicity in this state of affairs caused Beazley later to downplay Aussat's prominence in his considerations at the time. Graham Evans, however, recalls that the imperative to 'fix Aussat' was always central to the government's agenda, and Beazley's adviser, Costanzo, believes that solving Aussat was 'basically the benchmark on everything and [the reason] why we took particular actions'.[22]

Amid this, Hawke formally outlined his expectations to Beazley: to 'significantly increase competitive influences' in telecommunications, specifically regarding 'mobile phones; competition between the public carriers; and the future viability of Aussat', in order to realise 'benefits to the economy of the new technologies which characterise the sector'.[23] Hawke, along with his senior private secretary, Peter Harris,[24] and Rod Sims, until recently his economic adviser and now deputy secretary in the Prime Minister's Department with responsibility for economic, infrastructure and social policy,[25] also met with Beazley to emphasise to him the need for Telecom to face a potentially full-service competitor, for the government to accept Austel's recommendation for licensing two new mobile services providers, and for the liberalisation of rules around private network capacity resale.[26]

There was much contention over how Australia's future telecommunications sector should operate. Input was sought from key parties including Telecom, OTC,

Aussat, unions, industry associations and consumer groups. Notwithstanding ROSA's ostensibly structural focus, the issue of competition, whether as opportunity or threat, was at the top of everyone's mind.[27] Wielding a mix of old and new arguments, Telecom, OTC and Aussat each pushed their own interests. Telecom was open to competition, it said, by which it meant taking over OTC and Aussat and competing with a single new (presumably foreign) competitor in exchange for freer access to capital, greater operational autonomy and less telecommunications-specific regulation. OTC rolled out its traditional case against absorption by Telecom and advocated its own takeover of Aussat, citing technological synergies. In this plan, OTC-Aussat would immediately compete with Telecom across the board, but Telecom would be barred from OTC's international markets until the new entity was established domestically. For its part, Aussat wanted freedom from government ownership and freedom to compete against Telecom and OTC across all services over all networks in all locations, with no new competitors permitted to enter the market.[28]

The large users' association, ATUG, considered that Labor's 1989 reforms were serving 'the interests of … household telephone users and non-urban users on the one hand and employees and managers of monopoly carrier firms and their equipment suppliers on the other'; it wanted Telecom, OTC and Aussat to remain as separate entities and for the telecommunications sector to be fully opened to new competitors.[29] ATUG also proposed separating Telecom into three 'arms-length companies', respectively responsible for network infrastructure, fixed services and mobile, with the network company legally obliged to give non-discriminatory network interconnection to all access seekers (the new fixed-services company and any third-party providers) and provide full network data to Austel.[30] (It would later become abundantly apparent that effectively enforcing such regulations was devilishly difficult.)

The bottom line for ATUG was that whatever model the Hawke government ultimately adopted, the 'best chance' of effective competition required 'OTC to be kept separate from Telecom'.[31] In this it was destined to be disappointed. Less so were the big Telecom unions, the ATEA and APTU, which were unyieldingly opposed any form of liberalisation. They supported one change only: the merger of Australia's two 'dominant' carriers, Telecom and OTC; and they did so enthusiastically because it would mean a larger, stronger Telecom and the realisation of a long-term dream to capture OTC and its rivers of gold.[32] The new consumer group, the Consumers' Telecommunications Network, feared that the sector's liberalisation would benefit business at consumers' expense (a point privately acknowledged by Telecom). While conceding the inevitability of competition in more business-orientated and innovative services, the group wanted standard telephone services to remain 'reserved' and to be operated by a new Telecom-OTC-Aussat 'megacom'.[33]

On 10 April, Beazley sought Hawke's support for cabinet's swift consideration of an immediate capital injection to keep Aussat afloat until longer-term changes could be worked through as part of the broader ROSA process.[34] Hawke agreed that Aussat required 'urgent attention'. As he and Beazley readied themselves to travel to Turkey for the seventy-fifth anniversary of the Gallipoli landing, Hawke suggested the matter go to cabinet at its next meeting.[35] Virtually as the politicians' plane left the tarmac, Beazley's department was being warned by the Commonwealth Bank that Aussat required $100 million 'within the next two weeks'.[36] A handwritten note by Peter Harris was on the money: 'I foreshadow lots of telecommunications for Kim on return'.[37] Beazley had been in the job a fortnight.

Cabinet met on 1 May. Beazley informed his colleagues that Aussat was 'on the verge of technical bankruptcy' and, without an 'immediate capital injection' of $100 million, payable either upfront or in instalments, the company's bankers would disclose its financial situation and likely render it 'unable to meet its obligation[s]'.[38] Hawke came to the meeting with official advice that Aussat's equity base was 'grossly inadequate', but his department's preference was for cabinet to approve only $30 million (enough to cover Aussat's net operating loss for the year) with any further funding to be considered in light of ROSA.[39] For his part, Keating was armed with blunt advice from his senior adviser Ken Henry (later a long-term secretary of the Treasury): that if a $100 million payment to Aussat was 'the first micro reform decision taken by this government we might as well pack our bags now'. Henry accepted Aussat's need for capital but thought that $40 million would be adequate, with the proviso that any public announcement came with 'some pretty good cover'. This 'cover' should be to link the payment to the removal of Aussat's operating restrictions, which were, he said, the principal culprit in Aussat's 'failure'.[40] As it was, cabinet agreed to an immediate capital injection of $100 million, provided that it went entirely to retiring debt.[41] Consistent with their equity holdings in Aussat, the government paid $75 million and Telecom paid $25 million.[42] Three months later, the investment bank CS First Boston forecast that, even if Aussat gained full access to all markets, it would still require another $400 million in capital to 'become viable'.[43]

While all this was going on, the government finally released the Austel mobile competition report that recommended two new providers to compete with Telecom, preferably by year's end. At this, the caucus, the unions and Telecom erupted.[44] Roger Price, chairman of the telecommunications liaison committee, a former long-term Telecom employee and member of Labor's right, expressed caucus's opposition to ending Telecom's monopoly in mobile services. Left caucus member Bruce Childs went further, declaring that 'everything the Left has done has been to oppose the breaking up of Telecom control'. The ATEA condemned Austel's recommendation as 'Thatcherite', with the union's federal secretary Mick Musumeci arguing that Australia had 'already had one disastrously expensive mistake with competition in the telecommunications industry, Aussat … We don't need another'.[45]

Telecom's managing director, Mel Ward, also ramped up the pressure. Competition in mobile services would not stimulate anything 'new or different', he stated, whereas permitting new providers to access Telecom's mobile network could cost more than $1 billion over ten years. This cost, he vowed, would be passed on in full to customers. Both Ward and caucus condemned the prospect of any new mobile providers being foreign owned. Beazley also faced difficulties in the Senate, where the Australian Democrats, with the balance of power, were opposed to competition. Even Liberal senator Richard Alston indicated his preference for just one new mobile competitor, at least initially; though his view likely reflected the judgement that Telecom would in fact face tougher competition from one new entrant than from two.[46]

Problems and options

Beazley encouraged full and frank advice from his department, and he got it. In his first week as transport and communications minister, his top officials provided him with their assessment of Australian telecommunications' most significant problems: these were Aussat's financial crisis; inter-carrier cross-ownership arrangements, especially as they related to Telecom's hold over Aussat; the fact that Telecom, OTC and Aussat all operated in their own exclusive markets; and a fundamental lack of competition, which had produced high prices and low innovation and raised questions about the regulatory restrictions on the three government enterprises and the private sector.

A set of broad options was outlined to Beazley, sandwiched between the two impractical extremes of doing nothing or deregulating everything. They included maintaining the three carriers as separate entities, though with OTC potentially part-privatised, Aussat sold off entirely and all three allowed to compete with each other; merging OTC and Aussat to compete with Telecom; creating a new Telecom-OTC-Aussat 'megacarrier'; and breaking up Telecom. The megacarrier option came with warnings about the 'massive management problems' involved in merging three commercially 'weak' and mutually 'antagonistic' entities, and the risk that the 'worst practices' of each carrier—Telecom's poor customer service, OTC's excessive executive remuneration and Aussat's ineffective marketing—'could prevail'.[47] Conspicuously absent from these options was the model ultimately implemented, which rested on merging Telecom and OTC and privatising Aussat as the basis of a new full-service carrier.[48]

Beazley was 'very sensitive' to the views of important Labor stakeholders, according to Graham Evans, with the minister and his advisers carefully road-testing reform options with the unions and caucus.[49] Costanzo recalls the unions being 'very much at the forefront'. He says that Beazley gave him 'specific instructions to make sure that the unions were always on side, had someone who would listen to them at all times, and had the ear of the minister'.[50] The feedback from these rolling consultations fed into the policy parameters passed back to the Transport and Communications Department as part of an iterative process to construct a reform framework that Beazley could sell to Hawke and others as economically credible, and to caucus, unions and equipment manufacturers as a model that safeguarded their interests.[51]

The officials working on ROSA wanted as much competitive intensity in the telecommunications sector as possible. Graham Evans states that their preferred model (representing the 'strongest vehicle of competition') was for some form of structural separation of Telecom into discrete network and retail companies, the merger of OTC and Aussat to create a formidable full-service competitor, and measures to open the way for more private-sector providers, which were expected to be initially active in lucrative business market segments.[52]

According to Costanzo, structurally separating Telecom was viewed as the 'holy grail'.[53] Various break-up scenarios were floated by the Transport and Communications Department in early April: splitting Telecom into regional operating companies, either vertically integrated or divided into separate local, national, international and mobile entities; spinning off Telecom's MobileNet division; or breaking Telecom into separate network, services and mobile companies (ATUG's proposal). The key advantage of breaking up Telecom, departmental officials asserted, was to stimulate competition by eliminating its 'entrenched structural market dominance'. On the other hand, scale economies would be lost. This had implications for plans to compete in rapidly deregulating international markets.[54]

Following a meeting with ROSA officials on 11 April, Costanzo presented Beazley with a further option, which resonates strikingly with today's NBN. Under this scenario, a Telecom-OTC-Aussat 'megacom' would concern itself solely with network infrastructure and be 'prohibited' from retail markets, which would be open to competition. The underlying logic (as with the NBN) was that an infrastructure-only megacarrier would be commercially motivated to have as many retail service providers connected to its network as possible. This would render redundant the kind of 'special interconnection' regulations necessary to require a vertically integrated Telecom to provide non-discriminatory network access to its retail competitors.[55]

The Prime Minister's Department meanwhile was pressing Hawke to drive for 'comprehensive' reform that would place Australia 'on a par' with comparable countries and enhance the government's 'credibility' on microeconomic reform. Hawke was urged to push for the thorough investigation of two structural separation models: splitting Telecom into a network-plus-reserved-services company and a 'value-added' services company, or establishing MobileNet as a stand-alone business. This was the 'only guaranteed method', Hawke's departmental officials argued, that would stop Telecom from undermining competition by cross-subsiding competitive activities with monopoly profits.[56]

Peter Harris was also preparing his own paper on telecommunications reform for Hawke, on the 'basic approaches' open to the government; it was circulated to Beazley's office and department in early to mid-May.[57] The ideal approach, according to Harris, would be to reconfigure Telecom and OTC, either separately or as a new merged entity, into 'simple providers' of network infrastructure and basic services, with all 'value-added' services opened up to new competitors. This would remove the 'huge disincentive' for prospective new competitors to enter the Australian market because Telecom would no longer be able to 'adopt' and then dominate new services, nor would it have reason to obstruct access to basic network infrastructure. But, Harris conceded, there would be huge implementation challenges, not least of which was the need for Telecom and OTC to cooperate in 'hiving off' their value-added service operations.

A 'very effective second best' option outlined by Harris was to establish a joint-venture company, with OTC holding a 40 per cent stake, that would operate as a new full-service domestic carrier. The carrier could receive a new mobile licence, or Telecom's MobileNet could be spun off. Full network resale would enable the carrier, and any other market entrants, to compete across all services. This model had the advantage of practicality: Harris pointed out that OTC had a 'powerful desire to compete with Telecom' (or Telecom-Aussat), a well-resourced private-sector partner could 'scare Telecom … to lift its game', and crucially, implementation did not rely on Telecom's cooperation.[58]

Despite all this talk about Telecom's structural separation, the concept faced such hurdles that it never gained any real traction as a practical course of action (although it remained the subject of sometimes intense dialogue right up until cabinet's decision in September). Putting aside implacable caucus and union opposition, there was deep uncertainty among policymakers about the technical feasibility of splitting up Telecom, especially within the timeframe set by the government's political imperative to have its reforms up and running before the next election. A central problem was that the government depended on Telecom for technical advice about a path that the organisation had a strong vested interest in opposing.

Graham Evans's view was that, without Telecom's support, even an independent feasibility study would be unworkable. He considered it unrealistic for officials 'to persuade ministers to buy into something of a technical nature when the primary carrier had a different view on it'. Harris similarly recalls that it was impossible to 'sort out the truth from the fiction' because of polarised views about the concept and a lack of 'proper briefings from Telecom'.[59] Other advocates, such as ATUG, reached much the same conclusion.[60] But over and above all of this, there was another deal-breaker: Beazley himself.

12

A National Champion

*[We need] one very big Australian telecommunications company
... with the right to do whatever it wants in the field of domestic
and international telecommunications.*

Kim Beazley[1]

Reflecting on his period as transport and communications minister, Kim Beazley has said he was 'completely opposed' to all notions of structurally separating Telecom, though not because of the vexed political or technical challenges discussed in the previous chapter. According to Beazley, he believed that splitting Telecom's networks and services divisions would entrench its network monopoly and be 'a mechanism for freezing technology' as it would remove any incentive to invest in network upgrades or product development. To Beazley's mind, this was a particularly acute problem; he recalls advice that Telecom's network, far from being at the 'cutting edge of telecommunications engineering', as he had initially presumed, was actually being kept 'deliberately backward' by Telecom to make life 'as difficult as possible' for prospective new market entrants.[2] Beazley may also have worried that creating a new national network entity would further consolidate union leverage over critical infrastructure. His former adviser Costanzo suggests that memories of the rolling pain inflicted on the Fraser government by the ATEA remained fresh in the minds of Beazley and his advisers.[3]

There is some validity to Beazley's 'freezing technology' concern, but a more likely reason for his flat rejection of structural separation was that his vision for Telecom was heading completely in the opposite direction. Beazley was a true believer in Telecom's future as an Australian 'national champion'. He envisaged it as a home-grown state enterprise able to mix it with larger providers on the world stage, generating export revenues and underpinning Australia's equipment manufacturing sector.[4] This required Telecom not just to remain vertically integrated, but to increase in scale.

To the extent that Beazley was excited by the opportunities of telecommunications liberalisation, it was in foreign markets rather than at home. He was open to the potential benefits that Australia's economy and residents stood to gain from a vigorously competitive domestic sector, but this came second to setting up Telecom to take on global players such as Japan's Nippon Telegraph and Telephone Corporation or British Telecom.[5] Both of these competitors were active in the Asia-Pacific, where telecommunications was expected to be worth up to $130 billion by the mid-1990s.[6] While Telecom was a colossus in Australia, it was only about one-third British Telecom's size and half that of the Bell operating companies in the United States. According to Tony Shaw, so far as Beazley was concerned, 'the stronger [Telecom was] the better'.[7] Indeed, this was a key Beazley justification for Telecom's take-over of OTC. He wanted 'at least one very big Australian telecommunications company ... with the right to do whatever it wants in the field of domestic and international telecommunications'.[8]

Beazley's choice

With structural separation effectively off the table, attention turned to the alternatives. On 18 June, Graham Evans outlined to Beazley his department's 'preliminary thinking' on where ROSA would land. The preferred option was merging OTC and Aussat to form a full-service competitor to Telecom. The two carriers were operationally compatible (a point already made to Beazley by Costanzo, along with the caveat that 'OTC has funds while Aussat does not') and financial analysis by investment bankers CS First Boston was forecasting that the entity would be cashflow positive by 1995, earlier than any of the other merger scenarios. The proposed new company, to be at least partially privatised to prevent direct competition between two state-owned enterprises, would likely deliver 'the most competitive environment ... at an early stage', though Evans also foreshadowed (with a trace of understatement) 'some difficulties in gaining support' from various parties, not least Telecom, the unions and caucus.[9]

Costanzo says (and Evans confirms) that the OTC-Aussat option was debated 'long and hard' within Beazley's office, and between his office and senior officials, before Beazley ultimately concluded it 'was not something he could sell', at least in the timeframe available.[10] In a note to Beazley on 18 June, Evans outlined the department's 'second best' option: to retain the three government carriers as separate entities but with a privatised Aussat, granted a mobile licence and potentially one for pay-television too, given a free hand to compete against Telecom and OTC. Further competitive enhancements included splitting MobileNet from Telecom, awarding a third mobile licence, ending Telecom's first telephone handset monopoly, and permitting OTC to enter into a joint venture with a foreign telecommunications company to establish a new domestic operator.

Evans then came to 'the only other option that I am aware … being seriously discussed'. This was to merge Telecom and OTC and reconstitute Aussat along the lines above. This was the model favoured by Beazley (and ultimately what was implemented). His officials were discernibly cool. Evans's note pointed out that Telecom and OTC were both performing poorly in international markets and that Telecom had failed to provide any evidence to support its claim that joining the two carriers would improve efficiency. Indeed, analysis by ATUG, OTC and the Industry Commission (all opponents of the move) 'would point to a different conclusion'. Moreover, foreshadowing an argument that would soon be mounted by Paul Keating and Treasury, Evans asserted that Australia was most likely to succeed in foreign markets if it had 'a more competitive domestic environment rather than a marginally larger domestic/international carrier'.

If the government was 'nevertheless, still to choose to merge Telecom and OTC' (which Evans presumably surmised was a fair chance), then it would 'need to take a number of steps … to be able to claim that it was promoting competition'. These steps, which Evans acknowledged would be opposed by Telecom and the sector unions (among others), could include establishing Telecom-OTC's value-added services divisions and/or Telecom's MobileNet division as separate entities with their own boards and management teams; placing a regulatory obligation on Telecom-OTC to keep price rises below inflation; issuing a third mobile licence; and/or requiring Austel (as was the case with Britain's Oftel) to 'regulate the industry in favour of new competitors, specifically in this case Aussat'.[11] (Though the value-added services and MobileNet separation options were never pursued, an undated draft submission in Beazley's ministerial files indicates that his department did prepare for such an eventuality.)[12]

Political focus was soon coalescing around three options: to keep Telecom and OTC apart and merge Aussat with one or the other, or to merge Telecom and OTC and use a privatised Aussat as the basis of full-service competition. Beazley came reasonably swiftly to backing the Telecom-OTC versus Aussat model.[13] His view reflected a confluence of factors: accommodating established vested interests, resolving Aussat, satisfying his policy instincts, and judging how far he had to go to fulfil Hawke's instruction to 'significantly increase competitive influences'. In looking for a way to bring Telecom, the unions and caucus sufficiently on side to construct a reform package that was economically credible and could be up and running and showing results by the next election, OTC was Beazley's ace in the hole.

As we know, taking over OTC had long been a much-desired prize for Telecom (and the PMG). Telecom's unions felt the same way. Serendipitously for them, Beazley's 'nationalist view' (widely held at the time) meant that he was opposed to 'handing over' OTC to foreigners; he wanted Australia's international telecommunications assets to stay in Australian hands. Looking back, Beazley says that offering up OTC to Telecom, its unions and their caucus allies was one of the 'few incentives' he had to induce them to 'acquiesce' to the government's agenda.[14] Another factor, says Graham Evans, was that 'there was no way' that Telecom or its unions wanted to be lumbered with Aussat and its rivers of red ink.[15]

Resentment still lingered in the federal caucus about OTC's aggressively fought victory over the Whitlam government's attempt to merge it with Telecom in 1975. For some caucus members, there was an element of payback in their support for Beazley's plan. The South Australian senator Chris Schacht, for example, who during the battle had been principal private secretary to Whitlam's postmaster-general, Reg Bishop, was 'hell bent' on dealing with this unfinished business, according to Costanzo.[16] Keating, however, did not share Labor's general antipathy to OTC. Like many in the Liberal Party and business, he believed that OTC had the commercial 'mindset' to take on Telecom and, with its 'savvy and very well-connected' chairman, David Hoare, would soon be a force to be reckoned with.[17]

Beazley's departmental deputy secretary, Mike Hutchinson, was less persuaded, having served a stint as the acting chief executive of OTC. He considered its rich profits to be 'wholly due to its monopoly'.[18] He told Beazley that 'the people at OTC are prone to confuse their <u>willingness</u> to compete with their <u>ability</u> to do so. Their fairly easily-won success in the monopoly core business has tended to make them over-confident of their commercial abilities in a competitive environment.'[19] Beazley's adviser Constanzo had much the same view. According to him, 'a chimpanzee' could have made a success of OTC, because its monopoly 'was a licence to print money'.[20]

Selling the model

In June, Beazley's attention shifted to selling his preferred Telecom-OTC versus Aussat model. Costanzo recalls that Beazley had to work to convince his own department that it represented 'a real reform'.[21] His senior officials were disappointed but locked in behind him. They accepted that, given the political context in which they were working, Beazley's option represented a reasonable advance on the status quo and left the way open for further liberalisation down the track. The model also satisfied two immediate prerequisites: it dealt with Aussat and established a full-service competitor to Telecom.[22]

In Beazley's initial pitch to caucus's transport and communications committee on 25 June, he played up the virtues of a strong, vertically integrated state enterprise able to generate export dollars and safeguard Australia's equipment manufacturing sector. A privatised Aussat would provide Telecom with competition.[23] Labor's left and the ATEA, however, maintained the rage against change.[24] In July, about 5000 ATEA members took part in stop-work meetings in Melbourne and regional Victoria, committing to industrial action against the government 'should it become necessary'. The union's Queensland state secretary, Ian McLean, who was also Labor's federal vice-president, declared that any Labor politicians not actively opposing any move towards privatisation should be disendorsed.[25]

During this period, Beazley was frequently frustrated by leaks to journalists from what he termed caucus's 'Telecom alumni', comprising mostly former sector union officials. He recalls that 'they would walk straight out of … private briefings and immediately move through the press gallery'.[26] Beazley and his office were flooded with advice, opinions, lobbying, warnings and support from those fearful, excited or otherwise interested in the government's plans. Official files in the National Archives in Canberra bulge with correspondence from businesses and industry associations, unions, community and interest groups, Labor branches, individual party members and members of the public.[27]

Media reporting about the potential for Telecom to merge with OTC, or even with OTC and Aussat, triggered a flurry of activity. The ATEA's federal secretary, Mick Musumeci, thought establishing a Telecom-OTC-Aussat megacom but otherwise retaining the status quo would 'make sense', but allowing a new competitor to operate was 'the craziest proposition that anyone could put to the Australian people'. It would 'immediately' imperil Telecom, saddle it with 'a billion dollar liability' (that is, Aussat) and 'inevitably lead to increased phone call bills'.[28]

The ALP grass roots were similarly aggrieved. In early July, the secretary of Labor's Montrose Branch in outer suburban Melbourne wrote to Beazley expressing branch members' 'demand' that there be 'no further deregulation of the telecommunications industry in Australia', that 'current monopoly markets' be maintained, and that parliament control Telecom's service 'quality, cost and equity'.[29]

In the face of this incessant pressure, Beazley's department sought to fortify him with contrary views. One note from deputy secretary Mike Hutchinson offered a devastating assessment of Telecom's 'history of opposition to competition'. He outlined how Telecom had 'used its political influence, and the courts, to block would-be competitors'; how it had 'opposed all of the liberalisation measures' proposed by the government in 1988; and how it was still 'dragging its feet' on the government's directive to cost its community service obligations, with some Telecom executives being 'quite open in repudiating' the instruction. Beazley should be sceptical of Telecom's 'conversion' to competition, Hutchinson said; 'its genuineness and its depth and robustness within the Telecom culture has yet to be proven'. Beazley was reminded that the experience of reform in the United States, Britain and New Zealand had shown that an incumbent carrier was 'well able to delay, and even dilute [competitive safeguards] if it wishes to do so—even where it may overtly accept the merits of competition'.[30]

On the other hand, the PREIA, the union covering employees at OTC and Aussat, channelled OTC's traditional horror at the prospect of joining with Telecom. It called on the government to 'abandon' any plans for Telecom to 'swallow' OTC and, potentially, Aussat as well. The union's general secretary, Michael Roberts, warned that such an entity would be so overwhelmingly dominant in Australia that 'no new competitor—local or foreign—would be able to make a real impact other than in a few lucrative niches at the top end of the market'. If the Hawke government felt 'a need' to merge Aussat with anyone,

Roberts stated, then the 'clearly superior option' would be merging it with OTC. An OTC-Aussat combination 'could be a strong competitor to Telecom'.[31]

ATUG also expressed concern that the telecommunications reform debate seemed to be drifting away from focusing on 'maximising the benefit to all Australians' and was 'in danger of becoming simplified down to a contest between the existing carriers supported by different vested interests'.[32] In July, the proprietor of a small data company, Rosser Communications, contacted Beazley to 'object' to the creation of a new megacom because it would 'rip off Australians, especially Australian small business, even more than Telecom now is'.[33]

Beazley was also coming under sustained pressure from Keating. On 20 June, shortly before Beazley's initial pitch to caucus's transport and communications committee, the treasurer and Ken Henry met with Telecom's managing director, Mel Ward, and senior Telecom executives. Keating made it 'very clear' to Ward (according to Telecom's record of the meeting) that he was unhappy with the direction Beazley was heading and would be 'taking a strong personal position' on the government's telecommunications reforms. Keating's position was essentially the same as OTC's, which gave rise to speculation in Telecom's upper echelons that he was being influenced by his principal adviser, Don Russell, a friend of economist Henry Ergas, who was then consulting to OTC. Telecom's meeting note reports that Keating wanted to license an OTC-anchored joint venture as a full-service domestic competitor to Telecom and, at least for a time, allow OTC to retain its international monopoly.[34] Three days later, an impeccably-sourced account of the meeting appeared in the press.[35]

On 3 July, OTC, proclaiming itself 'Australia's worldwide telecommunications company', announced its 'blueprint' for a 'dynamic new Australian-controlled telecommunications carrier'. The carrier would comprise a consortium of OTC, Aussat and private-sector interests; it would compete with Telecom in long-distance calls and mobile facilities and services. The plan also envisaged OTC retaining its international operations while Telecom, in exchange for providing network access, would be permitted to compete with OTC in international calls. OTC's managing director, Stephen Burdon, promised cheaper calls (by 20–30 per cent), majority Australian ownership, and a 'Buy Australia' policy worth $900 million to the nation's manufacturing sector over the next ten years.[36]

OTC was already in consortium discussions with Britain's Racal Telecom (later Vodafone) and Australia's Pacific Dunlop, Exicom and AMP. In a public swipe at Beazley, OTC described these organisations as 'precisely the type of strong grouping of Australian companies that could participate with OTC in ensuring that robust competition was achieved'.[37] OTC's cockiness was being mocked within Telecom; according to an internal briefing note, 'most Australians think OTC is part of Telecom anyway!'[38]

Keating and Ward met again on 20 July. According to Telecom's file note, the treasurer 'openly' sought to 'pressure' Ward and his board to soften their 'position' on Beazley's Telecom-OTC model. If the merger went ahead, Keating would insist that Telecom pay $1.5 billion to 'take over' OTC and be forced 'to swallow' Aussat.[39]

The debate also played out in lively fashion between the two ministers' advisers and departments. The core bone of contention came from Keating's rejection of Beazley's vision of a bigger, bolder Telecom, enhanced by the addition of OTC, reborn as an Australian national champion successfully squaring up to its international peers on the world stage. In late June, for example, a rather acerbic Ken Henry blasted Beazley's plan in a personal note to the minister's senior private secretary, Patrick Walters. Henry described it as 'a blatant example of argument by association' that had no 'logical nexus'; the government's telecommunications reforms, he asserted, should be about 'getting cheaper services for Australian users, not about Australia providing cheaper services to Saudi Arabians'.[40]

There was fundamental disagreement about market structure. Keating and Treasury wanted full, open competition from the outset, while Beazley and his department pushed for a duopoly. Keating's position reflected ideology and practicality. Looking back, he says he had 'faith in markets, and I knew that in an open, competitive market, Telecom would be a very effective player'. It would 'defend itself immediately' and this would foster intense competition from new entrants. A duopoly, on the other hand, would require Telecom to 'gift' part of its market share to a nominated competitor, which he considered 'foolish'. Keating also found it incongruous that a duopoly in telecommunications was being contemplated just as one in airlines was being dismantled.[41] In meetings with Beazley's department, Treasury officials openly disdained the telecommunications duopoly idea as a model that 'smacks of the two airlines policy'.

With Beazley set on merging OTC with Telecom, his officials sought to find the 'best way' to place 'maximum pressure [on the new entity] as soon as possible', while also dealing with Aussat and working to mitigate the risk of union blow-ups.[42] They assessed Telecom-OTC's future market power as so overwhelming that the structural barriers to competition would likely be 'at least as great' as regulatory and technical ones; even if regulatory and technical issues were addressed fully, effective end-to-end competition would not develop for the foreseeable future.[43] Instead, an open market would likely comprise multiple niche operators servicing segments of the business market, with little to no benefit for everyday consumers.[44] Licensing a 'prominent, single, initial competitor', however, would allow for more effective regulated competitive safeguards and hopefully encourage a 'more restrained' union response.[45] Last but by no means least, the Transport and Communications Department feared that without a duopoly in which Aussat, bundled together with a mobile licence and other inducements, formed the basis of a second carrier, the financially distressed company was 'unlikely to attract any buyers'.[46]

Another difficult issue related to the persisting matter of Telecom's structural separation. In early August, senior Treasury official David Borthwick proposed to Keating that Telecom's 'core activities' (network operations and service lines) be divided into separately constituted and managed entities.[47] At a high-level meeting between officials from Treasury and Transport and Communications soon afterwards, this model was tabled as one of Keating's conditions for accepting a Telecom-OTC megacom.[48] Carving up Telecom was antithetical to Beazley's national champion plan. When briefing Beazley's office on the meeting, his department also stated that implementing a project 'on the scale envisaged' by Treasury could take four years (that is, well past the next election); his officials suggested that a system of internal accounting separation was more practical.[49]

Though an internal accounting separation model for Telecom was ultimately adopted, structural separation remained a live issue right through to September. Indeed, just days before cabinet was due to make its final decision on the government's telecommunications reforms, Mike Hutchinson warned Beazley that it seemed Keating 'may favour imposing a substantial degree of structural separation', by which he meant 'separate corporate entities, in common ownership, operating each layer of the network [and] with transparent inter-entity pricing arrangements'.[50] Reflecting on this period, Keating claims that he personally supported structurally separating Telecom, with its network infrastructure housed in a new entity, as the most effective way to get the organisation to 'stand up' as a leading services enterprise.[51] His contemporaneous notes and the official record just cited would seem to support this.[52] Beazley recalls it as an issue Keating 'thought about quite intensively'.[53]

Telecom stayed close to Beazley's office during this period, promptly forwarding file notes of meetings with Keating (and Ken Henry) and, in early August, sending Patrick Walters a dossier of internal papers detailing its view of the world 'in the great telecommunications debate'.[54] This included putting its case on what competition could look like and the benefits of such change, its vision for Australia's future in global telecommunications, how interconnection rules should apply to new market entrants, and why OTC should be merged with Telecom rather than being utilised as the basis for a new full-service domestic carrier.[55] Walters passed the documents to Beazley with a handwritten comment that they might provide 'some useful ammunition'.[56]

Several factors underlay Keating's decision to lead a full-blooded campaign for more ambitious telecommunications reforms than those sought by Beazley. First, the project was fundamental to the government's structural reform agenda, as promoted by Keating himself. Second, the treasurer (and by now also deputy prime minister) considered Telecom a 'behemoth' that operated as a 'dead-weight around the country's neck'. And third, he was becoming increasingly frustrated by Hawke's continued grip on the Labor leadership.[57]

The gloves in the Keating–Beazley contest really came off in mid-August, after Beazley's post-ROSA cabinet submission on structural relationships between the three government carriers was leaked to the *Australian Financial Review*. This was clearly intended to strengthen Beazley's hand at Keating's expense. Keating retaliated for this 'dirty pool' by personally approving the release to the *Financial Review* of a Treasury briefing paper that gave a scathing critique of Beazley's approach.[58]

Beazley's proposal rested on three principles: the pre-eminence of regulatory structure over market structure; the need to weigh telecommunications users' interests with those of the incumbent carriers and equipment manufacturers; and the importance of a stable and predictable transition to a more competitive sector, with government retaining a core role. The government's 'central consideration' was to reconcile the legitimate commercial interests of Telecom and OTC with their 'formidable' market power to a sufficient extent that private-sector operators would be willing to enter the market. As such, Beazley argued, regulatory settings were 'more important in determining the level of competition and its impact and viability than the actual carrier structure chosen'.[59] These views were informed partly by British precedent, though by contrast with the 1960s, the focus now was not on emulation but on avoiding unintended consequences.

Beazley recalls that executives of Mercury Communications, which had been established in 1981 to compete with British Telecom, provided 'very useful' insights about 'how they had been screwed by [British] Telecom and what our regulator would need to do to make sure that didn't happen' in Australia.[60] He was also influenced by the New Zealand Labour government's telecommunications competition reforms, which had seen prices drop by 21 per cent in real terms within twelve months.[61] Beazley's preferred model reflected his efforts to balance the need for liberalisation with traditional Labor sensitivities, while also serving his immediate political interests. It essentially said to those in cabinet, the caucus and the unions who opposed or were sceptical of the government's agenda that all the benefits of competition in telecommunications could be achieved without threatening Labor's traditional sacred cows. Indeed, Beazley's plan was to beef Telecom up.

Beazley rejected the open competition model advocated by Keating and Treasury, the John Hewson-led opposition and others. He wanted a 'simple, unambiguous and predictable' duopoly comprising a privatised Aussat-based full-service carrier competing in the domestic market and a merged Telecom-OTC able to operate as 'a one-stop-shop' for all of Australia's national and international needs and also take on global players.[62] Graham Evans points out that a duopoly also maximised Aussat's sale price by signalling to the market an implicit government guarantee that the new domestic carrier would not 'fall over' in the face of Telecom-OTC domination.[63]

Beazley maintains that Telecom was 'really worried' about the prospect of a second carrier able to 'pursue whatever it liked in telecommunications infrastructure and services', but the evidence for this is not strong. His former officials and staff independently concur that Beazley's main game at the time was to bulk up Telecom with OTC in readiness for offshore expansion. It has been suggested that the new Aussat-based carrier would essentially act as Telecom's 'sparring partner'; it was to be strong enough to give the incumbent 'a run for its money' and 'toughen it up' for Asia-Pacific markets, but not so strong as to threaten Telecom's dominance at home.[64] Financial analysis commissioned by the Department of Transport and Communications appears to support this contention. It found that under a duopoly structure, an Aussat-based carrier would achieve a far smaller market share than an OTC-based one (11 per cent of national calls and 5 per cent of international calls by 2000 versus 20 per cent and 45 per cent respectively); and perhaps more pertinently, that privatising OTC (under the second scenario) would raise up to $3.9 billion. Beazley's submission questioned the desirability of such an outcome, as it could mean OTC ultimately became more financially powerful than Telecom.[65]

The Treasury paper prepared in response to Beazley's leaked submission bluntly declared that his plan would 'fall far short of a good policy outcome' and would achieve 'at best … very limited competition'. Treasury argued that reform was essential in view of Australia's dysfunctional telecommunications regulatory framework, epitomised most damningly by the Aussat crisis; while regulated competitive safeguards would be needed to 'facilitate' a liberalised market, they could not 'substitute for competition'. Beazley's national champion concept was criticised for resting on a 'mistaken belief [that] creating uncompetitive domestic markets … would nurture the growth of large enterprises able to take on the world'.[66]

A political storm blew up after the Treasury paper's publication. In public, Keating sought to soften his officials' tone, though not their assessment, but it is abundantly clear from statements he made when reflecting on this episode, and his heavily annotated copy of the reproduced report, that he fully concurred with both the assessment and the tone. His handwritten notes from 1990 describe Beazley's justification for the Telecom-OTC merger as 'phoney'.[67] Looking back, Keating recalls arguing to caucus that a bulked-up Telecom lacking genuinely strong competition at home would not 'go out and slay the competition abroad [but] would waddle out and be slain themselves'.[68]

In Treasury's view, the 'principal aim' of the government's telecommunications reform project was to maximise domestic competitive intensity and drive 'the price and efficiency gains … which the community and the economy most need'.[69] This judgement was broadly consistent with that of the Transport and Communications Department, according to Graham Evans. He says that Beazley's officials 'basically agreed with Keating, and in a perfect world we would have done what he wanted'. But by this stage the policy caravan had moved on, and they were professionally (and sincerely) committed to executing the minister's decision.[70]

Treasury's disdain for Beazley's plan was apparent in its formal comments to Graham Evans two weeks later. Its views, if anything, had hardened, which was perhaps inevitable given the increasingly charged atmosphere. In view of the government's objective to lower telecommunications costs and increase efficiency and competitiveness, it was 'an odd reform, to say the least,' said Treasury deputy secretary A. J. Preston, to opt for 'a Megacom embedded in a protected David-and-Goliath duopoly'. It would be much better to dispense with the plan and use a wholly or partly privatised OTC as the basis for 'fast-track and more durable competition against Telecom'.

If a Telecom-OTC merger did ultimately go ahead, Preston argued, it would constitute a 'credible' reform only if accompanied by full contestability, including the removal of restrictions on network capacity resale and foreign investment, issuing three mobile licences and three international licences, and 'imposing structural separation of Megacom's activities into corporate arm's length subsidiaries'.[71] The tit-for-tat continued unabated; Beazley's office asked officials to prepare a point-by-point rebuttal, which they did, reiterating arguments that had already been made several times.[72]

So, who leaked Beazley's submission in the first place? Frustratingly, the available evidence does not say. The leak does not appear to have come from Beazley's department and, as to Beazley's office, Costanzo says it added 'a degree of complexity that we didn't need. [It] created a lot more work than we needed'.[73] Beazley initiated an internal departmental inquiry, encouraging it to seek cooperation from Treasury and other relevant departments but not requiring the participation of his personal staff or accepting requests by his acting secretary, Roger Beale, for a federal police investigation.[74] An incidental encounter between senior Transport and Communications Department official Vanessa Fanning and the journalist Geoff Kitney, which Fanning reported immediately to the departmental officer running the inquiry, made plain that she had no idea who the leaker was.[75] Costanzo passed a copy of Fanning's report to Beazley, with the handwritten comment, 'Kim, very interesting!'.[76]

Contest and conflict

Though the public contest between Keating and Beazley arose from genuine policy differences, the unusual intensity of Keating's campaign was influenced by the leadership tensions between him and Hawke, interplayed with Beazley's personal closeness to Hawke and his potential as a leadership rival. The differences caused serious friction between the two factionally aligned ministers. Gareth Evans for one recalls 'the air crackling with bloody tension between the two of them'.[77] But even before the battle went ballistic, Labor's national secretary, Bob Hogg, had become concerned that internal party dissension over telecommunications and aviation policy was gaining such a 'head of steam' that it risked derailing the government's reform agenda. Hogg also saw that cabinet's ultimate decisions on these issues would inevitably breach elements of Labor's platform because they related to competition and privatisation. He therefore set the ball rolling for a special national conference of the party.[78]

Labor's national executive resolved to broker a cross-factional consensus, but divisions immediately erupted. Broader fissures within cabinet also became increasingly apparent. Left caucus members released a statement announcing a tougher anti-liberalisation stance. This placed direct pressure on left cabinet ministers Brian Howe, Gerry Hand and Nick Bolkus, and triggered a public warning from the balance-of-power centre-left grouping that such a 'hard-line position of defending the platform [would make it] very hard for our people to support any changes'.[79] Centre-left ministers Michael Duffy (trade) and John Dawkins (employment) were already disagreeing with each other; Duffy called for Labor to 'seriously question what this deregulation push is all about and where it is taking us', while Dawkins observed that Beazley's plan 'doesn't appear to do anything about introducing effective competition quickly'. Hawke chastised them for debating policy options through the media, but the right's Ros Kelly (formerly Willis's junior communications minister) also entered the fray supporting OTC, saying it was 'very well placed to lead any competition'.[80]

Dawkins and his centre-left ministerial colleague John Button were more concerned about a foreign-owned competitor than whether it was based on OTC or Aussat (though on balance their faction favoured OTC to form the basis of Telecom's new domestic competitor).[81] Even the right, usually the most amenable bloc to pro-competition policy, was split over telecommunications, mainly because of pressure from its union base. Indeed, the convenor of caucus's telecommunications subcommittee, Roger Price, waged an unrelenting campaign against competition, methodically and colourfully ripping into Beazley's plan as being too hard on Telecom, too soft on a new competitor and too risky for everyone else. To Price, the proposed consumer safeguards were a 'communications sandcastle' that was bound to collapse; the proposed interconnect rules would be the 'world's toughest', causing 'a massive revenue haemorrhage for Telecom'; and the proposed industry policy was 'pathetic … sterile and bereft of any pretence of originality of thought'.[82] Even on the eve of cabinet's final decision, by which time the outcome was essentially assured, Price was broadcasting his 'massive revenue haemorrhage for Telecom' lines.[83]

Though the Keating–Beazley clash played out against a constantly shifting background of caucus and union resistance to the government's agenda, the trend inexorably favoured Beazley, because his plan represented the least-change option available. Beazley sought to win over Labor reform sceptics to his model by reiterating the merits of his vision; but he also sought to assuage concerns about Telecom's welfare in a more competitive future. A key point was that Telecom was highly profitable and could 'more than meet' (his words) its community service obligations. Telecom also needed to become more efficient to succeed in the technologically dynamic and diverse new world. It faced only 'modest pressure' to meet customer needs, improve processes, develop new products and manage costs. Its connection and fault rectification performance was relatively poor, and its administrative costs accounted for nearly half of its costs, compared with 10–30 per cent in similar organisations overseas. And what was more, he said, Telecom 'demanded' competition in exchange for gaining a free hand to compete offshore, where market growth was 'staggering'.[84]

Keating's increasingly strident campaign assisted Beazley by coaxing caucus members and union leaders into his tent. The ATEA shifted from threatening a 'holy war' against the government's reform project to reluctantly conceding support for Beazley over Keating because Telecom's 'slow strangulation' under the former was preferable to its quick 'garrotting' under the latter.[85] According to Labor MP John Saunderson, the ATEA also chose to back Beazley to ensure that 'the competitor got a liability, Aussat, not an asset, OTC'; without its own customer base, he added, an Aussat-based carrier would need to start from scratch, winning every customer from Telecom. While the Telecom unions were 'unhappy with a competitive model', Saunderson said, once it was clear that some form of competition was unavoidable they were 'not unhappy with the model they got'.[86]

Amid all this, the opposition released a new telecommunications policy, promising full and open competition as a precursor to the privatisation of Telecom, OTC and Aussat. This gave further impetus for Labor sceptics and opponents of competition to support Beazley, even if they did so through gritted teeth.

The Coalition's policy underlined the increasingly blurred distinctions between the major political parties in Australia and abroad. The shadow communications minister, Neil Brown, for example, favourably referenced the New Zealand Labour government's policy approach.[87] Opposition leader John Hewson, speaking with Keatingesque flair and in line with his position, declared Beazley's duopoly plan a 'two-phone policy' modelled on Australia's unravelling two-airline policy.[88] Hawke leapt on the opposition's pro-privatisation announcement, telling the government's internal critics that the surest way to keep Telecom in state hands was to support its reform agenda, which was designed to stimulate greater efficiency in Telecom by introducing an element of competition to the market.[89] To Labor's external critics, Hawke declared it 'thoroughly unreal' to expect its telecommunications policy debate 'not [to] raise differences of opinion' within the government; but he promised, 'at the end of the debate there will be the clearest possible distinction between the Labor Party and the Tories'.[90]

Beazley and Keating had long sought to downplay any difficulties between them, but they now concede that their relationship suffered during this period. It was 'not good', says Beazley (with some understatement). It was 'terrible', says Keating; 'for a long time, he never spoke to me at all'. Hawke recalls Beazley being especially galled that Keating was intervening so directly in his portfolio, though Keating's view remains that telecommunications policy was of such central importance to the government's structural reform agenda that it fell legitimately within his remit as treasurer.[91] Doubtless Keating's frustration with Hawke's determined hold on the Labor leadership (and prime ministership) was key to the combative way he prosecuted what he considered, with good reason, better policy, to the short-term detriment of his support in cabinet.

Hawke later acknowledged the economic superiority of Keating's proposal, but observed that caucus was already edgy, having just sanctioned the Commonwealth Bank's partial sale and with the aviation privatisation issue still ahead; he said that for this reason he supported Beazley's plan as 'the only practical conclusion'.[92] Other senior Labor figures reached similar verdicts.[93] Gareth Evans, Keating and Beazley all assumed that Telecom would probably be privatised at some stage. Evans and Keating were comfortable with this. Beazley was not; he says he 'confidently expected that I would be well out of politics by then. I was obviously wrong'.[94] Notwithstanding this, Hawke's deliberations were probably influenced by his desire to deny Keating a policy win. Certainly Beazley's senior officials, and Keating, operated throughout this period on the understanding that Hawke backed Beazley. According to Graham Evans, Hawke 'gave Beazley the support and authority to push [his plan] within the party and cabinet and not be overrun by Keating'.[95]

Hawke faced some cabinet criticism for his hands-off approach to the Beazley-Keating battle, though Costanzo says that various three-way discussions did take place at the time. Shortly before cabinet was to deliberate on telecommunications in early September, Hawke called Beazley and Keating to his office to 'settle it', Costanzo says; Hawke 'lit a cigar, put his feet on his desk' and invited Beazley to kick off first. According to Keating, Hawke 'played it as subtly as he could, sitting Solomon-like, listening to me, listening to Beazley'. He considered it inevitable that Hawke would back Beazley, but resolved 'not to let Bob or Beazley have this debate free, without cost or real pressure'. Costanzo recalls the discussion occurring 'over beers and potato chips' and wrapping up 'in the small hours of the morning' with Hawke acknowledging the respective merits of both proposals before coming down on Beazley's side.[96]

Cabinet decisions and Labor's national conference

Cabinet met at least three times from late August to decide the government's telecommunications reform measures.[97] Beazley went to these meetings prepared to cover the full gamut of already well-ventilated issues. Though some form of competition was inevitable by this stage, most likely consistent with Beazley's plan, there remained much devil in the detail for ministers to work through, along with the expectation that Keating's alternative ideas would be forcefully expressed. On the duopoly, a five-year timeframe was again suggested by Beazley's department as a 'workable compromise'. His officials advocated a five-year review process over a sunset clause; they felt this would offer potential market entrants 'some prospect of the duopoly continuing' and therefore improve the likelihood of 'attracting a well-resourced initial competitor'. Anticipating a final push by Keating for 'a substantial degree' of structural separation for Telecom, Mike Hutchinson reminded Beazley that a key argument against splitting up Telecom—that it would be 'too easy for a future Coalition government to privatise parts of the system'—had lost currency since the opposition had committed to selling Telecom in its entirety.[98]

As to a third mobile licence, the key challenge was one of timing. The Transport and Communications Department knew that there were parties keen to make mobile-only bids and believed that offering a third licence concurrent with trying to sell an Aussat-plus-mobile package would depress (if not destroy) the price the government could attract for Aussat. Indeed, Beazley was already being lobbied by a consortium that included Racal Telecom (later Vodafone) and Exicom, a major Australian equipment manufacturer; it argued that its 'viable proposition' was to acquire a 'mobile licence separate from the Aussat package', to be achieved either by unbundling the second licence from Aussat or simultaneously offering a third.[99]

The ambivalence of Beazley's own department about merging Telecom and OTC was apparent in its pre-cabinet advice to him. Hutchinson noted pointedly that 'you have taken the view' that the competitive advantages of a Telecom versus OTC-Aussat model 'are not sufficient to outweigh political opposition', and that a merged Telecom-OTC would have the scale to compete internationally and grow Australia's export revenues. On this, Hutchinson said, the evidence 'remains inconclusive'. He suggested that if Beazley could not win cabinet's support for the merger, he might propose maintaining Telecom and OTC as separate entities, confined to their existing geographic markets and competing against a privatised Aussat-based full-service operator. While the odds that Beazley would go for such a compromise so late in the piece were not high, Hutchinson laid out some advantages (which were also implicit criticisms of Beazley's preferred model): it would avoid the considerable operational and management disruption of integrating 'radically different OTC and Telecom cultures' and dealing with inevitable union 'friction', and it would reduce the risk (of which Hutchinson said he was 'personally aware') of OTC 'losing the last of the key people [with] personal status [and] established interpersonal relationships' in international forums. Hutchinson argued that a compromise along these lines, combined with full third-party resale (which Beazley, at this stage, did not support) and strong competitive safeguards, would constitute 'presentationally a highly competitive outcome in world terms'.[100]

On 6 September, cabinet committed to Telecom's retention in state ownership and its community service obligations, 'the maximum participation of Australian industry' and 'effective competition' in the telecommunications sector from whatever reforms were ultimately agreed, and the enactment of regulations to 'ensure that such competition delivers the lowest possible prices to consumers, the highest possible quality of services and the early introduction of new technologies'.[101] Four days later, on the same day that cabinet was due to make its final decision, Beazley received implicit public backing from the ACTU and ATEA. The ACTU's president, Martin Ferguson, said that in acceding to the partial privatisation of Qantas, the full privatisation of Australian Airlines and the Telecom-OTC merger, the union movement had gone as far as it could. He stated, 'if cabinet makes a decision to go any further it will lose the lot'; Telecom's unions 'have already told us' that anything more would trigger massive industrial action and possibly a 'split in the Labor Party'. The ACTU's assistant secretary (and recently the ATEA's federal secretary), Bill Mansfield, similarly foreshadowed a 'savage split' between Labor and union movement if Hawke's cabinet went beyond Beazley's plan.[102]

The 10 September cabinet meeting was a lengthy and fiery affair, from which Costanzo recalls Beazley eventually emerging 'quite exhausted', having taken ministers 'chapter and verse' through his proposed reform package.[103] Once it was clear that Beazley would prevail, Keating famously lost his temper ('a spectacular tantrum', recalled Hawke), vividly lambasted his colleagues, received some lambasting in return, and stormed out of the room.[104] Keating has since conceded that his approach was 'a bit manic'.[105] He maintains that cabinet backed Beazley's plan because it had become conflated with Hawke's leadership authority and cabinet 'simply wouldn't' roll the prime minister on this issue. He claims that cabinet's other economic ministers endorsed Hawke's support for Beazley with 'a kind of resignation'.[106] Once cabinet had agreed the key elements of Beazley's model and deferred other 'detailed decisions' until after Labor's special conference, the way was paved for two weeks of last-ditch deal-making. With unenthusiastic ministers of all factions likely in mind, cabinet's official record of the meeting noted its commitment to 'the principles of collective responsibility ... leading up to the Special Party Conference ... and thereafter'.[107]

On the very day of cabinet's decision, as Labor minds turned to the forthcoming conference, Beazley's top officials, worried about the potential consequences of Beazley precipitately involving the unions in scoping competitive safeguards, began pushing him to focus on broader issues related to implementation planning. It was 'essential', said acting deputy secretary Vanessa Fanning, to involve 'all sections of the industry ... Telecom, the potential entrant(s), major users, industry bodies and the unions' in this process from the outset, as had occurred in 1989. But, before this, it was 'vital' that the government provide explicit 'ground rules' about the parameters of competitive safeguards to forestall union manoeuvres to 'frustrate' the government's program. She argued that 'potential new entrants will not commit themselves to bid for entry to the Australian market unless it is absolutely clear that the terms and conditions of interconnection are favourable to a new entrant'.[108]

Graham Evans makes the point that, to be effective, policy reform must be not only the 'most appropriate for the intended outcomes, but also workable'. This goes beyond political compromise. He says it is 'also about institutional capabilities' and ensuring that, whatever changes are implemented, they 'work and can be measured'. Achieving these outcomes is the responsibility of the relevant minister and their department. It meant that in 1990 Beazley and his department had more policy skin in the game than any of the other parties engaging in the debate, and it helps explain why Beazley's officials so consistently engaged in detailed public consultations about reform options and 'the specifics of proposed implementing legislation'.[109]

OTC was also quick out of the blocks, expressing concerns to Beazley about the 'impression … being conveyed in some media' that Telecom was 'taking over' OTC, and pressing him for a 'quick decision' confirming OTC's 'separate status' within the new enterprise. The consequences of inaction could be severe, warned OTC's chairman, David Hoare; he claimed that major overseas and domestic contracts were already being delayed by customer 'nervousness' about OTC's future and by 'prospective joint venture partners' seeking clarity. Dusting off OTC's merger mitigation plan from 1975, Hoare informed Beazley that the OTC board 'highly favours a separate business entity model' in which OTC, under the auspices of 'an umbrella holding company subject to a senior board', would retain its own board and 'brand' and have 'autonomy and accountability' for its business plans, budget and capital funding. Its finances would be 'segregated' to prevent the deployment of any funds 'for other purposes'. OTC also made a play for Telecom's long-distance services and networks, value-added services, private network management services and its international subsidiary company. These steps, Hoare asserted, 'would go a considerable way' to alleviating the concerns of OTC customers and staff.[110]

OTC was doubtlessly displeased by Beazley's affirmation at Labor's conference shortly afterwards that the government's reform plan represented 'a process of strengthening' Telecom by 'giving it' OTC. Beazley methodically walked delegates through his well-honed arguments. Technological advances and the pace and scale of international growth had rendered the status quo unsustainable. The decision was not whether to have competition, but how it 'should be controlled'. The government's plan would 'protect the ordinary consumer [and] advance the interests of the business consumer'. By creating a bigger, better state enterprise able to generate 'well in advance of $1 billion net of community service obligations', Australia would become 'an effective participant in the global telecommunications environment over the next few decades'. And, over and above this, Telecom itself wanted 'to experience across the board competition in order to make it more effective'; this would safeguard it from privatisation, Beazley declared.[111]

Over the preceding month, Beazley had reportedly spent just two nights at home in Perth, such was his schedule of meetings with factional and union figures, caucus members and conference delegates.[112] The tenacity and conviction with which he prosecuted his case earned him kudos then and now from officials, advisers and politicians, regardless of their own views about its policy merits.[113] Conference delegate (and Queensland premier) Wayne Goss later claimed, for example, that Beazley's impeccable grasp of the policy detail convinced him that 'whatever this bloke wants, I'll vote for that'.[114] But getting the factions over the line was still uncertain on conference eve. The left remained resolutely opposed and the centre-left was in 'turmoil', according to Graham Richardson.[115] Beazley offered further assurances to the centre-left—that Telecom would 'not be disadvantaged' by any new measures, that network interconnection arrangements would 'at least' cover Telecom's provisioning costs, and that there would be no timed local calls—and the faction's delegates were granted a free vote. In the end, the government's proposals were ratified by 58 votes to 43, with the centre-left dividing 13–6 in favour.[116]

Most of the heat from the debate quickly dissipated after Labor's conference, though Hawke was compelled to slap down some 'rather belligerent statements' made immediately afterwards by the ATEA.[117] There remained much unhappiness in the party, though, and ministers received plenty of representations from branch members deploring government policy. A particularly succinct example was provided by one electorate council secretary who wrote to Beazley in late October to condemn 'the disturbing trend of ALP Ministers following the advice of senior Public Servants, and in the process ignoring Party policy and the wishes of Party rank and file'.[118] But outside Labor, the government's measures were more often criticised for their timidity. Economist Rodney Maddock's assessment was typical: they were 'the very least that might be considered a reform'.[119] For the journalist Paul Kelly, Labor's new telecommunications (and aviation) policies were 'a dramatic purging of Labor ideology', but, in the context of contemporary governance, they were 'merely orthodox'.[120] Hawke and Beazley themselves seemed to swing between understating and over-egging their telecommunications reforms. For Hawke, they were both 'real world solutions to real world problems' and 'the greatest ever in this critically important industry'.[121] For Beazley, they were 'standard, average, common-sense, democratic socialist policy' but also 'the most radical restructuring of this key industry ever undertaken in Australia'.[122]

Next Steps

Attention immediately shifted to the formidable task of turning the government's policy decisions into reality. A regulatory framework had to be developed and legislated, quality bids had to be attracted for Aussat and a second carrier licensed, and Telecom and OTC had to be joined together. A series of committees and steering groups was established, led by Transport and Communications and including Treasury, Finance and the Prime Minister's Department, along with a ministerial advisory committee chaired by two prominent caucus opponents of liberalising telecommunications, Roger Price and Neil O'Keefe.[123] The officials from Transport and Communications, most of them veterans of Labor's first-wave reforms under Gareth Evans and Ralph Willis, were sensitive to the substantial risk of unintended consequences inherent in enshrining such technically and operationally complex issues into law, particularly in a technologically dynamic environment. They strongly supported genuinely consultative processes with key parties and experts, including from the three government carriers, Austel, the ACTU, sector unions, industry and user groups, and potential bidders for Aussat.

Beazley's officials were initially cool towards his advisory committee concept for fear it would be 'tainted' (in Mike Hutchinson's words) by vested interests, but in the event the ministerial advisory committee proved valuable in progressing Labor's reforms by co-opting disparate interests—the caucus and unions, consumer, business and user groups, equipment manufacturers, Telecom and OTC—into what became an effective clearing house for dealing with difficult political and technical issues as they arose.[124] Graham Evans notes that the Transport and Communications Department also viewed 'the telecommunications reform process, in terms of consultations, exposure of legislation and above all evaluation' as something of a precedent-setting test case; 'if we were able to demonstrate better services at reduced prices, this gave us credibility for other reforms in broadcasting, radiocommunications, aviation, shipping and road and rail transport'.[125]

The legislative drafting process was an enormous undertaking of great complexity carried out within a tight timeframe, though it could not start properly until the cabinet decided on a number of issues that had been held over pending Labor's conference. These included determining the terms for merging Telecom and OTC, issuing a third mobile licence, foreign ownership of the second carrier, and the duopoly. Even at this late stage, Beazley's department was anticipating pressure from 'some ministers' for the 'full structural separation' of Telecom-OTC (though as already noted, Beazley's accounting separation proposal was confirmed).[126] On the duopoly, cabinet's decision reflected Keating's position—a hard deadline of five years, after which the sector would open to all comers—though Hawke and Keating both claim credit for this outcome at Beazley's expense. Hawke recalls in his memoirs persuading 'a reluctant Beazley' to accept a 'sunset clause'.[127] Keating claims that Beazley asked him to drop the clause as 'a personal favour' but he declined and 'got my way' in cabinet.[128] For his part, Beazley tells a different tale. Although he had previously gone to cabinet recommending a seven-year review of the duopoly (the option preferred by his department to boost Aussat's sale price), he says a five-year deadline 'didn't worry me because that's what I thought was a sensible model anyway'.[129] Indeed, his officials had repeatedly raised this option as a workable compromise since at least mid-August.[130]

The government's telecommunications policy statement (known colloquially as the 'red book') was the bible for officials and advisers tasked with implementing its reform program and the go-to source for industry, unions, consumer representatives, journalists and anyone else engaged in the issue.[131] It systematically detailed eighty-three government decisions covering competitive safeguards; network interconnection, access charges and operational arrangements; accounting separation; pricing arrangements, including price caps on local, national and international calls; Austel's new powers and functions; the Telecom-OTC merger; arrangements for Aussat's sale and the second carrier licence; resourcing for

189

new carrier arrangements; a new Universal Service Obligation; mobile services licensing arrangements; excess network capacity resale and policy for private networks; the first telephone monopoly; satellite services, including arrangements with global satellite groups Intelsat and Inmarsat; and the duopoly sunset clause.[132] It comprised, Hutchinson commented, a 'fairly daunting' workload.[133]

A fair slice of that workload went to Austel. Leo Dobes, a Treasury official who moved to Transport and Communications in 1990 to work on telecommunications reform, recalls that matters considered 'too difficult or time-consuming to tie down in legislation' were often referred to the regulator 'to fix later'.[134] Between late 1990 and mid-1991, Austel conducted a range of public consultations and released numerous reports addressing a variety of economic, commercial and technical aspects of Australia's forthcoming telecommunications regime; this included, in one three-month period alone, four reports about network interconnection and equal access arrangements.[135] These settings would underpin how (and if) meaningful competition developed. It was an issue close to Austel's heart, not least because from July 1991 promoting the growth of competition was to be one of the regulator's new responsibilities in its 'central and greatly enhanced role' (Beazley's words). Beazley made clear to Austel chairman Robin Davey that 'the success of the government's objectives of developing a truly competitive, export-orientated industry depends to a large extent upon [Austel's] sound formulation and expert management of the pro-competitive safeguards'. But, Beazley said, with 'hard work, and a degree of goodwill from all concerned', and some additional funding and staff, he felt sure that Austel was up to the job.[136]

Beazley also made his expectations clear to Telecom and OTC. He wanted detailed reports on their plans for network interconnection, 'prompt and comprehensive' provision of information to third parties bidding for Aussat, 'full cooperation' with Austel and other government officials, the observance of 'mutually non-intrusive and harmonious relationships' and, to Telecom, an end to 'public debate [and] lobbying on policy matters' now that the government had 'settled its policy position'.[137]

His officials focused on working out the interim measures to precede OTC's merger with Telecom and the new carrier's post-amalgamation organisational and structural arrangements. They were acutely aware of the enterprises' 'very different cultures' and, more challenging at least in the short term, the mutual 'antipathy between [their] senior executives'. They were also concerned that 'untrammelled

Telecom hegemony' over OTC risked the much smaller but lucrative international agency 'withering away'. In this light, Mike Hutchinson proposed to Beazley that he give responsibility for settling the nuts and bolts of the merger and a new corporate structure to 'the major interested groups' by way of a 'supra-board' comprising Telecom deputy chairman Bill Dix, OTC chairman David Hoare, an ACTU nominee (Bill Mansfield was appointed) and the Transport and Communications Department's secretary, Graham Evans. The alternative approach, placing this task solely in the hands of officials, would 'amount to little more than "amateur brain surgery"'.[138]

On 8 November, Beazley introduced to parliament the Aussat Amendment Bill, an interim legislative measure that removed all legal barriers to Aussat's sale and allowed the company to compete with Telecom and OTC across all services.[139] The bill passed the Senate a month later with the Coalition's support, though Richard Alston labelled Beazley's policy win over Keating 'a tragedy for Australia'.[140] As Beazley had foreshadowed at Labor's special conference, potential bidders for Aussat were intensely invested in the legislative and regulatory details around Australia's new competitive arrangements. None of them would commit funds without clarity on the specifics.

With the Aussat Amendment Act in place, the stricken satellite company was readied for sale. The government reacquired Telecom's 25 per cent stake in Aussat for $25 million. This was less than half Telecom's valuation, but Finance Minister Willis and Beazley deemed the price 'fair and reasonable' given Aussat's 'accumulated losses', 'dubious future prospects' and the lack of a 'current market value'.[141] Aussat's two Telecom-nominated directors were removed, and, with remarkable irony given the catalytic role Aussat's financial plight had played in stampeding the government's second-wave reforms, the commonwealth assumed direct responsibility for the company's $798 million debt.[142]

During 1991, two further steps were taken to fatten Aussat for market. In September, Beazley obtained cabinet's reluctant assent to roll exclusive satellite-based pay-television rights into the deal. (He had reportedly been told by at least one potential Aussat bidder, Hong Kong's Hutchison, that it would only participate under these terms.) Pay television had long been a fraught policy area; the powerful free-to-air networks fiercely opposed its introduction and the idea of voters being forced to pay to watch sport sent chills down politicians' spines. The Aussat arrangement was to run from October 1992 until the duopoly ended in

June 1997, with concessions to the free-to-airs including an ongoing advertising monopoly for five years.[143]

The other market-fattening step was to go slow on a third mobile licence. This was Beazley's fallback option after cabinet rejected his proposal for a duopoly in mobile services until 'initial competition is firmly established, say in 1995'.[144] Once expressions of interest were invited for Australia's second carrier licence, it soon became obvious that potential bidders were attracted to mobile, not Aussat. The Transport and Communications Department immediately reaffirmed its view that Beazley should delay a third licence 'as far as possible' so that bidders would 'focus first on the sale of Aussat and are not side-tracked by subordinate issues ... such as mobile licensing'.[145] When Beazley publicly reported in March that the second carrier licence had elicited more than thirty expressions of interest from 'many of the world's leading telecommunications enterprises [and] major Australian industrial and finance companies', he also noted that a third mobile licence would be postponed to 'a later date'.[146] Hawke's senior private secretary, Peter Harris, immediately went to Hawke with his view that this approach was 'completely wrong', but no response from Hawke is evident.[147]

In November 1991 it was announced that Optus Communications, an American-British-Australian consortium that included Bell South and Cable and Wireless, was the successful bidder for Australia's second carrier licence. Any windfall the government hoped to gain from the sale was cancelled out, however, by the mountain of Aussat debt it had assumed. Optus paid $804 million, barely more than the quantum of Aussat's debts, having reportedly assessed the company's value at just $100 million (and therefore the licence at about $700 million).[148] The government would receive $504 million upfront, the rest by 1997.[149] The politically explosive potential of this simple calculation was anticipated in government circles and there was some surprise when it did not face detailed questions about it.[150]

The Hawke government legislated its telecommunications reforms in May and June of 1991. From late 1990, Beazley and his advisers and department maintained an open dialogue with the Coalition's Warwick Smith (in the House of Representatives) and Richard Alston (in the Senate), who had carriage of the issue for the opposition. Beazley had personal regard for Smith and Alston, and they received detailed briefings from officials, who recall constructive discussions with both men in spite of their reservations about Labor's approach. Costanzo believes Beazley was 'very lucky' to have had Smith as his shadow in the lower house, describing their engagement as 'very collaborative'.[151] Labor depended on opposition votes in the Senate to pass its Telecommunications Bill, which dealt with competition and privatisation, both moves that the Australian Democrats unequivocally rejected. It also helped that ATUG accepted that these reforms were the best deal available and encouraged the Coalition to back them. Meanwhile, the government's Australian and Overseas Telecommunications Corporation Bill, which dealt with the Telecom-OTC merger, passed the Senate with Democrats support. The two bills had been structured this way to achieve this result.[152]

The parliamentary debate underlined the extent to which the central policy contest over Australian telecommunications reform had played out within Labor rather than between Labor and the Coalition. Indeed, once Beazley's plan was confirmed by cabinet and ratified at Labor's conference, the government's principal parliamentary opposition in all matters other than the Telecom-OTC merger came from the Australian Democrats in the Senate. The Coalition's parliamentary critiques of Labor's reform measures were barely distinguishable from those previously mounted from within sections of the government and bureaucracy, most prominently by Keating, who, amid the debate, unsuccessfully challenged Hawke for the Labor leadership and moved to the backbenches. There was disquiet among some Coalition MPs about the implications of a more competitive telecommunications sector on rural communities (former Nationals leader and Fraser communications minister Ian Sinclair acknowledged that his preference was for keeping liberalisation 'at the small end'). Nevertheless, the debate between government and opposition was not about the need for market liberal reforms but about how far they should go and how best to achieve them. The opposition's view (expressed by Alston) was that 'Mr Keating got it right'.[153]

Warwick Smith described the government's plan as 'a step in the right direction taken in the worst possible way'. Labor's Telecommunications Bill, he said, was 'full of compromises which defer the problems sure to appear down the track'. This was prescient. Pivotal to these compromises were a 'David and Goliath' duopoly and the 'gigantic juggling efforts' needed 'to make it possible for a new entrant to be taken on'.[154] Over forty Coalition amendments to Labor's bills were agreed to in the Senate; among them were measures to further bolster these gigantic juggling efforts, for example by more explicitly describing Austel's consumer protection functions and expanding its enforcement powers, including doubling penalties for non-compliance.[155] Consistent with Peter Harris's earlier advice to Hawke, Smith criticised the plan to delay a third mobile licence and, as had Keating and Treasury, dismissed out of hand the prospect of Telecom developing into a successful global player while it did not face any significant competitive pressure at home.[156]

Nonetheless, the Hawke government's telecommunications bills gained parliamentary approval on 20 June 1991, amid grumbling from Beazley about 'flaws in the drafting … and flaws in the policy', in time for the new regime to commence as promised on 1 July.[157] Eighteen months later, a third mobile licence was awarded to global operator Vodafone. It began operating in Australia in September 1993. A new era had begun.

13

Lessons and Legacies

It is not too much to say that for telecommunications one should read innovation, the free flow of ideas, individual fulfilment and economic progress. In short, for 'telecommunications' read 'freedom'.

Michael Kirby[1]

The new framework legislated by the Hawke government in 1991 was a transformational development and marks the birth of Australia's modern telecommunications era. Since then, federal governments of all persuasions have looked to competition as the sector's core energising force and sought to buttress it to stimulate innovation and efficiency for economic and social benefit. In exploring the politics of Australian telecommunications policy over the quarter-century leading up to this reform, this book has interrogated the key dynamics, decisions and actions that cumulatively saw the nation transition from a system of rigid state monopolies in the 1960s to a competition-based model in the 1990s.

I have argued that this long transition began in 1967 when, responding to a confluence of technological, sectoral and structural factors placing pressure on the telecommunications and postal systems, the Whitlam-led Labor opposition committed to a program of fundamental change. For the first time since federation, a major political party had repudiated the political consensus over how best to deliver these essential services. This move initiated a period in which national policy objectives and deeply embedded structural and institutional arrangements were repeatedly challenged in an environment being disrupted by relentless technological change.

As the sole operator of Australia's vast network of national telecommunications infrastructure and services, the PMG was able to deploy its technical expertise and its insider knowledge of the system, particularly regarding politically and socially sensitive issues such as the cost and durability of cross-subsidy arrangements, to fortify its monopoly and shape favourable policy outcomes. In 1975, this power and influence were handed on to its successor, the statutory authority Telecom. In the latter 1970s, and particularly from the late 1980s, Telecom's unique access to information, combined with the telecommunications system's presence in just about every Australian community, business and economic sector, proved an obstacle to even modest competitive reform.

A particular barrier to change arose from the opaque, politically infused system of cross-subsidies that supported the provision of services to rural and regional areas. It had long been a bipartisan objective in Australian social policy that affordable services should be provided to Australians wherever they lived, but over time this structure gave rise to a powerful sectional lobby on behalf of country interests. Throughout the Coalition's long postwar period of government, the Country Party was an especially fierce defender of subsidies for rural users. With support from rural Liberal MPs, it wielded its control of the postmaster-general's portfolio from 1949 to 1963 and its strength in cabinet through to 1972 to push successfully for expanded subsidies and services to non-metropolitan areas. Successive Liberal prime ministers Holt, Gorton and McMahon appear not to have engaged with this vast area of government expenditure, perhaps symptomatic of the Coalition's general lethargy regarding administrative reform.

This inertia was abetted by the telecommunications system's continued capacity to deliver improvements to service quality and functionality and to network performance. These advances were made possible by the rapid technological change that telecommunications was undergoing in the 1960s. There were also rising community expectations, reinforced by demographic shifts. As Australia's population grew and its cities spread outwards, household demand for telephone services surged. New data applications also became increasingly indispensable to business. From the 1970s, businesses began to demand more innovative and responsive services to meet their changing needs.

The accelerating pace of technological change, combined with demand growth well beyond the PMG's capacity to serve, placed the department under operational and financial pressure during the 1960s and strained the governance arrangements under which the system ran. The magnitude of rural subsidies contributed significantly to the PMG's troubles; they stimulated demand for commercially unviable services in country areas, placing pressure on the PMG's capital budget. By the early 1970s, it was clear that the status quo was financially and administratively unsustainable.

This in turn intensified the political pressure for reform, but the Coalition government undertook no significant change. The Liberal and Country parties had no political imperative to embark upon major reform and no desire to do so. Liberal Postmaster-General Alan Hulme, cognisant of the need to provide the PMG with greater autonomy, was prepared to make incremental adjustments, but he was personally convinced that it was necessary to maintain existing institutional structures and direct ministerial authority to fulfil policy objectives in rural areas. He actively discouraged proposals for more significant changes, even when they came from within the PMG. The Coalition lacked the collective will to grapple with the complex political and policy challenges that faced it.

For the Labor Party under Whitlam, the lie of the land was different. The new opposition leader was personally committed to administrative reform, including specifically in telecommunications, and he led from the front. Developing a politically pragmatic across-the-board reformist policy program was a principal priority. The APWU, the largest of the PMG's unions, had long pushed within Labor for the PMG to be recreated as an autonomous state enterprise freed from public service strictures. This aligned with Whitlam's agenda and prevailing international trends. Labor committed to the reform of telecommunications and post based on this model. It refined the policy during its last five years in opposition, advocating for change in parliament and at the 1969 and 1972 elections.

In government, Labor adopted a generally evidence-based, transparent and consultative approach to its reform program. Whitlam actively co-opted respected, politically conservative business figures into important leadership roles. This reflected his essentially non-partisan outlook on telecommunications policy and his genuine intent to inject business expertise and practices into the system. His government's early measures included moves to rebalance service charges in response to the PMG's urgent financial problems. These changes were also consistent with Whitlam's long-stated aim of making Australian telecommunications more self-sufficient and his support for user-pays principles in this area to free government funds for other policy priorities.

Labor's program received broad backing from key stakeholders. Caucus and the unions, despite reservations, supported the shift to more autonomous statutory authorities for mostly industrial reasons, while senior PMG officials supported Telecom's establishment for the commercial freedoms and opportunities it offered. The government also achieved sufficient consensus with the Coalition to facilitate Telecom's establishment. A crucial factor in this was the Vernon commission's scrupulous report into the PMG, which showed irrefutably that the present state of affairs was not fit for purpose.

But Whitlam and other members of his government also acted in ways that cut across Labor's policy objectives and worked against its political interests. They took a needlessly inflammatory approach to rural concerns about reduced government funding and services, although in reality the government continued to provide significant support to country areas. Substantial subsidies continued to sustain the bipartisan telecommunications policy of affordable universal service.

Whitlam aroused hostility with a peremptory vow to abolish OTC and transfer its functions to the new telecommunications authority. This sparked opposition from a broadly based and well-resourced coalition of interests, comprising OTC's top management, unions, large business customers and the Liberal and Country parties, which comprehensively defeated the government on this issue. In the course of this fight, while scrambling to secure Coalition Senate support to inaugurate Telecom and Australia Post on time, Labor attempted to allay the opposition's concerns about rural service provision by expanding discretionary ministerial powers over the new statutory authorities, unintentionally undermining the independence it had long sought for them.

Notwithstanding the uneasy collaboration between Labor and the Coalition over establishing Telecom, the parties' different ideological and political perspectives were clear. The Whitlam government argued for an autonomous statutory authority because it wanted to improve the financial efficiency and operational effectiveness of Australia's telecommunications system. But Labor refused to acknowledge legitimate concerns that its approach could strengthen the unions and put upward pressure on operating costs, which would be passed on to households and businesses. For its part, the Coalition professed support for business management principles and improved productivity, though in reality this meant little more than cutting fixed labour costs by employing more contractors. At no point did it acknowledge the financial consequences of its previous mismanagement of the system.

The Liberals in particular struggled to reconcile their support for 'businesslike' efficiency with their commitment to universal, affordable rural services. In parliamentary debates about the mooted telecommunications and postal authorities, the Coalition pushed hard for more legislative prescription and wider ministerial powers to ensure that commercial considerations did not outweigh social policy objectives. The struggle intensified markedly after Whitlam's government was dismissed and replaced by the Fraser-led Coalition.

The Fraser government came to office having given little thought to telecommunications, but before long it confronted an unanticipated set of political and policy dilemmas that ultimately it could not resolve. A key problem was that the emergence of new business-orientated communications equipment and data services was creating a level of demand that Telecom was not set up to meet. In particular, businesses were looking for a level of customer service and choice that cut across Australia's one-size-fits-all system. This posed a critical challenge because it pitted the interests of business, a core Coalition constituency, against the concerns of its rural supporter base. The dilemma was compounded by hitherto latent tensions over the role of Telecom. Whereas the Coalition took the view that the proper economic role of the public sector, including a statutory authority such as Telecom, was not to crowd out the private sector, Telecom (as Labor had intended) was keen to exploit new commercial opportunities, including in competition with business.

Amid these difficulties, the Fraser government decided to establish Aussat, a state-owned company to develop and operate a national satellite system. This marked an unintended turning point in the politics of telecommunications reform. It inserted an inherently disruptive force into the system, principally because satellite had the technical potential to replicate Telecom's monopoly landline services. But the Coalition did not set out with an agenda to fundamentally change Australia's telecommunications arrangements. Indeed, telecommunications, though always in the policy mix, was a secondary consideration for the government, which was primarily focused on broadcasting and on satellite's transformative blue-sky potential. In fact, the post and telecommunications minister, Tony Staley, initially wanted Telecom to have responsibility for satellite to promote policy and operational simplicity, and the Fraser cabinet ensured that Telecom's core monopoly and cross-subsidies were protected for fear of endangering service delivery to rural areas.

In the early 1980s, the Fraser government increasingly struggled to reconcile the forces pressing for liberalisation in telecommunications with its continued commitment to traditional universal service objectives. The Australian policy debate was shifting in complex and contentious ways, becoming less about how to improve the existing telecommunications system's efficiency and more about whether the system itself needed to change. The Coalition could not resolve these conundrums, and Labor had little appetite to try. There was neither a clear evidence-based policy path forward nor a broadly accepted economic framework within which to assess the dilemmas being thrown up. Competing interest groups could and did make plausible arguments for and against change. Telecom also leveraged its technical expertise and inside knowledge of the system to shape government decision-making. The practical and policy implications of the Davidson inquiry's recommendation to open the entire telecommunications sector to competition reinforced this quandary. Embarking on significant reform at this point would have required a public policy leap of faith and a reserve of political capital that the Fraser government did not have.

Following the Hawke government's election in 1983, its telecommunications policy went through two distinct phases; essentially, it was two different governments. In its first four years, Labor favoured established interests, especially Telecom and its unions. Its first-term priority was to kill off the nascent market liberalism tentatively explored under Fraser. There was little meaningful engagement with the complex issues challenging the system's integrity. Hawke and his economic ministers had other priorities. The government's approach to Aussat was especially significant; by constraining its operations and allowing Telecom to occupy a powerful position on its board, Labor not only hobbled the company but complicated and distorted its own political and policy options.

During Labor's second governing phase, from 1987, wider national economic imperatives drove a telecommunications policy pivot. Economic and political pressures meant that business as usual was no longer an option. The Hawke government's telecommunications reforms did not reflect an ideological conversion to market liberalism analogous to the ideological shift that had occurred in the Liberal Party from 1983, but once committed to change, the government was open to co-opting these ideas to advance its policy objectives, as it had been with its earlier economic reforms.

Five critical interrelated elements explain the Hawke government's reform of telecommunications. First, Hawke and Labor's key economic ministers were politically committed to the project and provided clear direction and support. Hawke wanted real competition in the sector and later boasted of his reformist ambition. In practical terms, however, his appetite for change was contingent on removing Aussat as a political and financial problem, ensuring that caucus and the unions were on side, and adopting a model that would be operational and showing returns by the next election. Cabinet and the machinery of government were reorganised to align with new priorities.

Secondly, policy was developed and executed by a new cohort of public servants not beholden to earlier government decisions. Successive ministers Gareth Evans, Ralph Willis and Kim Beazley each encouraged robust policy discussions with their officials. Mutual respect was high. Though officials would have preferred the government's measures to go further and faster, they accepted that Labor's program was an inherently incremental process dependent on caucus assent, which at best was ambivalent, and the acquiescence of hostile sector unions.

The third element was that the Hawke government pursued telecommunications reform as part of a centrally coordinated across-the-board program of structural reform. This meant that it could concurrently deal with broader countervailing forces as they arose, such as the negative impacts of liberalisation on the protected local equipment manufacturing sector.

Fourthly, and closely related, was the government's commitment to meaningful consultations with the parties to be affected by changes, especially potential losers such as the sector unions and their members. The need for caucus backing and the associated determination to avoid industrial action meant that progress was at times glacial, but the government maintained momentum by setting out clear transition paths and taking specific strategic steps, such as establishing a telecommunications regulator and corporatising state enterprises. A true breakthrough was the achievement of independent costings for Telecom's community service activities. This provided the government (and everyone else) with hard evidence that Australia's cross-subsidy-funded universal service objectives were compatible with full competition. It thus removed the core political risk that had long been associated with dismantling Telecom's monopoly—a risk that had immobilised both Coalition and Labor cabinets.

The fifth element related to timing. Labor benefited from having a first-mover advantage. Though liberalisation was patently a complex and challenging process, the government could accommodate vested interests and its core supporter groups by way of staged, targeted changes and assistance measures while still producing economic productivity gains and consumer benefits within the 1987–90 and 1990–93 electoral cycles. Also important was that, notwithstanding the Coalition's strong criticism of specific Labor measures, the opposition consistently facilitated the passage of government legislation as long as it at least pointed in the general direction of providing for greater openness, flexibility and competition.

The government's decisions in 1990 reshaped Australian telecommunications. Labor's model was built on strengthening Telecom (later Telstra) and exposing it to the potential for national competition in all services, initially within a highly regulated duopoly shared with a re-birthed, privatised Aussat. Competition between rival service providers would now provide the principal stimulus for innovation in the high-tech communications sector. The model established an underlying structure that remained in place at least until the NBN, which itself was a legacy of this original structure.

From the late 1980s a shift to full competition was highly probable, perhaps inevitable, but the timing and the model to be adopted were uncertain. Contingency and agency were significant in shaping Labor policy outcomes during 1990. Aussat's financial crisis, which was largely a consequence of the Hawke government's earlier decisions, drove the urgent timing of its review into the structural arrangements of the three state telecommunications enterprises. Solving the Aussat problem, both politically and financially, remained a central government priority. Gifting OTC to Telecom and using Aussat as the basis for a new competitor satisfied caucus, Telecom and its unions, advanced Beazley's national champion ambitions for Telecom and retained Australian assets in Australian hands. The competitive model Beazley selected and tirelessly prosecuted was clearly the product of political deal making, but it also reflected his genuine policy views, which were imbued with traditional Labor values.

This book has highlighted the crucial role of particular interest groups in shaping Australian telecommunications policy. Rural communities had been at the centre of the telecommunications system since federation, and dedicated, influential interest groups mobilised around the issue of cross-subsidies. In opposition, Coalition politicians representing regional and rural areas railed against the Whitlam government's subsidy rollback. The Coalition's agreement to facilitate Telecom's establishment was conditional on the new enterprise being subject to explicitly codified obligations towards country Australia and to stronger ministerial discretion to direct its activities.

Rural Australia was a core constituency of the Fraser government. Indeed, a key reason for the government's enthusiasm about a national satellite system was the technology's potential to solve the perennial problem of how to provide city-comparable services to country areas. Universal service provision also remained a central policy objective under the Hawke government from 1983. When Labor launched its telecommunications liberalisation project, however, traditional rural interests were less effectively defended by National Party MPs than, perhaps ironically, by the Telecom unions, their caucus allies and Telecom itself, as part of the sector establishment's fight to preserve the status quo.

The large Labor-affiliated telecommunications unions played a consistently significant role in the direction and scope of policy reform. The unions' political and industrial strength was derived from their coverage of the essential services staff who exclusively operated and maintained critical infrastructure. They single-mindedly leveraged this power in pursuit of their sectional interests. In the 1960s, the APWU's advocacy for liberalising telecommunications and postal arrangements was key to Whitlam-led Labor's 1967 commitment to major governance and institutional reform of the PMG. But from the latter 1970s the unions fought resolutely against further change.

The industrial disputes that occurred under Fraser had significant unintended consequences. They confronted business with its vulnerability to unilateral union action just as it was becoming increasingly reliant on more advanced, innovative services and frustrated with its inescapable dependence on Telecom. This spurred the sector to organise collectively to lobby for liberalisation. The disputes also prompted Fraser's cabinet to consider options to mitigate the industrial risks associated with maintaining a monopoly over essential communications infrastructure. Significantly, this occurred at a time when satellite technology seemed to offer the potential for a degree of network redundancy, and market liberal ideas and practical options for increased competition in telecommunications were emerging.

The unions maintained a central role under the Hawke government by virtue of their institutional relationship with Labor and their industrial strength. But like other groups with vested interests in preserving the status quo in telecommunications, they could not ultimately withstand the forces for change—

in this case because the government was determined to proceed with reform. Nonetheless, they fundamentally shaped the parameters of Labor's reform project, including the timing and scope of measures taken and, most importantly, the new market structure and arrangements introduced in 1991.

The business sector was also represented in the debates over telecommunications. The emergence of new telecommunications-focused business interests in the latter 1970s introduced two well-resourced and well-connected lobby groups, Business Telecommunications Services and ATUG, to the policy environment. In pressing for greater flexibility, openness and competition, both groups brought a new and fundamentally disruptive dynamic into what had been, in effect, a closed system that did not, and most likely could not, serve business needs, but was sustained by subsidies funded in large part by business.

Although business stood to gain the greatest immediate benefit from liberalisation, its lobby had less direct impact on government decision-making than did rural Australia, the Telecom unions or the state-owned telecommunications enterprises themselves. This reflected in part the extent to which the interests of these established groups were already embedded in the system and in bipartisan policy assumptions. The Hawke government was never especially responsive to business calls for liberalising telecommunications. Rather, its reforms were driven mostly by wider national imperatives to improve economic productivity and competitiveness, though in practice the outcomes broadly aligned with pre-existing business objectives.

The government telecommunications enterprises, especially Telecom but also OTC and Aussat at particular junctures, played pivotal roles in the reform process. Telecom's ability to reinforce the established structures and norms of Australia's telecommunications arrangements was especially evident. It consistently leveraged its scale and ubiquity in virtually all areas of national affairs and economic activity, and its intimate understanding of the telecommunications system, as previously discussed. This was ably shown during the contentious, long-running corporatisation debate involving Hawke government ministers, officials and state enterprises.

In hindsight, the changes in telecommunications policy that occurred between the late 1960s and the early 1990s can appear as inevitable responses to the impact of technological change. The consequences of actions taken can seem obvious, but this was not the case. The status quo was under near-constant strain during these years, and the decisions taken by successive governments and others were based on incomplete and often contradictory information, usually in the context of strongly contested interests and perspectives, competing policy priorities and whatever transitory political issues were also then at play. Matters were for the most part technically complex, with policy advisers and decision-makers dependent on the expertise of specialists with vested interests in the outcomes. Institutional capacity was uncertain.

Significant change only occurred under Whitlam and Hawke, but this does not mean that telecommunications reform was naturally a Labor project. In fact, from the early 1980s, during Fraser's final term, the opposite was the case. Implementing significant reform depending on a convergence of factors that, while presenting differently to Labor and the Coalition, went beyond party politics. They included an unambiguous imperative for change; clear, committed prime ministerial leadership; consensus among decision-makers about what to do; and a sufficiently broad bloc of stakeholders favouring reform or at least prepared to tolerate it. The pressures for change consistently pushed governments toward enabling greater flexibility and autonomy, but specific policy responses were never set and always carried a real risk of unintended consequences, whether financial, social, economic, industrial, administrative or political.

* * *

While it would be simplistic and incorrect to draw a direct causal link between the decisions taken by the Hawke government in 1990 and the NBN that has been exercising Australians for well over a decade, it is nonetheless the case that had the debate within Labor played out differently then, we would not be where we are now.[2] On winning office in 1996, the Howard government focused on strengthening the legal framework governing telecommunications to constrain Telstra from exploiting its market dominance. At the same time, consistent with Labor's plan, it opened the sector to full competition. A substantively new Telecommunications Act and significantly amended Trade Practices Act were enacted, which provided additional safeguards to new competitors, including a requirement that Telstra negotiate network access on reasonable terms and a more interventionist arbitration role for the Australian Competition and Consumer Commission (ACCC).

But the sources of Telstra's power were simply too pervasive and entrenched to be curbed by these actions. It owned Australia's core network infrastructure and dominated the retail space. Its retail competitors were also its wholesale customers, dependent on access to its network. Telstra could outmanoeuvre, outspend and outlast all comers on the market and legal battlefields.[3] And its insider knowledge continued to mean that ministers were, in Richard Alston's words, 'essentially beholden' to it for information critical to policy decisions.[4]

A competitive local telecommunications sector was important to the Howard government but, as had been the case with Labor, there was a higher priority. For the Coalition, it was maximising Telstra's sale price to pay down debt and fund key election commitments, not least a $1 billion environmental program crafted before the election to win new voters and sweeten the bitter privatisation pill.[5] Just over a quarter of the electorate at the time, and barely a third of Coalition voters, supported selling Telstra.[6] With echoes of Whitlam's focus on redirecting commonwealth monies from the PMG to other priorities, Telstra's privatisation was also about putting tens of billions of public-sector dollars to better use and freeing the telecommunications giant to access equity markets.

During the 1996 election campaign, the Coalition had tackled Labor's anti-privatisation 'save Telstra' drive with ads targeting Paul Keating's role in privatising other government-owned enterprises, namely the Commonwealth Bank and Qantas, and his public musings about selling off Telstra's mobile services and directories businesses. The Coalition's counterattack also involved promising not to break up Telstra in government. This was successful politically but had the major strategic consequence of taking the option of Telstra's structural separation off the table.[7]

So there was a fundamental conflict at the heart of the Howard government's policy, and it was there for a long time, with Telstra's privatisation ultimately taking three stages over ten years to complete. Competition was important, but even more so was protecting Telstra's privileged position in order to maximise its value to investors and thus the funds to pass into state coffers. As always, rural interests featured prominently. Each privatisation tranche involved hundreds of millions of dollars for country programs, including grants, funding for new mobile and fixed networks, enlarged untimed local call zones and extended public broadcasting coverage. There was also a requirement for Telstra's board to contain at least two directors with knowledge of the needs of rural communities.

When Labor's shadow communications minister, Lindsay Tanner, sought to initiate debate on the future of Telstra and telecommunications competition, including specifically the prospect of Telstra's structural separation, he was shut down by the government. The government also rejected an ACCC recommendation that Telstra be required to divest its hybrid fibre coaxial cable network and its half share of pay-television company Foxtel. In hindsight we can say the Hawke government created a telecommunications market structure handicapped by an unsurmountable power imbalance, and the Howard government consolidated it.

From the mid-2000s, cheaper, faster broadband services started becoming more available and market demand began expanding beyond business and boffins. Led by a newly arrived American chief executive, Sol Trujillo, and with the Howard government looking to sell its final 50.1 per cent stake in the company, Telstra launched a series of audacious gambits. It offered to build a new broadband network if the government gave it a regulatory free hand, including relief from access rules and the obligation to operationally separate its wholesale and retail divisions. Such a model made commercial sense to Telstra but ran counter to the pro-competition direction of telecommunications policy since the 1980s. Alarmed at the implications of Telstra's plans and fearing that its siren song would seduce the Coalition, an alliance of smaller competitors led by Optus developed an alternative proposal: an explicitly open-access national broadband network, owned by a consortium of industry players and other investors. To work, the plan needed regulated access to key elements of Telstra's network infrastructure.

Notwithstanding moments of temptation, especially as political pressure for a broadband 'solution' intensified in the lead-up to the 2007 election, Telstra's ask was too great for the Coalition, as it would also have been for Labor. The company's strikingly bellicose approach towards the government was typified by Trujillo's communications director Phil Burgess; his over-the-top rhetoric was frequently riveting but ultimately worked against Telstra's objectives. One outcome, however, was the fortuitous availability of competing broadband models for new Labor leader Kevin Rudd, who was on the lookout for exciting big-bang policies aligned with his Kevin07 brand. He announced that a Rudd government would spend up to $4.7 billion in partnership with private-sector investors to build a commercially viable open-access national broadband network covering 98 per cent of Australia's population.

Caught short, the Coalition launched its own plan soon after, awarding $958 million to a joint venture between Optus and agribusiness company Elders to build a rural broadband network. By this stage, relations between Telstra and senior Coalition figures were poisonous. Telstra openly barracked for a Labor win, confident that it was the only company able to build and operate the mooted national broadband network.

For most of 2008, after Labor's victory, the assumption prevailed that, one way or another, Telstra would build and operate the network. The Howard government's communications minister in its final term, Helen Coonan, publicly conceded as much before the 2007 election when she said that for Australia to develop a national fibre network 'in the foreseeable future, it would have to be Telstra' because the obstacles to anything else seemed 'almost insurmountable'.[8] But Telstra became worried that a side-effect of running the new government's national broadband network might be its structural separation, and it stopped playing ball. In a confrontational and misjudged game of brinkmanship, Telstra sought to wrest sweeping regulatory concessions from Labor. When that failed, it effectively torpedoed the government's project by lodging a blatantly non-compliant response to the formal process seeking proposals from parties interested in building the network. This left the government with little choice but to exclude Telstra from the process, which collapsed shortly afterwards.

Telstra overreached, assuming Labor would have to commission it to build and operate the network. But cornered and politically humiliated, the Rudd government doubled down. In April 2009, Rudd stood alongside his treasurer and finance and communications ministers to announce the establishment of a state-owned national broadband network company, NBN Co, to build 'the most ambitious, far reaching and long-term nation building infrastructure project ever undertaken by an Australian government'.[9] This represented a step change from Labor's earlier defunct policy. Rudd now promised much faster broadband over a more extensive network using superior technology. He also foreshadowed an eightfold increase in public spending, from less than $5 billion to more than $40 billion, though neither of these figures meant much; the first reflected a flawed understanding of an earlier Telstra proposal and the second was, in the government's own words, just a 'preliminary estimate'.[10] This was political shock and awe by Labor, not the outcome of orderly, rigorous policy-making. A politically red-faced government had taken the Year Zero option and, in a radical post-GFC intervention, set out to remake Australia's telecommunications sector afresh by grafting a new state-run monopoly onto existing structures.

One consistency between both Labor plans was that the network would be open-access and wholesale-only. The logic was that, with no skin in retail, the NBN operator's overriding commercial incentive would be to drive as much business as possible over its network. It would be configured so that the telecommunications, internet and media companies using it could meaningfully differentiate their product and service offerings to the market. This approach was reminiscent of various proposals doing the rounds in Canberra throughout 1990. Rudd proclaimed that creating a new, wholesale-only NBN company 'solves, once and for all, the core problem created when the previous Prime Minister privatised Telstra a decade ago without ever resolving the conflict of a private monopoly owning the network infrastructure and dominating the retail market'.[11] His combative communications minister, Stephen Conroy, said more bluntly that the new industry structure would fix 'a mistake by the Hawke government taken further by the sale of Telstra'.[12]

Channelling his inner Godfather a few months later, Conroy held a legislative gun to Telstra's head and made it an offer it couldn't refuse. Telstra could get with the program and voluntarily separate its wholesale and retail functions, or the government would do it itself, in which case Telstra might also find itself banned from acquiring new wireless spectrum for its mobile business and forced to sell its majority stake in Foxtel, thus losing control of the company's strategically important cable network. There was political payback in Conroy's approach, but he was also protecting NBN Co's future viability. Telstra chose option A, though it extracted its pound of flesh. Following lengthy negotiations, NBN Co agreed in 2011 to pay Telstra more than $10 billion (in 2011 dollars) over at least thirty years to rent its network assets and, in an orderly form of structural separation, migrate its customers to the new network. Telstra extracted further concessions in 2014, after the election of the Abbott Coalition government.

One might consider the Rudd government's 2009 NBN policy Whitlamesque in its audacity, but as this book has shown, the Whitlam government's approach to telecommunications was for the most part prudent, evidence-based and the product of years of incremental policy development. A closer parallel is the Fraser government's establishment of Aussat. In both cases there was excitement and faith among top decision-makers about the transformative potential of a dramatic new technological solution to deliver economic and social benefits across the nation and bridge Australia's city-country divide. There was also an initial pragmatic preference by government for the domestic incumbent to run the project; its recalcitrance was followed by politically infused decisions to create entirely new state-owned enterprises, Aussat and NBN Co respectively, to carry out the government's politico-policy objectives.

When the NBN was announced during the still heady days of Kevin07, it excited the popular imagination and was integral to Labor projecting as the party to take Australia to a technologically advanced, innovative twenty-first-century future. After the inconclusive 2010 federal election, the NBN was pivotal to Labor (now led by Julia Gillard) retaining government, being specifically cited by the independent MPs who backed the party on the floor of parliament. But over the last decade, as prime ministers, governments and NBN Co chief executives have come and gone, and as corporate plans, technology choices and operational priorities have chopped and changed, the project has frequently been mired in controversy and recrimination. Labor's level of political investment in the NBN meant that money, and arguably time, was no object in realising its dream of a gold-plated fibre-to-the-premises network. After winning government in 2013, the Coalition had NBN Co adopt a more commercially rational strategy, utilising less premium technology options to accelerate the rollout, reduce upfront costs and bring forward positive cashflows.

Amid all the impassioned arguments on both sides, by politicians, industry players, technology enthusiasts and the public, what is striking is that, boiled down, the issues in contention are precisely those that have reverberated for well over the last half century: tensions between economic and social policy objectives, city and country interests and, more recently, business and households; debate over governance arrangements for the sector; and the relentlessly disruptive pressure from constant technological developments that, in the NBN's case, have now appeared in the form of 5G. In this context, NBN Co's announcement in 2020 of a $4.5 billion network upgrade to connect 8 million premises with fibre by 2023, to provide capacity for services up to one gigabit per second, gave proponents on all sides of the debate a burst of renewed energy to argue the merits of their case.[13]

Continuous disruption, whether technological or political, is the only real certainty in telecommunications. Nonetheless, there are short odds of an NBN sale process commencing within the next decade, despite the Albanese Labor government's announcement in late July 2022 that it would 'retain NBN Co in public ownership for the foreseeable future'.[14] If—or when—privatisation kicks off, the most likely scenario is that Telstra will be first in line. The company has made no secret of wanting 'a seat at that table', and has been progressively splitting its vast portfolio of assets and operations into separate businesses.[15] One of these, InfraCo Fixed, will comprise Telstra's domestic physical infrastructure, including fibre, data centres and exchanges.[16] It is plainly primed for a future full or partial NBN sale, though further separation from Telstra would still need to occur. The company's former chief executive, Andy Penn, has acknowledged that 'being vertically integrated is clearly not going to fly'.[17] But be that as it may, if Telstra, in some form or other, does ultimately emerge as the inheritor of this great state project, the echo of our telecommunications past will resonate once again across the land.

Acknowledgements

Much of the research and early writing for this book was done while completing my PhD. So, no PhD, no book, and for that reason alone (though there are countless others) I am indebted to Judith Brett and Nicholas Barry, my supervisors, for their unstinting support, guidance and steadfast good humour throughout that arduous and ultimately exhilarating experience—and then for being there when I needed them as the PhD project became a book project.

During the book's long gestation, I received encouragement and assistance from many people. Thank you to Richard Alston, Andrew Bedogni, John Besemeres, Frank Bongiorno, Nicholas Brown, Henry Ergas, Brian Galligan, Carolyn Holbrook, Nathan Hollier, Michael Lee, David Lowe, Stuart Macintyre, Robert Manne, Race Mathews, Jane McCabe, Phillipa McGuiness, George Megalogenis, Richard Prebble, Holly Raiche, Gary Smith, John Stanton, James Walter and Clare Wright. Particular thanks to Paul Fletcher, who has consistently supported my professional endeavours over the years, and true to form did so in numerous ways throughout this multi-phased exercise.

For agreeing to be interviewed, and generously making available their time and recollections, I am grateful to Kim Beazley, Neil Brown, Jim Carlton, Chris Cheah, Paddy Costanzo, Robin Davey, Leo Dobes, Gareth Evans, Graham Evans, Vanessa Fanning, Malcolm Fraser, Peter Harris, Paul Keating, Tony Shaw, Ian Sinclair and Tony Staley. I additionally thank Graham Evans and Tony Shaw for reading parts of the manuscript and providing incisive comments, and also Kim Beazley and Gareth Evans for their support as the book neared publication. Of course, any errors are entirely my responsibility.

I acknowledge the professional services received from staff at the National Archives in Canberra, La Trobe University's Borchardt Library and the State Library Victoria. I especially thank Andrew Cairns, Lisa Donnelly and Tim Mifsud. Colleen Graham, Susan Grusovin and Amy Smith also provided valuable assistance, as did staff from the Victorian division of the Liberal Party and the New South Wales National Party, for which I'm grateful.

A big thank you to Gavin McLean and Louise Saw for their warm welcome and indispensable assistance when I was a PhD newbie at La Trobe University some ten years ago. And an equally big call out to Dominic Kelly, Jim Vale and Gijs Verbossen, whose comradeship I greatly valued then and whose friendship I do today. Thanks also to Gwenda Tavan for her encouragement and support.

Nick Walker at Australian Scholarly Publishing responded with enthusiasm to my book proposal all the way back in 2018, and was supportive, wise and calmingly unflappable during the many fits-and-starts of this enterprise. I'm greatly appreciative, Nick, thank you. Thanks also to ASP's Anna Nechkina and David Morgan for resolutely shepherding the book to physical form. My editor, indexer and all-round go-to person, Jenny Lee, has been an absolute delight to work with and to learn from. This book is so much better for her dedication and expertise. Jenny, I can't thank you enough.

To family and friends far and wide, who in one way or another have been on this ride with me, thanks for your interest and encouragement. To Tom and James, who have been part-and-parcel of this frequently intense and seemingly never-ending project for between a half and two-thirds of their lives, thank you from the bottom of my heart for sticking it out with me. My hope is that you're proud of me for writing this book. My dream is that one day you'll actually read it.

And now to Aneetha. How can I possibly express the sweep of my emotions for all that's transpired for us since we embarked on our great new adventure a decade ago? Truth is, I can't. My depth of gratitude—for your unwavering encouragement and support, your unshakeable belief in this enterprise and in me, and your quite extraordinary patience—is simply beyond words. Without you, I could never have started this project, and most certainly I could never have finished it. Thank you so very, very much.

Notes

Introduction

1 Michael Kirby, Foreword in Mark Armstrong (ed.), *Telecommunications Law: Australian Perspectives* (Media Arm, Melbourne, 1990), xvii.

2 Tony Staley in CPD (Reps) (18 October 1979), 2229.

3 Tony Staley, interview with author, 3 March 2014.

4 Staley in CPD (18 October 1979), 2224–9.

5 Malcolm Fraser, interview with author, 14 February 2014; Staley, interview.

6 Staley in CPD (18 October 1979), 2229.

7 Harold White, quoted in S. R. Paltridge, 'Aussat: the social shaping of a satellite system', PhD thesis (University of Wollongong, 1989), 162.

8 Newspaper editorials in the *Australian* and the *Age* quoted in Trevor Barr, *The Electronic Estate: New Communications Media and Australia* (Penguin, Melbourne, 1985), 160.

1. A Vast Concern

1 Robert Anderson, *Report on the Business Management of the Postmaster-General's Department of the Commonwealth of Australia* (Commonwealth of Australia, August 1915), 5. The report was known colloquially as the Anderson report.

2 This chapter draws from John Doyle, 'Conceiving of Telecom: The Politics of Australian Telecommunications Reform, 1967–1972', *Australian Journal of Politics and History*, 61/2 (2015), 201–16.

3 N. G. Butlin, A. Barnard and J. J. Pincus, *Government and Capitalism: Public and Private Choice in Twentieth Century Australia* (George Allen & Unwin, Sydney, 1982), 295.

4 K. T. Livingstone, *The Wired Nation Continent: The Communication Revolution and Federating Australia* (Oxford University Press, Melbourne, 1996), 183–5.

5 Butlin *et al.*, *Government and Capitalism*, 297–8; Ann Moyal, *Clear Across Australia: A History of Telecommunications* (Thomas Nelson, Melbourne, 1984), 259.

6 Drake and Best quoted in Moyal, *Clear Across Australia*, 90–1.

7 Moyal, *Clear Across Australia*, 97–106, 260. The inquiries were the Royal Commission on Postal Services (1908–10), the Inquiry on the Business Management of the Postmaster-General's Department of the Commonwealth of Australia (Anderson Inquiry, 1915), and the Royal Commission Appointed to Consider and Report upon the Public Expenditure of the Commonwealth of Australia with a view to effecting Economies (1918–21).

8 Royal Commission on Postal Services quoted in PMG, *Australian Post Office Commission of Inquiry: Submission by the Postmaster-General's Department*, I (Canberra, 1973), 23–9.

9 See G. P. Walsh, 'Anderson, Sir Robert Murray McCheyne (1865–1940)', *Australian Dictionary of Biography*.

10 Anderson, *Report on Business Management of the PMG*, 40.

11 Butlin *et al.*, *Government and Capitalism*, 297; Moyal, *Clear Across Australia*, 106; James Vernon, James Kennedy and Bernard Callinan, *Report of the Commission of Inquiry into the Australian Post Office* (AGPS, Canberra, 1974), 53–5. Billy Hughes quoted in Ian McLean, *Telephone Pricing and Cross-Subsidization Under the PMG, 1901–1975*, Working Papers in Economic History, 27 (ANU, Canberra, September 1984), 24.

12 Butlin *et al.*, *Government and Capitalism*, 301–18; Moyal, *Clear Across Australia*, 258; PMG, *Australian Post Office Commission: Submission*, IV, 442–9, 482; TFCEP, *Review of the Continuing Expenditure Policies of the Previous Government* (AGPS, Canberra, 1973), 125–7.

13 Judith Brett, 'Fair share: country and city in Australia', *Quarterly Essay*, 42 (June 2011), 23; Paul Davey, *Politics in the Blood: The Anthonys of Richmond* (UNSW Press, Sydney, 2008), 82.

14 Anderson, *Report on Business Management of the PMG*, 5.

15 Moyal, *Clear Across Australia*, 225; PMG, *Community Telephone Plan 1960* (AGPS, Melbourne, 1960), 9.

16 PMG, *Australian Post Office Commission: Submission*, IV, 412.

17 Moyal, *Clear Across Australia*, 280–4.

18 PMG, *Australian Post Office Commission: Submission*, I, 46–51; and IV, 412; TFCEP, *Review of Continuing Expenditure Policies*, 131–2; Vernon *et al.*, *Report of Commission*, 12–13, 51.

19 PMG, *Australian Post Office Commission: Submission*, I, 50; Grant Fleming, David Merrett and Simon Ville, *The Big End of Town: Big Business and Corporate Leadership in Twentieth-Century Australia* (Cambridge University Press, New York, 2004), 15.

20 Tony Maiden, 'Managing a giant with clouded responsibilities', *Australian Financial Review*, 19 December 1972.

21 B. F. Jones, 'The Post Office and the Community', *Australian Journal of Public Administration*, 26/2 (June 1967), 113; PMG, *Australian Post Office Commission: Submission*, III, 300–2; and V, 218; PMG, *Australian Post Office Commission of Inquiry: Statements by the Postmaster-General's Department on Submissions by Other Parties*, III: *Statement by the Postmaster-General's Department on Submission by the Public Service Board* (Canberra, 1974), 12; Vernon *et al.*, *Report of Commission*, 13; Roger Wettenhall, 'The Post Office', *Current Affairs Bulletin*, 45/9 (23 March 1970), 137.

22 Vernon *et al.*, *Report of Commission*, 36–7.

23 Moyal, *Clear Across Australia*, 259–60; PMG, *Australian Post Office Commission: Statements*, III: *Public Service Board*, 4.

24 PMG, *Australian Post Office Commission: Submission*, V, 512–13; Frank Waters, *Postal Unions and Politics: A History of the Amalgamated Postal Workers' Union of Australia* (University of Queensland Press, St Lucia, 1978), 118, 158–85, 239.

25 'Don't call me—I'll call you', *Bulletin*, 22 January 1972.

26 Ian Allan in CPD (Reps) (2 May 1968), 1069.

27 T. A. Housley, 'Communications in modern society', *Australian Journal of Public Administration*, 26/2 (June 1967), 112.

28 W. K. Hancock, *Australia* (Jacaranda, Brisbane, 1961 [1930]), 106–7.

29   Gough Whitlam in CPD (Reps) (19 August 1965), 234.

30   Moyal, *Clear Across Australia*, 262.

31   John Harper, *Monopoly and Competition in British Telecommunications: The Past, the Present and the Future* (Pinter, London, 1997), 14; PMG, *Australian Post Office Commission: Submission*, I, 43; and IV, 464.

32   PMG, *Australian Post Office Commission: Submission*, I, 43; Vernon *et al.*, *Report of Commission*, 27.

33   Alan Hulme in CPD (Reps) (4 April 1968), 840.

34   Wettenhall, 'The Post Office', 140.

35   Moyal, *Clear Across Australia*, 258; PMG, *Australian Post Office Commission: Submission*, I, 43; Vernon *et al.*, *Report of Commission*, 27.

36   Moyal, *Clear Across Australia*, 260–2; PMG, *Australian Post Office Commission: Submission*, V, 524–5.

37   Hulme in CPD (4 April 1968), 840–1.

38   Dugald Munro in CPD (Reps) (1 May 1968), 1009.

39   Moyal, *Clear Across Australia*, 206; Waters, *Postal Unions and Politics*, 120, 278. Quote is from Doug Anthony in CPD (Reps) (12 September 1973), 838.

40   PMG, *Australian Post Office Commission: Submission*, IV, 449–50.

41   Hulme in CPD (16 September 1971), 1490; PMG, *Australian Post Office Commission: Submission*, V, 580–4, 593–4.

42   PMG, *Australian Post Office Commission: Submission*, IV, 412.

43   PMG, *Australian Post Office Commission: Submission*, I, 80.

44   Doug Anthony, 1972 election policy speech (Lismore, 20 November 1972).

45   TFCEP, *Review of Continuing Expenditure Policies*, 125–7.

46   Moyal, *Clear Across Australia*, 251; Vernon *et al.*, *Report of Commission*, 117, 136–7; Waters, *Postal Unions and Politics*, 239–40.

47   PMG, *Australian Post Office Commission: Submission*, V, 514, 533; Vernon *et al.*, *Report of Commission*, 128; Waters, *Postal Unions and Politics*, 118–24, 170–85.

48   Moyal, *Clear Across Australia*, 260; Waters, *Postal Unions and Politics*, 239.

49   Waters, *Postal Unions and Politics*, 197.

50   ALP, *Official Reports of the 27th Commonwealth Conference and Special Conference and the 28th Commonwealth Conference* (Melbourne, 1969), 22, 85–6.

51   See Jenny Hocking, *Gough Whitlam: A Moment in History* (Miegunyah Press, Melbourne, 2008), 279; Gough Whitlam, *The Whitlam Government, 1972–1975* (Viking, Melbourne, 1985), 4–7.

52   Whitlam in CPD (2 May 1968), 1066.

53   Whitlam, *Whitlam Government*, 215.

54   Whitlam in CPD (19 August 1965), 233–6.

55   ALP, *Official Reports of 27th Commonwealth Conference*, 22, 85–6.

56   Harry Webb in CPD (Reps) (10 May 1967), 1951.

57   PMG, *Australian Post Office Commission: Submission*, IV, 465, 489.

58   Whitlam in CPD (2 May 1968), 1066.

59   Whitlam in CPD (19 August 1965), 233–6; Whitlam, *Whitlam Government*, 215.

60   Whitlam in CPD (2 May 1968), 1066.

61   Webb in CPD (1 May 1968), 1004.

62   Whitlam in CPD (2 May 1968), 1066.

63   Webb in CPD (1 May 1968), 1000.

64   Whitlam in CPD (2 May 1968), 1066.

65   Webb in CPD (1 May 1968), 1003–5.

66   Hulme in CPD (1 May 1968), 1005–7.

67   Bob Cotton in CPD (Senate) (28 May 1968), 1150.

68   See CPD (Reps) (23 September 1970), 1509–19, 1528–32; (8 September 1971), 913–14; (13 September 1971), 1163–94, 1203, 1215.

69   Gough Whitlam, 'Into the Seventies with Labor', 1969 election policy speech (Sydney, 1 October 1969).

70   Gough Whitlam, 'It's time for leadership', 1972 election policy speech (Sydney, 13 November 1972).

2. Reform and Renovation

1   Whitlam in CPD (19 August 1965), 233.

2   David Humphries, 'Labor's anchor through turbulent era', *Sydney Morning Herald*, 3 April 2012; C. J. Lloyd and G. S. Reid, *Out of the Wilderness: The Return of Labor* (Cassell, Melbourne, 1974), 52–4.

3   'Lionel Bowen: the model deputy', *ABC News*, 1 April 2012.

4   Bowen quoted in Fred Brenchley, 'Lionel Bowen: Labor's "Mr. Fixit" is quietly moving up the ladder', *National Times*, 3–8 December 1973.

5   Cabinet submission no. 8, 3 January 1973, NAA: A5915, 8; Bowen quoted in Christopher Dawson, 'Industry that loses mail and money', *Sydney Morning Herald*, 3 May 1973.

6   Cabinet submission no. 8, 3 January 1973, NAA: A5915, 8.

7   Paul Kelly, 'The Whitlam legacy' in Troy Bramston (ed.), *The Whitlam Legacy* (Federation Press, Sydney, 2013), 391–2.

8   Cabinet submission no. 8, 3 January 1973; Cabinet decision no. 26, 9 January 1973, NAA: A5915, 8.

9   Cabinet ad hoc committee decision no. 44, 9 January 1973, NAA: A5915, 8.

10   Cabinet decision no. 112, 30 January 1973, NAA: A5915, 8; Lloyd and Reid, *Out of the Wilderness*, 244.

11   Cabinet ad hoc committee decision no. 44, 9 January 1973, NAA: A5915, 8.

12   Cabinet decision no. 26, 9 January 1973, NAA: A5915, 8.

13   Edgar Harcourt, *Taming the Tyrant: The First One Hundred Years of Australia's International Telecommunications* (Allen & Unwin, Sydney, 1987), 249, 282–92, 308–43; Moyal, *Clear Across Australia*, 182.

14   Quoted in Tony Maiden, 'Customers must adapt to standards set by the line of least resistance', *Australian Financial Review*, 21 December 1972.

15   Vernon to Whitlam, 6 December 1972; Whitlam to Vernon, 12 January 1973, NAA: M503, 20134; Whitlam, *Whitlam Government*, 697.

16 Moyal, *Clear Across Australia*, 266; Vernon *et al.*, *Report of Commission*, 1–4.

17 Australian Post Office Commission of Inquiry, submission files, NAA: CA 2040, A4066; Vernon *et al.*, *Report of Commission*, 1–4.

18 PMG, *Australian Post Office Commission: Statements*, I: *Australian Country Party*, 1–3, 7–11.

19 DURD, *Submission to the Australian Post Office Commission of Inquiry* (Canberra, 16 May 1973), 1–2, NAA: A4066, 361.

20 PMG, *Australian Post Office Commission: Statements*, I: *Australian Country Party*, 1–10.

21 PMG, *Australian Post Office Commission: Statements*, II: *Department of Urban and Regional Development*, 2–4.

22 See Eber Lane to Hugh Payne, 2 August 1973, NAA: A4066, 455.

23 PMG, *Australian Post Office Commission: Statements*, III: *Public Service Board*, 1–4.

24 PMG, *Australian Post Office Commission: Statements*, II: *Treasury*, 1–2; Treasury, *The Australian Post Office Commission of Inquiry: Submission by the Department of the Treasury* (Canberra, 1973), 3–6, NAA: A4066, 434.

25 Waters, *Postal Unions and Politics*, 233–4.

26 APWU submission to Vernon commission quoted in Waters, *Postal Unions and Politics*, 243–5; PMG, *Australian Post Office Commission: Statements*, I: *Amalgamated Postal Workers' Union*, 9–12; also Hugh Payne to James Vernon, 6 July 1973, NAA: A4066, 289.

27 Slater to Payne, 1 June 1973, NAA: A4066, 289.

28 PMG, *Australian Post Office Commission: Statements*, I: *Amalgamated Postal Workers' Union*, 2.

29 PMG, *Australian Post Office Commission: Statements*, III: *Overseas Telecommunications Commission*, 1–5.

30 Whitlam quoted in TFCEP, *Review of Continuing Expenditure Policies*, v.

31 TFCEP, *Review of Continuing Expenditure Policies*, 15–19, 26–8, 59–62.

32 TFCEP, *Review of Continuing Expenditure Policies*, 39–42.

33 TFCEP, *Review of Continuing Expenditure Policies*, 119–32.

34 Graham Freudenberg, *A Certain Grandeur: Gough Whitlam in Politics* (Macmillan, Melbourne, 1977), 280–1.

35 Whitlam, *Whitlam Government*, 263–4, 275–6.

36 Freudenberg, *A Certain Grandeur*, 280–1.

37 Lionel Bowen in CPD (Reps) (21 August 1973), 173–4.

38 Bowen in CPD (12 September 1973), 847.

39 Bowen in CPD (21 August 1973), 174–6.

40 Frank Stewart in CPD (Reps) (29 August 1973), 542; and Fred Daly, 588; and Bob Katter (sr.), 579–80; and Ian Robinson, 1094; and Gil Duthie, 583.

41 See CPD (Reps) (29 August 1973), 540–1; (19 September 1973), 1255–7; and CPD (Senate) (25 and 27 September 1973).

42 Vernon *et al.*, *Report of Commission*, xiii-xiv.

43 Vernon *et al.*, *Report of Commission*, 237–40.

44 Vernon *et al.*, *Report of Commission*, 198–203.

45 Vernon *et al.*, *Report of Commission*, 208–12.

46 Vernon *et al.*, *Report of Commission*, 251–2.

47 Vernon *et al.*, *Report of Commission*, 297–9. See also Paltridge, 'Aussat', 158.

48 Vernon *et al.*, *Report of Commission*, 23.

49 Vernon *et al.*, *Report of Commission*, 197–8.

50 Vernon *et al.*, *Report of Commission*, 182–201, 228–35.

51 Vernon *et al.*, *Report of Commission*, 57–8.

52 Vernon *et al.*, *Report of Commission*, 189.

53 Gough Whitlam, 'Report of the Commission of Inquiry into the Post Office', media release, 24 April 1974.

54 Gough Whitlam, 1974 election policy speech (Sydney, 29 April 1974).

55 Snedden quoted in Allan Barnes, 'Govt plans to split Post Office', *Age*, 25 April 1974.

56 Liberal Party, *The Way Ahead with a Liberal Country Government* (Canberra, March 1974), 106.

57 'New structure: fresh outlook?', *Age*, 26 April 1974.

58 Maiden, 'Managing a giant with clouded responsibilities'; Moyal, *Clear Across Australia*, 278, 294; Ian Reinecke and Julianne Schultz, *The Phone Book: The Future of Australia's Communications on the Line* (Penguin, Melbourne, 1983), 19.

59 'Establishment of separate posts and telecommunications corporations', *Queensland Postal Worker*, December 1974.

60 Quoted in Reinecke and Schultz, *Phone Book*, 20.

61 CPD (Senate) (20 May 1975), 1573, 1606; Harcourt, *Taming the Tyrant*, 355, 381–2; Moyal, *Clear Across Australia*, 296.

3. Escalating Challenges

1 Whitlam, 1974 election policy speech.

2 Alan Reid, *The Whitlam Venture* (Hill of Content, Melbourne, 1976), 215.

3 Cabinet submission no. 1066, 28 June 1974, NAA: A5915, 1066.

4 Reg Bishop in CPD (Senate) (20 May 1975), 1604; Cabinet decision no. 2365, 22 July 1974, NAA: A5925, 2365.

5 Tim Colebatch, 'Gibbs loves a challenge', *Age*, 7 June 1973; Moyal, *Clear Across Australia*, 295.

6 Cabinet decision no. 2422, 5 August 1974, NAA: A5915, 1066.

7 Cabinet submission no. 1117, 18 July 1974; Cabinet decision no. 2363, 22 July 1974, NAA: A5915, 1117; Michael Easson, 'Industrial relations policy' in Bramston (ed.), *Whitlam Legacy*, 230; John O'Mahony, 'Economic policy' in Bramston (ed.), *Whitlam Legacy*, 170–2; Waters, *Postal Unions and Politics*, 248.

8 Cabinet submission no. 1117, 18 July 1974, NAA: A5915, 1117.

9 Cabinet decision no. 2363, 22 July 1974, NAA: A5915, 1117.

10 Whitlam, *Whitlam Government*, 698.

11 Bowen in CPD (23 July 1974), 511–12.

12 Peter Morris in CPD (Reps) (25 July 1974), 681.

13 Peter Nixon in CPD (Reps) (25 July 1974), 680; Robinson in CPD (25 July 1974), 693. The 'profitable' quote is from Nixon; the 'bitter' quote is from Robinson.

14 Whitlam in CPD (31 July 1974), 842.

15 Brett, 'Fair share', 22; Robert Manne, 'The Whitlam revolution' in Robert Manne (ed.), *The Australian Century: Political Struggle in the Building of a Nation* (Text, Melbourne, 1999), 201.

16 See CPD (Senate) (30 July 1974), 591–3.

17 *Australian Financial Review*, 31 July 1974, quoted in CPD (Reps) (17 September 1974), 1427.

18 'Postal losses must be faced', *Age*, 1 August 1974.

19 Crean quoted in O'Mahony, 'Economic policy' in Bramston (ed.), *Whitlam Legacy*, 172.

20 Bowen in CPD (17 September 1974), 1427.

21 Peter Durack in CPD (Senate) (26 September 1974), 1461.

22 IWGCI, *Report of the Interdepartmental Working Group*, attachment B, 3 October 1974, NAA: A5915, 1490.

23 IWGCI, *Report of the Interdepartmental Working Group*, D, NAA: A5915, 1490.

24 Cabinet submission no. 1490 [undated], NAA: A5915, 1490.

25 IWGCI, *Report of the Interdepartmental Working Group*, D, NAA: A5915, 1490.

26 Moyal, *Clear Across Australia*, 296, 410.

27 See CPD (Senate) (30 October 1974), 2117; (20 November 1974), 2563–4; and (26 November 1974), 2714–5.

28 Cabinet decision nos. 2924, 14 November 1974, NAA: A5925, 2924; and 2925, 14 November 1974, NAA: A5925, 2925.

29 Bishop in CPD (23 April 1975), 1262; Cabinet submission no. 1490 [undated], NAA: A5915, 1490.

30 Whitlam in CPD (17 July 1974), 278.

31 Bishop in CPD (23 April 1975), 1256–8.

32 Durack in CPD (20 May 1975), 1569.

33 See CPD (Senate) (21 May 1975), 1671–2.

34 See CPD (Senate) (23 April 1975), 1261.

35 Durack in CPD (20 May 1975), 1571.

36 See CPD (Senate) (20 May 1975), 1587, 1591.

37 Durack in CPD (20 May 1975), 1569–70.

38 Durack in CPD (20 May 1975), 1573–4, 1591–2.

39 Bishop in CPD (20 May 1975), 1592.

40 Durack in CPD (20 May 1975), 1593; Alan Reid, *The Gorton Experiment* (Shakespeare Head Press, Sydney, 1971), 14.

41 Steele Hall in CPD (Senate) (20 May 1975), 1593.

42 Durack in CPD (20 May 1975), 1573.

43 Ron McAuliffe in CPD (Senate) (11 June 1975), 2536.

44 Bishop in CPD (23 April 1975), 1258.

45 Nixon in CPD (3 June 1975), 3259.

46 Durack in CPD (11 June 1975), 2531–2.

47 Bowen in CPD (29 May 1975), 3030.

48   Whitlam, *Whitlam Government*, 698–9.

49   Moyal, *Clear Across Australia*, 263, 300–2; Reid, *Whitlam Venture*, 215; Brian Toohey, 'Bureaucrats' wage splurge', *Australian Financial Review*, 18 July 1975.

50   Bishop in CPD (21 August 1975), 146–7; Reinecke and Schultz, *Phone Book*, 27.

51   Quoted in Moyal, *Clear Across Australia*, 300.

52   Moyal, *Clear Across Australia*, 301–3, 307–8; Reinecke and Schultz, *Phone Book*, 21; Toohey, 'Bureaucrats' wage splurge'. Cooley quoted in Moyal.

53   Peter Samuel, 'PMG charges set hot pace', *Bulletin*, 9 August 1975; Toohey, 'Bureaucrats' wage splurge'. The 'fat cat' quote is from Samuel.

54   Bishop in CPD (19 August 1975), 14; Durack in CPD (19 August 1975), 14; and (21 August 1975), 146–7.

4. A Fast-changing Area

1   Fraser, interview.

2   Fraser quoted in D. M. White and D. A. Kemp (eds), *Malcolm Fraser on Australia* (Hill of Content, Melbourne, 1986), 120–2.

3   Philip Ayres, *Malcolm Fraser: A Biography* (William Heinemann, Melbourne, 1987), 304.

4   Fraser, interview.

5   Ian Sinclair, interview with author, 12 March 2014; Staley, interview.

6   Neil Brown, *On the Other Hand: Sketches and Reflections from Political Life* (Poplar Press, Canberra, 1993), 178.

7   Liberal Party, *The New Government Policies* (Canberra, 1976), 56–7.

8   Cabinet submission no. 485, June 1976, NAA: A12909, 485; Moyal, *Clear Across Australia*, 306–12.

9   Cabinet decision nos. 1181, 15 July 1976, NAA: A12909, 485; 2691, 27 April 1977, NAA: A13075, 2691; and 5836, 21 June 1978, NAA: A12933, 470; Australian Telecommunications Commission (Telecom), *Submission to Public Inquiry into Telecommunications Services in Australia* (Melbourne, February 1982), C17.

10   Doug Anthony, 'Protect your future', 1977 election policy speech; Malcolm Fraser, 1977 election policy speech (21 November 1977).

11   Gough Whitlam, 'A program for Australia's recovery', 1977 election policy speech (Sydney, 17 November 1977).

12   Barr, *Electronic Estate*, 201–3; Reinecke and Schultz, *Phone Book*, 6, 48, 91–6.

13   Moyal, *Clear Across Australia*, 313; Reinecke and Schultz, *Phone Book*, 80.

14   ATUG, *Submission to the Public Inquiry into Telecommunications Services in Australia* (Sydney, February 1982), 36; ATUG, *Telecommunications Policy: Increasing Efficiency Through Competition* (Sydney, February 1990), 3–4.

15   John Langdale, 'Competition in the Australian telecommunications industry? The Davidson inquiry', *Australian Quarterly*, 54/2 (Winter 1982), 176–80; C. D. Trengrove, *Telecommunications in Australia: Competition or Monopoly?*, Special Study, 4 (Centre of Policy Studies, Monash University, Melbourne, 1982), 51.

16   DOC, *Capital and Policy Requirements for the 1980s: Telecom Australia: A Report Prepared by McKinsey and Company* (AGPS, Canberra, 1981 [June 1980]), v–vii, 2.10–11.

17   Moyal, *Clear Across Australia*, 359–60.

18 Staley quoted in *Australian Financial Review*, 3 July 1980.

19 Moyal, *Clear Across Australia*, 359–60; Telecom, *Submission to Public Inquiry*, B40, E11.

20 Telecom, *Submission to Public Inquiry*, E11.

21 Hawke quoted in Blanche d'Alpuget, *Robert J. Hawke: A Biography* (Schwartz, Melbourne, 1982), 350.

22 Tim Dare, 'A leap into the electronic future', *Sydney Morning Herald*, 24 January 1978; Moyal, *Clear Across Australia*, 319–20.

23 Cabinet submission no. 2935, 26 January 1979, NAA: A12909, 2935; Moyal, *Clear Across Australia*, 323–8.

24 Hawke quoted in d'Alpuget, *Robert J. Hawke*, 350–1.

25 Moyal, *Clear Across Australia*, 328–9.

26 Michael Doyle, 'Bans move on Telecom', *Age*, 4 October 1979; Moyal, *Clear Across Australia*, 331–3, 375–8; Reinecke and Schultz, *Phone Book*, 164–6.

27 BTS, *Submission to the Public Inquiry into Telecommunications Services in Australia* (Sydney, December 1981), 1, annex 1. Holmes à Court quoted in Barr, *Electronic Estate*, 121–2.

28 ATUG, *Submission to Public Inquiry*, 36.

29 Cabinet submission no. 2935, 26 January 1979, NAA: A12909, 2935.

30 Staley, interview.

31 Cabinet submission no. 2935, 26 January 1979; Cabinet decision no. 7596, 13 February 1979, NAA: A12909, 2935.

32 Cabinet decision no. 9114, 3 July 1979, NAA: A12909, 3302.

33 Cabinet submission no. 3302, 29 June 1979, NAA: A12909, 3302.

34 Cabinet decision no. 17284, 15 December 1981; ICVTS, *Report*, 33–7, NAA: A12909, 5218.

35 Cabinet submission no. 5218, 27 November 1981, NAA: A12909, 5218.

36 Cabinet decision no. 17284, 15 December 1981. See also ICVTS, *Report*, 33–4, NAA: A12909, 5218.

37 Cabinet submission no. 2966, 21 February 1979, NAA: A12909, 2966.

38 Cabinet decision no. 5836, 21 June 1978, NAA: A12933, 470; Staley, interview.

39 Cabinet submission no. 2966, 21 February 1979, NAA: A12909, 2966.

40 DOC, *Capital and Policy Requirements*, v, x, 5.1.

41 Cabinet decision no. 16323, 20 July 1981, NAA: A12909, 4852.

42 Treasury, *Public Monopolies: Telecom and Australia Post: Submission to the Committee of Inquiry into Telecommunications Services in Australia and into the Monopoly Position of the Australian Postal Commission*, Treasury Economic Paper no. 10 (AGPS, Canberra, 1983), 35.

43 Cabinet submission no. 4852, 3 June 1981, NAA: A12909, 4852; Sinclair, interview.

44 Telecom, *Submission to Public Inquiry*, B62–B63.

45 Cabinet decision no. 15503, 11 June 1981, NAA: A13075, 15503.

46 Cabinet decision no. 15477, 10 June 1981, NAA: A13075, 15477; Moyal, *Clear Across Australia*, 377. Quote is from Patrick Weller, *Malcolm Fraser PM: A Study in Prime Ministerial Power* (Penguin, Melbourne, 1989), 138.

47   Cabinet decision no. 15503, 11 June 1981, NAA: A13075, 15503.

48   Ian Sinclair and Wal Fife, 'Telecom dispute', media statement, 11 June 1981, NAA: A13075, 15503.

5. Blue Sky Dreaming

1   Staley, interview.

2   Paltridge, 'Aussat', 77–8.

3   Fraser, interview.

4   See Donald Bond, *The Opportunity for Television Program Distribution in Australia Using Earth Satellites* (Television Corporation Limited, Sydney, 1977).

5   Paltridge, 'Aussat', 78.

6   Cabinet decision no. 3931, 22 September 1977, NAA: A13075, 3931.

7   White quoted in Paltridge, 'Aussat', 159.

8   Commonwealth Government Task Force on the National Communications Satellite System (White taskforce), *Report on the National Communications Satellite System* (AGPS, Canberra, July 1978), 114–23.

9   SSWG, *National Communications Satellite System: Working Group Report* (AGPS, Canberra, August 1979), vii–viii, 180–205.

10   Cabinet decision no. 3931, 22 September 1977, NAA: A13075, 3931; Paltridge, 'Aussat', 158.

11   White taskforce, *Report on National Communications Satellite*, 45–7, 56–65.

12   Moyal, *Clear Across Australia*, 339–43; Reinecke and Schultz, *Phone Book*, 104–5.

13   Telecom, *National Satellite Communications System* (Melbourne, October 1977), 10.

14   White taskforce, *Report on National Communications Satellite*, 123.

15   Harcourt, *Taming the Tyrant*, 381–2; Paltridge, 'Aussat', 159.

16   Staley, interview.

17   See Reinecke and Schultz, *Phone Book*, 8, 99.

18   Staley quoted in Paltridge, 'Aussat', 91.

19   The 'encourage' quote is from Moyal, *Clear Across Australia*, 344–5; the 'important factor' quote is from Ann Nevile, 'Politicians, media moguls and pay-TV: policy-making in Australia 1977–1995', *Australian Journal of Public Administration*, 59/2 (June 2000), 64.

20   Cabinet submission no. 3520, 28 September 1979, NAA: A12909, 3520.

21   Staley, interview.

22   Paltridge, 'Aussat', 88–91.

23   Cabinet submission no. 3520, 28 September 1979, NAA: A12909, 3520.

24   Lansdown quoted in Moyal, *Clear Across Australia*, 348.

25   Coleman quoted in Paltridge, 'Aussat', 162.

26   Staley, interview.

27   Cabinet submission no. 4158, 26 June 1980, NAA: A12909, 4158.

28   Staley quoted in *Australian Financial Review*, 26 August 1980, quoted in Allan Brown, 'Golden bird or white elephant? Australia's Aussat satellite system', *Telecommunications Policy* (June 1991), 260.

29   Barr, *Electronic Estate*, 161–71.

30   Cabinet submission no. 4156, 26 June 1980, NAA: A12909, 4156.

31   Paltridge, 'Aussat', 132.

32   SSWG, *National Communications Satellite System*, 156.

33   Cabinet submission no. 4156, 26 June 1980, NAA: A12909, 4156.

34   Paltridge, 'Aussat', 140.

35   Holmes à Court quoted in Paltridge, 'Aussat', 140.

36   Cabinet submission no. 5218, 27 November 1981, NAA: A12909, 5218.

37   Cabinet decision no. 17284, 15 December 1981, NAA: A12909, 5218.

38   ICVTS, *Report*, 20, NAA: A12909, 5218.

39   Cabinet decision no. 17284, 15 December 1981, NAA: A12909, 5218.

40   Paltridge, 'Aussat', 92–108.

41   Curtis quoted in Paltridge, 'Aussat', 111.

42   Cabinet memorandum no. 929, 31 July 1980, NAA: A12930, 929.

43   Curtis quoted in Paltridge, 'Aussat', 109.

44   Charles Jones in CPD (Reps) (22 September 1977), 1511–12.

45   Paltridge, 'Aussat', 209–18; Susan Ryan in CPD (Senate) (27 September 1978), 975; (1 May 1979), 1530; and (29 May 1979), 2300.

46   ALP, *Platform, Constitution and Rules as Approved by the 33rd National Conference* (Adelaide, 1979), 18.

47   Ian Sinclair in CPD (Reps) (6 May 1982), 2410.

48   DOC, *Project: National Communications Satellite System* (AGPS, Canberra, 1982); Sinclair in CPD (6 May 1982), 2406–7.

49   Sinclair, interview.

50   Addendum to Cabinet submission no. 811, 15 June 1984, NAA: A13977, 811.

6. Intractable Conundrums

1   Jim Davidson *et al.*, *Report of the Committee of Inquiry into Telecommunications Services in Australia* (AGPS, Canberra, 1982), 7.

2   Malcolm Fraser in CPD (Reps) (30 April 1981), 1830–1.

3   Fraser quoted in Patrick Bowers, 'Fraser adamant: industrial chaos must stop', *Sydney Morning Herald*, 13 July 1979.

4   Weller, *Malcolm Fraser PM*, 247.

5   Cabinet submission no. 4852, 3 June 1981; Cabinet decision no. 16323, 20 July 1981, NAA: A12909, 4852.

6   Sinclair in CPD (23 September 1981), 1678.

7   Sinclair quoted in Deborah Snow, 'Telecom inquiry terms of reference revealed', *Australian Financial Review*, 7 September 1981.

8   Sinclair, interview.

9   Sinclair in CPD (23 September 1981), 1678.

10   Sinclair in CPD (13 October 1981), 1866.

11   Jim Carlton in CPD (Reps) (13 October 1981), 1990.

12   See Davidson *et al.*, *Report of Committee of Inquiry*, 1–2.

13   Snow, 'Telecom inquiry terms of reference revealed'.

14   See Barr, *Electronic Estate*, 123–40; Moyal, *Clear Across Australia*, 380–4; Reinecke and Schultz, *Phone Book*, 199–225.

15   See BTS, *Submission to Public Inquiry*, 39–40.

16   BTS, *Submission to Public Inquiry*, 10, 21–5, 57, 72–5.

17   ATUG, *Submission to Public Inquiry*, 30, 62–4.

18   Telecom, *Submission to Public Inquiry*, D16.

19   Treasury, *Public Monopolies*, 29–30, 34.

20   BTS, *Submission to Public Inquiry*, 72–4.

21   ACOA and APTU, *Joint Telecom Unions' Submission to Telecommunications Inquiry* (Melbourne, February 1982), 29–30.

22   ACOA and APTU, *Joint Telecom Unions' Submission*, 2, 12–13, 21–4.

23   John Button, *Submission to the Committee of Inquiry into Telecommunications in Australia* (December 1981), 1–3, 11–20.

24   Slater quoted in Reinecke and Schultz, *Phone Book*, 176–8.

25   John Button, *Supplementary Submission to the Committee of Inquiry into Telecommunications Services in Australia* (February 1982), 2–4.

26   ALP, *Platform, Constitution and Rules as Approved by the 35th National Conference* (Canberra, 1982), 17.

27   Moyal, *Clear Across Australia*, 380–1.

28   Telecom, *Submission to Public Inquiry*, D16, E8, E19–E20, E26–E27.

29   Brown, *On the Other Hand*, 126–8.

30   DOC, *Selected Issues in Telecommunications Policy: A Submission to the Committee of Inquiry into Telecommunications Services in Australia* (Canberra, March 1982), 17–22.

31   Davidson *et al.*, *Report of Committee of Inquiry*, 6–7.

32   Davidson *et al.*, *Report of Committee of Inquiry*, 7–10, 22, 46–50, 230–9.

33   Davidson *et al.*, *Report of Committee of Inquiry*, 21–2, 127, 233

34   Davidson *et al.*, *Report of Committee of Inquiry*, 19.

35   Davidson *et al.*, *Report of Committee of Inquiry*, 230–3.

36   Davidson *et al.*, *Report of Committee of Inquiry*, 19, 153, 368–9.

37   Davidson *et al.*, *Report of Committee of Inquiry*, 137, 148–52, 230. Also Robert Albon, 'Evaluating Telecom's cross-subsidies: political favours at a heavy cost', *Australian Economic Papers*, 30 (June 1991), 11–12.

38   Davidson *et al.*, *Report of Committee of Inquiry*, 23, 233–7, 330, 346, 368–9.

39   Beesley inquiry quoted in Harper, *Monopoly and Competition in British Telecommunications*, 139.

40   Neil Brown in CPD (Reps) (28 October 1982), 2710.

41   Judith Hoare, 'Davidson report opens Telecom door', *Australian Financial Review*, 29 October 1982.

42   Quoted in Deborah Snow, 'Blueprint for Telecom's reduced role', *Australian Financial Review*, 29 October 1982.

43   Snow, 'Blueprint for Telecom's reduced role'.

44 Moyal, *Clear Across Australia*, 383.

45 See CPD (Reps) (8 December 1982), 3099; (14 December 1982), 3416; and (3 May 1983), 75.

46 Telecom, *Initial Response to Davidson Inquiry Recommendations* (January 1983), 1, NAA: A13977, 448.

47 Cabinet submission no. 5965, 3 February 1983, NAA: A12909, 5965.

48 Cabinet submission no. 5974, 4 February 1983, NAA: A12909, 5974.

49 Cabinet submission no. 5965, 3 February 1983, NAA: A12909, 5965.

50 Cabinet submission no. 5974, 4 February 1983, NAA: A12909, 5974. See also Telecom, *Initial Response to Davidson*, 21, NAA: A13977, 448.

51 Telecom, *Initial Response to Davidson*, 1, 14, 18, NAA: A13977, 448.

52 PM&C, 'Bradley (Post) and Davidson (Telecom) Reports', 4 February 1983, NAA: A10756, LC5104 Part 1.

53 PM&C, 'Note on cabinet submission no. 5965', 4 February 1983, NAA: A10756, LC5104 Part 1.

54 Cabinet coordination committee decision no. 19642(C), 6 February 1983, NAA: A12909, 5965; Cabinet decision no. 19654, 8 February 1983, NAA: A13075, 19654.

55 Brown quoted in Moyal, *Clear Across Australia*, 384.

56 Neil Brown, interview with author, 19 December 2014.

57 See Moyal, *Clear Across Australia*, 384.

58 See Doug Anthony, 1983 election policy speech (21 February 1983); Malcolm Fraser, 'We're not waiting for the world', 1983 election policy speech (15 February 1983).

59 Liberal Party, '1983 policy speech supplementary statements' (Canberra, 1983), 55–8.

60 Bob Hawke, 1983 election policy speech (Sydney, 16 February 1983), 18.

61 Julianne Schultz, 'Deregulation by default or design', *Media, Culture and Society*, 7 (1985), 42–4; Moyal, *Clear Across Australia*, 384.

7. Turning Back the Tide

1 Cabinet submission no. 2802, 17 April 1985, NAA: A14039, 2802.

2 Cabinet memorandum no. 67, 6 May 1983, NAA: A11116, CA232 Part 1.

3 ERC decision no. 361(ER), 9 May 1983; Cabinet decision no. 417, 16 May 1983, NAA: A11116, CA232 Part 1.

4 Cabinet memorandum no. 38, 29 April 1983; Cabinet decision no. 416, 16 May 1983, NAA: A13978, 38.

5 Quoted in Greg Earl, 'Paul Keating's media masterstroke', *Australian Financial Review*, 23 February 1987.

6 Bob Hawke, *The Hawke Memoirs* (William Heinemann, Melbourne, 1994), 121–2, 157, 424.

7 Cabinet submission no. 448, 26 September 1983, NAA: A13977, 448.

8 Telecom, 'Managing the new telecommunications era in Australia' (1983), 1–4, NAA: A13977, 448.

9 Cabinet submission no. 448, 26 September 1983, NAA: A13977, 448.

10 Handwritten note by PM&C official on letter from Duffy to Hawke, 20 December 1983, NAA: A1209, 1988/1239 Part 1.

11 Cabinet decision no. 2309, 20 October 1983, NAA: A13977, 448.

12 Cabinet submission no. 274, 7 July 1983, NAA: A13977, 274.

13 PM&C, 'Notes on cabinet submission no. 274, 13 July 1983; ASTEC, briefing paper to Hawke, 13 July 1983, NAA: A11116, CA461 Part 1; Cabinet submission no. 274, 7 July 1983; Cabinet decision no. 918, 13 July 1983, NAA: A13977, 274; Paltridge, 'Aussat', 236.

14 Cabinet submission no. 495, 27 October 1983, NAA: A11116, CA204 Part 1.

15 Robert Brack to Duffy, 24 August 1983, NAA: A11116, CA204 Part 1.

16 Paltridge, 'Aussat', 218–20.

17 Cabinet submission no. 495, 27 October 1983, NAA: A11116, CA204 Part 1.

18 Paltridge, 'Aussat', 232.

19 Arndt to Bowen, 7 November 1983, NAA: A463, 1987/G1290. A handwritten note on the letter states, 'Mr Bowen does not wish to meet delegation.'

20 ASTEC, 'Refer cabinet submission no. 495', 8 November 1983; Cabinet submission no. 495, 27 October 1983; PM&C, 'Notes on cabinet submission no. 495', 3 November 1983, NAA: A11116, CA204 Part 1.

21 Hoare to Duffy, 25 August 1983, NAA: A11116, CA204 Part 1.

22 Gosewinckel quoted in Barr, *Electronic Estate*, 145–6.

23 ERC decision no. 2438(ER), 14 November 1983; Cabinet decision no. 2447, 14 November 1983, NAA: A11116, CA204 Part 1.

24 See Cabinet submission no. 5703, 22 April 1988, NAA: A11116, CA3107 Part 1.

25 Peter Leonard, 'Footprints down a narrow path: the regulation of AUSSAT', *Media Information Australia*, 58 (November 1990), 38–9.

26 See Bruce Lloyd in CPD (Reps) (8 March 1984), 697.

27 Bob Hawke, 1984 election policy speech (Sydney, 13 November 1984).

28 Liberal and National parties, *Communications Policy* (November 1984), 1, 5–7.

29 Gareth Evans, *Inside the Hawke–Keating Government: A Cabinet Diary* (Melbourne University Press, 2014), 154–5, 172.

30 Keating quoted in Paul Kelly, *The End of Certainty: Power, Politics and Business in Australia* (Allen & Unwin, Sydney, 1994), 196.

31 Cabinet decision no. 5779, 13 May 1985, NAA: A14039, 2820.

32 ERC decision no. 5540(ER), 2 May 1985, NAA: A14039, 2820.

33 Walsh to Duffy, 25 June 1985, NAA: A11116, CA204 Part 1.

34 ERC amended decision no. 8100(ER), 25 July 1986, NAA: A13979, 8100/ER; ERC decision no. 9136(ER), 29 March 1987; Cabinet decision no. 9469, 8 May 1987, NAA: A14039, 4674.

35 Brack to Duffy, 5 August 1986, NAA: A9488, I1985/29 Part 10; Keating to Duffy, August 1986, NAA: A9488, I1985/29 Part 9.

36 Paul Keating, interview with author, 16 April 2015.

37 Cabinet memorandum no. 3694, 26 March 1986, NAA: A11116, CA204 Part 1.

38 PM&C, 'Notes on cabinet memorandum no. 3694', 7 April 1986, NAA: A11116, CA204 Part 1.

39   Kelly, *End of Certainty*, 237–9.

40   Kelly, *End of Certainty*, 391.

41   ERC decision no. 7618(ER), 19 May 1986; ERC decision no. 8215(ER), 31 July 1986, NAA: A11116, CA204 Part 1.

42   Cabinet submission no. 3580, 20 February 1986, NAA: A11116, CA204 Part 1.

43   Cabinet memorandum no. 4675, 25 March 1987; PM&C, 'Notes on cabinet memorandum no. 4675', 27 March 1987, NAA: A11116, CA204 Part 1.

44   ERC decision no. 9138(ER), 29 March 1987, NAA: A11116, CA204 Part 1; Paul Kelly, 'Labor and globalisation' in Manne (ed.), *Australian Century*, 247.

8. Imperatives for Change

1   Keating, interview.

2   J. R. Nethercote, 'Public service reform: its course and nature' in Alexander Kouzmin *et al.* (eds), *Australian Commonwealth Administration 1983: Essays in Review* (Canberra College of Advanced Education, 1984), 32; Roger Wettenhall, 'Statutory authorities' in Kouzmin *et al.* (eds), *Australian Commonwealth Administration 1983*, 105–9; Roger Wettenhall, 'Guidelines for statutory authorities', *Australian Journal of Public Administration*, 45/4 (December 1986), 299; TFCEP, *Review of Continuing Expenditure Policies*, 26–7. See also Royal Commission on Australian Government Administration, *Report* (AGPS, Canberra, 1976).

3   Cabinet decision no. 19645, 8 February 1983, NAA: A12909, 5963.

4   During the Fraser government, the committee was the Senate Standing Committee on Finance and Government Operations.

5   Wettenhall, 'Statutory authorities' in Kouzmin *et al.* (eds), *Australian Commonwealth Administration 1983*, 130–1.

6   Cabinet submissions nos. 457 and 459, 12 October 1983, NAA: A11116, CA882 Part 1.

7   Dawkins to Hawke, 2 April 1984, NAA: A9488, I1985/29 Part 1.

8   Roger Wettenhall, 'Statutory authorities' in J. R. Nethercote *et al.* (eds), *Australian Commonwealth Administration 1984: Essays in Review* (Canberra College of Advanced Education, 1985), 74.

9   Cabinet submission no. 5048, 11 August 1987, NAA: A11116, CA882 Part 5.

10   Cabinet submission no. 459, 12 October 1983, NAA: A11116, CA882 Part 1.

11   See Treasury, *Australian Post Office Commission of Inquiry: Submission*, NAA: A4066, 434.

12   John Dawkins, 'Précis of introductory comments by the Minister for Finance to the Legal and Administrative Committee on the package of submissions and memorandum on statutory authorities', 16 November 1983, NAA: A11116, CA882 Part 1.

13   Dawkins to Harold Heinrich, 19 December 1983, NAA: A9488, I1985/29 Part 1. The 'profit motive' comment is a handwritten note on the filed memorandum.

14   PM&C, 'Notes on Submission no. 459', 20 October 1983, NAA: A11116, CA882 Part 1; PM&C, 'Notes on Submission no. 1051', 28 September 1984, NAA: A11116, CA882 Part 2.

15   Duffy and Morris to caucus members, 10 May 1985, NAA: A9488, I1985/29 Part 5. The official's comment is handwritten on Treasury's copy of the letter.

16   Cabinet submission no. 1051, 18 September 1984, NAA: A11116, CA882 Part 2.

17   Halton to Keating, 14 July 1986, NAA: A1209, 1988/2742 Part 3.

18   Robert Brack, seminar presentation, University of Sydney (September 1986), NAA: A9488, I1985/29 Part 10.

19   ATEA, 'A response by the Australian Telecommunications Employees Association to the proposed policy guidelines for statutory authorities and government business enterprises (The Green Paper)' (September 1986), 1, NAA: A1209, 1988/2742 Part 3.

20   Cabinet submission no. 3398, 11 November 1985, NAA: A11116, CA882 Part 4.

21   Brack to Walsh, 14 August 1986, NAA: A1209, 1988/2742 Part 3.

22   David Hoare to Michael Duffy and Peter Walsh, 19 August 1986; Aussat, *Statutory Authorities and Government Business Enterprises: Paper by Aussat Pty Ltd* (August 1986); OTC, *Policy Discussion Paper on Statutory Authorities and Government Business Enterprises: Response of the Overseas Telecommunications Commission (Australia) Board of Commissioners* (September 1986), NAA: A1209, 1988/2742 Part 3. Maltby quotes are from George Maltby, 'Response to the proposed guidelines by the Overseas Telecommunications Commission', *Australian Journal of Public Administration*, 45/4 (December 1986), 339–43.

23   Duffy to Walsh, 5 August 1986, NAA: A9488, I1985/29 Part 9.

24   Cabinet memorandum no. 2710, 3 April 1985, NAA: A11116, CA882 Part 3.

25   Cabinet submission no. 3398, 11 November 1985, NAA: A11116, CA882 Part 4.

26   Cabinet submission no. 2802, 17 April 1985, NAA: A14039, 2802.

27   Duffy to Rolfe, 23 August 1984, NAA: A14039, 2802.

28   Cabinet submission no. 2802, 17 April 1985, NAA: A14039, 2802.

29   Cabinet decision no. 6878, 25 November 1985, NAA: A14039, 2802.

30   Edward Brunetti, 'Public bodies need competition, says EPAC report', *Age*, 16 October 1986; EPAC, *Summary of BCA Response to Government Discussion Paper on Proposed Policy Guidelines for Statutory Authorities and GBEs* (AGPS, Canberra, 21 November 1986), NAA: A9488, I1985/29 Part 12.

31   Duffy quoted in Kelly, *End of Certainty*, 238.

32   Brack to Walsh, 14 August 1986, NAA: A1209, 1988/2742 Part 3.

33   Sedgwick to Hawke, 15 November 1985, NAA: A11116, CA882 Part 4.

34   Cabinet submission no. 3931, 9 May 1986; Cabinet decision no. 7607, 13 May 1986, NAA: A11116, CA882 Part 4; Hawke, *Hawke Memoirs*, 420–1; J. R. Nethercote, 'Changing climate of public service' in Roger Wettenhall and J. R. Nethercote (eds), *Hawke's Second Government: Australian Commonwealth Administration, 1984–1987* (Canberra College of Advanced Education, 1988), 2–3.

35   Neil Hyden to Ted Mathews, 28 November 1986, NAA: A9488, I1985/29 Part 12.

36   K. Kang to Ted Delofski, 15 October 1986, NAA: A9488, I1985/29 Part 11.

37   K. Kang, file note, 21 October 1986, NAA: A9488, I1985/29 Part 11.

38   Cabinet submission no. 4861, 1 May 1987, NAA: A14039, 4861.

39   See ERC decision no. 9368(ER), 2 May 1987, NAA: A14039, 4861.

40   Hawke, *Hawke Memoirs*, 420–1.

41   Bob Hawke in CPD (Reps) (25 September 1986), 1448.

42   Keating, interview.

43   Evans, *Inside the Hawke–Keating Government*, 379.

44   Cabinet submission no. 4048, 24 June 1986; Cabinet decision no. 7987, 21 July 1986, NAA: A14039, 4048.

45   Anne Davies, 'The origins of the Act' in Armstrong (ed.), *Telecommunications Law*, 53–4.

46   Staley to Duffy, 3 December 1986, NAA: A1209, 1985/554 Part 1; Staley, interview.

47   Davies, 'Origins of the Act' in Armstrong (ed.), *Telecommunications Law*, 53; Greg Earl, 'Users' group steps up campaign against Telecom', *Australian Financial Review*, 11 May 1987.

48   Staley to Duffy, 3 December 1986, NAA: A1209, 1985/554 Part 1.

49   Davies, 'Origins of the Act' in Armstrong (ed.), *Telecommunications Law*, 54.

50   Paul Austin, 'Telecom viability "depends on freedom from controls"', *Australian*, 26 May 1987; Annette Young, 'Telecom might lose its monopoly: Duffy', *Age*, 5 May 1987. Ward quoted in Young.

51   Young, 'Telecom might lose its monopoly'.

52   Davies, 'Origins of the Act' in Armstrong (ed.), *Telecommunications Law*, 54.

53   Arndt to Duffy, Hawke and Willis, 4 May 1987, NAA: A463, 1987/G1290

54   Brett quoted in Janet de Silva, 'Deregulation plan lifts a few hackles', *Australian Financial Review*, 8 May 1987.

55   Neil Hyden to Paul Keating, 27 May 1987, NAA: A9488, I1985/29 Part 14.

56   ALP, *Platform, Resolutions and Rules as Approved by the 37th National Conference* (Hobart, 1986), 19–24.

57   ALP, 1987 election policy statement (23 June 1987), 11.

58   Brown, *On the Other Hand*, 30.

59   Paul Austin, 'Telecom at heart of Macphee dispute', *Australian*, 23 April 1987; Liberal Party, 'Get in front again', 1987 election policy statement (25 June 1987), 12. Duffy quoted in Young, 'Telecom might lose its monopoly'.

60   National Party, 1987 election policy summary (Canberra, June 1987), 30.

9. A New Agenda

1   Gareth Evans, interview with author, 10 February 2015.

2   Keating, interview; Kelly, *End of Certainty*, 392.

3   Bob Hawke, 1988 Garran Oration, published as R. J. L. Hawke, 'Challenges in public administration', *Australian Journal of Public Administration*, 48/1 (March 1989), 9.

4   Hawke, *Hawke Memoirs*, 160.

5   Gareth Evans, interview.

6   Evans quoted in Keith Scott, *Gareth Evans* (Allen & Unwin, Sydney, 1999), 206.

7   Gareth Evans, interview.

8   Gareth Evans, interview.

9   Paddy Costanzo, interview with author, 7 April 2015; Vanessa Fanning, interview with author, 1 April 2015; Tony Shaw, interview with author, 1 April 2015; Roger Wettenhall and Ian Beckett, 'Movements in the public enterprise and statutory authority sector' in John Halligan and Roger Wettenhall (eds), *Hawke's Third Government: Australian Commonwealth Administration, 1987–1990* (University of Canberra, 1992), 181.

10   Gareth Evans, interview.

11   Cabinet memorandum no. 5089, 17 August 1987, NAA: A14039, 5089.

12   Cabinet memorandum no. 5089, 17 August 1987, NAA: A14039, 5089.

13   SAC decision no. 9803(SA), 19 August 1987. See also Cabinet submission no. 9896, 25 August 1987, NAA: A14039, 5089.

14   Hawke and Evans quoted in Shaun Carney, 'Government will consider ending Telecom monopoly', *Age*, 4 September 1987.

15   Carney, 'Government will consider ending Telecom monopoly'.

16   Evans quoted in Scott, *Gareth Evans*, 205–6.

17   Scott, *Gareth Evans*, 206.

18   Gareth Evans, interview.

19   Murray Goot, 'Public opinion, privatisation and the electoral politics of Telstra', *Australian Journal of Politics and History*, 45/2 (1999), 216–9.

20   See Mark Armstrong, 'Introduction' in Elizabeth More and Glen Lewis (eds), *Australian Communications Technology and Policy* (Centre for Information Studies, Kuring-gai College of Advanced Education, Australian Communications Association, Australian Film and Radio School, Sydney, 1988), 3–5.

21   Davies, 'Origins of the Act' in Armstrong (ed.), *Telecommunications Law*, 54; Rodney Maddock, 'Microeconomic reform of telecommunications: the long march from duopoly to duopoly' in Peter Forsyth (ed.), *Microeconomic Reform in Australia* (Allen & Unwin, Sydney, 1992), 244; Holly Raiche, *A History of Telecommunications Policy*, research paper (Faculty of Law, University of NSW, 1997), Chapter 2, pp. 3–4.

22   Gareth Evans, interview.

23   Shaw, interview.

24   Donald Greenlees, 'ALP gets in early for big sell-off', *Australian*, 14 August 1987.

25   See Anne Davies, 'Govt curbs Telecom deregulators', *Australian Financial Review*, 4 November 1987.

26   Leo Dobes, interview with author, 31 March 2015; Gareth Evans interview; Fanning, interview.

27   WGCR, 'Telecommunications regulation: initial information paper', 27 November 1987, 37, NAA: A14039, 5439.

28   Telecom, *Discussion Paper on Aspects of Telecom Australia's Non–Commercial Trading Activity* (Melbourne, 1987), NAA: A1209, 1987/1506 Part 3.

29   Keating, interview.

30   Rolf Gerritsen, 'The politics of microeconomic reform: structuring a general model', *Australian Journal of Public Administration*, 51/1 (March 1992), 69–76.

31   Kelly, *End of Certainty*, 390.

32   Peter Wilenski, 'Technological change and policy planning' in More and Lewis (eds), *Australian Communications Technology and Policy*, 70–1.

33   Graham Evans, interview with author, 1 June 2015.

34   Davies, 'Govt curbs Telecom deregulators'; Davies, 'Origins of the Act' in Armstrong (ed.), *Telecommunications Law*, 56; Raiche, *History of Telecommunications Policy*, Chapter 2, p. 4; Fanning, interview; Shaw, interview.

35   Richard Alston in CPD (Senate) (4 November 1987), 1716; Davies, 'Govt curbs Telecom deregulators'; Fanning, interview; Shaw, interview. Quote is from Alston in CPD.

36 Gareth Evans, interview; Fanning, interview; Shaw, interview.

37 WGCR, 'Telecommunications regulation', 27 November 1987, 4–5, 10–11, 23, NAA: A14039, 5439.

38 PM&C to Hawke, 14 December 1987, NAA: A11116, CA2979 Part 1.

39 WGCR, 'Telecommunications regulation', 27 November 1987, 11, 24, NAA: A14039, 5439.

40 N. Hyden to B. Primrose, 13 November 1987, NAA: A1209, 1987/1506 Part 3.

41 E. Mathews to B. Primrose, 13 November 1987, NAA: A1209, 1987/1506 Part 3.

42 PM&C to Hawke, 14 December 1987, NAA: A11116, CA2979 Part 1.

43 Cabinet memorandum no. 5439, 27 November 1987, 4, NAA: A14039, 5439.

44 Mathews to Primrose, 13 November 1987, NAA: A1209, 1987/1506 Part 3.

45 WGCR, 'Telecommunications regulation', 27 November 1987, 6–7, 23–4, NAA: A14039, 5439.

46 Cabinet memorandum no. 5439, 27 November 1987, NAA: A14039, 5439.

47 WGCR, 'Telecommunications regulation', 27 November 1987, 15–16, 25–6, NAA: A14039, 5439.

48 Maddock, 'Microeconomic reform of telecommunications' in Forsyth (ed.), *Microeconomic Reform in Australia*, 250.

49 See Michael Duffy to Hawke, 21 December 1983; and John Dawkins to Hawke, 19 January 1984; NAA: A1209, 1985/554 Part 1.

50 WGCR, 'Telecommunications regulation', 27 November 1987, 26, NAA: A14039, 5439.

51 Cabinet submission no. 5742, 5 May 1988, NAA: A14039, 5742.

52 AEIA, *The Role and Importance of the Australian Telecommunications Network to Local Equipment Suppliers* (Canberra, October 1987); Telecom, *Telecom's Outlook* (1987), NAA: A1209, 1987/1506 Part 3.

53 Cabinet memorandum no. 5439, 27 November 1987, NAA: A14039, 5439.

54 WGCR, 'Telecommunications regulation', 27 November 1987, 19–20, NAA: A14039, 5439.

55 AIIA, *Opportunity and Efficiency – The Compelling Case for More Competition in the Telecommunications Environment* (October 1987), NAA: A1209, 1987/1506 Part 3; WGCR, 'Telecommunications regulation', 27 November 1987, 28, NAA: A14039, 5439. ATUG quote is by Wally Rothwell, quoted in Bronwen Martin and Julietta Jameson, 'Taking on Telecom', *Business Review Weekly*, 29 May 1987.

56 R. Maddock to B. Primrose, 13 November 1987, NAA: A1209, 1987/1506 Part 3.

57 Cabinet memorandum no. 5439, 27 November 1987, NAA: A14039, 5439.

58 PM&C to Hawke, 14 December 1987, NAA: A11116, CA2979 Part 1.

59 SAC decision no. 10631(SA), 15 December 1987, NAA: A11116, CA2979 Part 1.

60 Gareth Evans, interview.

10. Creating Momentum

1 Gareth Evans, interview.

2 Davies, 'Origins of the Act' in Armstrong (ed.), *Telecommunications Law*, 57.

3   Gareth Evans, interview.

4   Pilita Clark, 'Caucus backlash on timed phones', *Sydney Morning Herald*, 18 December 1987; David Kennedy, 'Union may block timed calls', *Sydney Morning Herald*, 16 December 1987. See also Davidson *et al.*, *Report of the Committee of Inquiry*, 148–52.

5   'Staley backs timed calls', *Age*, 5 February 1988. Hawke quoted in Keith Scott, '9pc swing to the Liberals', *Canberra Times*, 7 February 1988.

6   Gareth Evans, interview; Fanning, interview; Shaw, interview; Raiche, *History of Telecommunications Policy*, Chapter 2, p. 8. Quotes are from Evans interview.

7   Gareth Evans, interview; Fanning, interview; Shaw, interview; Scott, *Gareth Evans*, 207–8. Quotes are from Evans interview.

8   Cabinet submission no. 5742, 5 May 1988, NAA: A14039, 5742.

9   Gareth Evans, interview.

10   Cabinet amended decision no. 11070(SA), 9 May 1988, NAA: A14039, 5742.

11   Cabinet submission no. 5742, 5 May 1988, NAA: A14039, 5742.

12   Gareth Evans, interview.

13   Cabinet submission no. 5742, 5 May 1988, NAA: A14039, 5742.

14   Gareth Evans, *Australian Telecommunications Services: A New Framework: Summary* (AGPS, Canberra, 1988), 2–3.

15   ALP, *Platform, Resolutions and Rules as Approved by the 38th National Conference* (Hobart, 1988), 21–2.

16   Cabinet submission no. 5048, 11 August 1987, NAA: A11116, CA882 Part 5.

17   Cabinet memorandum no. 5310, 2 October 1987, NAA: A14039, 5310.

18   PM&C, 'Notes on cabinet memorandum no. 5310', 6 October 1987, NAA: A11116, CA882 Part 6.

19   PM&C, 'Notes on cabinet memorandum Nos. 5405, 5397, 5398, 5395, 5406, 5407, 5403 and 5401', 17 November 1987, NAA: A11116, CA882 Part 6.

20   Cabinet decision no. 10386(SA), 8 October 1987, NAA: A14039, 5310.

21   Peter Walsh in CPD (Senate) (4 November 1987), 1705–7.

22   John Stone in CPD (Senate) (4 November 1987), 1708.

23   Gareth Evans, interview.

24   Gareth Evans in CPD (Senate) (25 May 1988), 2922.

25   Cabinet submission no. 5705, 25 April 1988, NAA: A14039, 5705.

26   Gareth Evans, *Reshaping the Transport and Communications Government Business Enterprises* (AGPS, Canberra, 1988), 5–6, 22–3.

27   Cabinet decision no. 11185, 23 May 1988, NAA: A11116, CA3107 Part 1; Alex Arena, 'What the government expects from the GBEs' in Armstrong (ed.), *Telecommunications Law*, 51; Wettenhall and Beckett, 'Movement in the public enterprise and statutory authority sector' in Halligan and Wettenhall (eds), *Hawke's Third Government*, 184–8, 238.

28   PM&C, 'Notes on cabinet submissions Nos 5705, 5704, 5703, 5702', 27 April 1988, NAA: A11116, CA3107 Part 1.

29   Evans, *Reshaping the Transport and Communications Government Business Enterprises*, 23.

30 Arena, 'What the government expects from the GBEs' in Armstrong (ed.), *Telecommunications Law*, 50; Evans, *Reshaping the Transport and Communications Government Business Enterprises*, 8, 24–5. See also Ian Beckett, 'To privatise or not?' in Halligan and Wettenhall (eds), *Hawke's Third Government*, 272; and Wettenhall and Beckett, 'Movement in the public enterprise and statutory authority sector' in Halligan and Wettenhall (eds), *Hawke's Third Government*, 187–8.

31 Arena, 'What the government expects from the GBEs' in Armstrong (ed.), *Telecommunications Law*, 48; Wettenhall and Beckett, 'Movement in the public enterprise and statutory authority sector' in Halligan and Wettenhall (eds), *Hawke's Third Government*, 186.

32 David Lindsay, 'Select legislative history of telecommunications' in Armstrong (ed.), *Telecommunications Law*, 33; Wettenhall and Beckett, 'Movement in the public enterprise and statutory authority sector' in Halligan and Wettenhall (eds), *Hawke's Third Government*, 222–3.

33 Cabinet submission no. 5705, 25 April 1988, NAA: A14039, 5705.

34 Cabinet submission no. 5397, 11 November 1987, NAA: A14039, 5397.

35 PM&C, 'Notes on cabinet submissions Nos 5705, 5704, 5703, 5702', 27 April 1988, NAA: A11116, CA3107 Part 1.

36 Cabinet decision no. 11000(SA), 27 April and 6 May 1988, NAA: A14039, 5703.

37 Cabinet submission no. 5705, 25 April 1988, NAA: A14039, 5705; decision no. 11000(SA), 27 April and 6 May 1988, NAA: A14039, 5703.

38 Gareth Evans, interview.

39 Evans quoted in Davies, 'Origins of the Act' in Armstrong (ed.), *Telecommunications Law*, 55.

40 Graham Evans, interview.

41 Dobes, interview; Fanning, interview; Shaw, interview.

42 Ralph Willis, *Implementation of GBE Reforms and Telecommunications Pricing* (AGPS, Canberra, 1989), 2.

43 Vanessa Fanning, 'Issues faced in drafting the regulatory legislation' in Armstrong (ed.), *Telecommunications Law*, 39.

44 Mark Armstrong, 'The regulatory environment' in Armstrong (ed.), *Telecommunications Law*, 9, 23; Fanning, 'Issues faced in drafting the regulatory legislation' in Armstrong (ed.), *Telecommunications Law*, 41–5.

45 Alston in CPD (4 November 1987), 1716–7.

46 Alston in CPD (5 June 1989), 3327–8.

47 Alston in CPD (4 November 1987), 1716.

48 Alston in CPD (5 June 1989), 3329.

49 Tony Staley, 'Perspectives of some users' in Hazel Ramsden (ed.), *Competition and Competitiveness in Telecommunications* (Centre of Policy Studies symposium, Monash University, 5 August 1987), 92–4. See Hugh Morgan, 'A castle in France' in Ramsden (ed.), *Competition and Competitiveness in Telecommunications*, 77–9.

50 Armstrong, 'Regulatory environment' in Armstrong (ed.), *Telecommunications Law*, 7–9; Michael Hutchinson, 'Restructuring Australia's telecommunications' in Anna Bodi, Anthony Newstead and Peter White (eds), *Telecommunications Management and Policy: Australian and International Perspectives* (Monash University, 1992), 43; Ros Kelly in CPD (Reps) (23 April 1989), 1624.

51 Beverley Head, 'Austel chief appeals for goodwill', *Australian Financial Review*, 24 April 1989.

52 Davey quoted respectively in Head, 'Austel chief appeals for goodwill' and Stewart Fist, 'AUSTEL – a legal minefield?', *Australian Communications* (August 1989), 16.

53 Robert Albon, 'A new age in telecommunications? An assessment of the May ministerial statement 1988', *ACC/Westpac Economic Discussion Papers*, 4 (December 1989); Ian Cuncliffe, 'AUSTEL: functions and powers' in Armstrong (ed.), *Telecommunications Law*, 246; Geoffrey Heenan, 'Regulation of the Australian telecommunications industry', *Economic Papers: A Journal of Applied Economics and Policy*, 8/4 (December 1989), 70–1; Raiche, *History of Telecommunications Policy*, Chapter 3, p. 3.

54 Alston in CPD (5 June 1989), 1330–2.

55 Beverley Head, 'Legal hurdles in Telecom reform', *Australian Financial Review*, 1 August 1990.

56 Robin Davey, interview with author, 1 April 2015.

57 Robin Davey, email to author, 10 February 2015.

58 Davey, interview.

59 Paul Austin and Tracey Aubin, 'Cabinet faces revolt over phone reform', *Australian*, 10 April 1990; Liz Fell, 'Interview with Reg Coutts', *Telecommunications Journal of Australia*, 53/2 (2003), 3–10.

60 Cabinet submission no. 7329, 2 August 1990, NAA: A14039, 7329; Davey, interview. See also Tracey Aubin, 'Mobile telephone "to cost $1bn"', *Australian*, 11 April 1990; Davies, 'Origins of the Act' in Armstrong (ed.), *Telecommunications Law*, 57–8.

61 Davey, interview.

62 Davey, interview.

63 Shaw, interview; Albon, 'Evaluating Telecom's cross-subsidies', 13–4; Peter White, 'Community service obligations' in Armstrong (ed.), *Telecommunications Law*, 354.

64 BTCE, *The Cost of Telecom's Community Services Obligations* (AGPS, Canberra, 1989), iii, 9–11.

65 Shaw, interview.

11. Competitive Influences

1 Hawke to Beazley, 8 April 1990, quoted in Hawke, *Hawke Memoirs*, 601.

2 Graham Evans, interview.

3 Brown, 'Golden bird or white elephant?', 255–7; Raiche, *History of Telecommunications Policy*, Chapter 4, p. 4.

4 BTCE, *Financial Performance of Government Business Enterprises in the Transport and Communications Portfolio 1977–78 to 1988–89* (AGPS, Canberra, 1990), 90.

5 Gosewinckel quoted in Brown, 'Golden bird or white elephant?', 255.

6 Graham Evans, email to author, 14 May 2015, and interview; Shaw, interview.

7 Vanessa Fanning to Beazley, 'Telecommunications carriers: Review of Ownership and Structural Arrangements (ROSA)', Attachment A: 'Scope of review', 10 April 1990, NAA: M3365, 7/4 Part 1.

8 Kim Beazley, interview with author, 15 July 2015.

9 Costanzo, interview.

10   Hawke, *Hawke Memoirs*, 487.

11   Beazley, interview; Costanzo, interview; Peter Harris, interview with author, 16 March 2015; Peter FitzSimons, *Beazley: A Biography* (HarperCollins, Sydney, 1998), 301.

12   Beazley, interview.

13   Costanzo to Walters, 'Comments on PM&C reform paper', 8 May 1990; Fanning to Beazley, 'Telecommunications carriers', Attachment D: 'Aussat financial position and the implications for the second generation of satellites', 10 April 1990, NAA: M3365, 7/4 Part 1.

14   N. T. Cleary to Gosewinckel, 3 April 1990, NAA: M3365, 7/4 Part 1.

15   Fanning to Beazley, 'Telecommunications carriers', Attachment D: 'Aussat financial position', 10 April 1990, NAA: M3365, 7/4 Part 1.

16   Fanning to Beazley, 'Aussat: capital injection', 5 April 1990, NAA: M3365, 7/4 Part 1.

17   Fanning to Beazley, 'Telecommunications carriers', 10 April 1990, NAA: M3365, 7/4 Part 1.

18   Costanzo, interview.

19   See cabinet submission no. 5703, 22 April 1988; Beazley to Hawke, 10 April 1990, paraphrased in H. V. J. Moir to Hawke, 'Aussat's financial position', 18 April 1990, NAA: A11116, CA3107 Part 1.

20   Fanning to Beazley, 'Telecommunications carriers', Attachment F: 'GBE cross ownership and cross board membership', 10 April 1990, NAA: M3365, 7/4 Part 1.

21   Beazley, interview.

22   Costanzo, interview; Graham Evans, interview.

23   Hawke to Beazley, 8 April 1990, quoted in Hawke, *Hawke Memoirs*, 489, 601.

24   Harris was later secretary of the federal Department of Broadband, Communications and the Digital Economy (2009–12) during the early years of the NBN, and chairman of the Productivity Commission (2012–19).

25   Sims was subsequently chair of the ACCC for nearly eleven years, retiring in March 2022.

26   Harris, interview; Hawke, *Hawke Memoirs*, 489, 601.

27   Graham Evans, interview; Fanning to Beazley, 'Telecommunications carriers', 10 April 1990, 4–6, NAA: M3365, 7/4 Part 1.

28   Fanning to Beazley, 'Telecommunications carriers', 10 April 1990, 6–7, NAA: M3365, 7/4 Part 1; Raiche, *History of Telecommunications Policy*, Chapter 4, pp. 6–7.

29   ATUG, 'Review of structural arrangements submission', 3 July 1990, NAA: M3365, 7/8 Part 1.

30   ATUG, *Telecommunications Policy*, iv–ix; Raiche, *History of Telecommunications Policy*, Chapter 4, pp. 6–7.

31   ATUG, 'Review of structural arrangements submission', 3 July 1990, NAA: M3365, 7/8 Part 1.

32   Fanning to Beazley, 'Telecommunications carriers', 10 April 1990, 7, NAA: M3365, 7/4 Part 1.

33   Raiche, *History of Telecommunications Policy*, Chapter 4, pp. 5–7; T. A. Cutler, 'Notes of meeting with Treasurer, 20 June 1990', 21 June 1990, NAA: M3365, 7/8 Part 1.

34   Beazley to Hawke, 10 April 1990, paraphrased in Moir to Hawke, 'Aussat's financial position', 18 April 1990, NAA: A11116, CA3107 Part 1.

35   Hawke to Beazley, 19 April 1990, NAA: A11116, CA3107 Part 1.

36 N. T. Cleary to Vanessa Fanning, 23 April 1990, Attachment F to Cabinet submission no. 7018, 27 April 1990, NAA: A11116, CA3107 Part 1.

37 Handwritten note by Harris dated '19.4' on Moir to Hawke, 'Aussat's financial position', 18 April 1990, NAA: A11116, CA3107 Part 1.

38 Cabinet submission no. 7018, 27 April 1990, NAA: A11116, CA3107 Part 1.

39 H. V. J. Moir to Hawke, 'Notes on submission no. 7018', 27 April 1990, NAA: A11116, CA3107 Part 1.

40 Henry to Keating, 1 May 1990, NAA: A11116, CA3107 Part 1.

41 Cabinet decision no. 13678, 1 May 1990, NAA: A11116, CA3107 Part 1.

42 Brown, 'Golden bird or white elephant?', 255–7.

43 See Vanessa Fanning to Patrick Walters, 'Treasury minute on telecommunications reform', 3 August 1990, NAA: M3365, 7/11/1 Part 2.

44 Aubin, 'Mobile telephone "to cost $1bn"'.

45 Childs, ATEA and Musumeci quoted in Austin and Aubin, 'Cabinet faces revolt over phone reform'.

46 Aubin, 'Mobile telephone "to cost $1bn"'; Davies, 'Origins of the Act' in Armstrong (ed.), *Telecommunications Law*, 58.

47 Fanning to Beazley, 'Telecommunications carriers', 10 April 1990, 4–15, NAA: M3365, 7/4 Part 1.

48 See SAC memorandum no. 7007, April 1990, 5–7, NAA: A14039, 7007; Fanning to Beazley, 'Telecommunications carriers', 10 April 1990, 8–15, NAA: M3365, 7/4 Part 1.

49 Graham Evans, interview.

50 Costanzo, interview.

51 Dobes, interview; Graham Evans, interview; Fanning, interview; Shaw, interview.

52 Graham Evans, interview; Fanning, interview; Shaw, interview; also Glenn Milne, 'Aussat–OTC merger preferred', *Australian*, 2 July 1990.

53 Costanzo, interview.

54 Fanning to Beazley, 'Telecommunications carriers', 10 April 1990, 12–13, NAA: M3365, 7/4 Part 1.

55 Costanzo to Beazley, 'Review of structural arrangements—megacarrier option', 12 April 1990, NAA: M3365, 7/4 Part 1.

56 H. V. J. Moir to Hawke, 'Notes on SAC memorandum no. 7007: discussion paper: micro–economic reform—strategic paper on telecommunications', 27 April 1990, NAA: A11116, CA3666 Part 1.

57 See Paddy Costanzo to Patrick Walters, 'Comments on PM&C reform paper', 8 May 1990, NAA: M3365, 7/4 Part 1.

58 Peter Harris, 'Telecommunications Reform', 15 May 1990, NAA: M3365, 7/4 Part 1.

59 Graham Evans, interview; Harris, interview.

60 D. M. Rowell to Beazley, 21 July 1990, NAA: M3365, 7/8 Part 3.

12. A National Champion

1 Beazley quoted in FitzSimons, *Beazley*, 308.

2 Beazley, interview.

3   Costanzo, interview.

4   Costanzo, interview; Graham Evans, interview.

5   Chris Cheah, interview with author, 2 April 2015; Costanzo, interview; Dobes, interview; Graham Evans, interview; Fanning, interview; Shaw, interview.

6   Kim Beazley in CPD (Reps) (7 May 1991), 3094.

7   Shaw, interview.

8   Beazley quoted in FitzSimons, *Beazley*, 308.

9   Evans to Beazley, 'Review of structural arrangements between Australia's telecommunications carriers', 18 June 1990; Costanzo to Beazley, 'Domestic competition', 8 June 1990, NAA: M3365, 7/8 Part 1.

10 Costanzo, interview; Graham Evans, interview.

11 Evans to Beazley, 'Review of structural arrangements between Australia's telecommunications carriers', 18 June 1990, NAA: M3365, 7/8 Part 1.

12 See draft cabinet submission, 'Structural relationship among the three telecommunications carriers', undated, NAA: M3365, 7/4 Part 2.

13 Costanzo, interview; Graham Evans, interview; Fanning, interview; Shaw, interview.

14 Beazley, interview.

15 Graham Evans, interview.

16 Costanzo, interview.

17 Keating, interview.

18 Michael Hutchinson, 'Telecom structural separation clarified', *Australian Financial Review*, 19 June 2018.

19 Hutchinson to Beazley, 'Telecommunications: structural relationships and competition', 5 September 1990, NAA: M3365, 7/8 Part 5. (Text underlined in original.)

20 Costanzo, interview.

21 Costanzo, interview.

22 Graham Evans, interview; Fanning, interview; Shaw interview.

23 Geoff Kitney, 'Beazley wants Telecom-OTC merger', *Australian Financial Review*, 26 June 1990.

24 Glenn Milne, 'Left warns Hawke: no asset sales', *Australian*, 9 July 1990.

25 Chris Wallace and Ewin Hannan, 'NZ push for rival role over Telecom', *Australian*, 27 July 1990.

26 Beazley, interview.

27 See M3365, 7/8 Part 1, NAA, Canberra.

28 Mick Musumeci, media interview, ABC 'PM' program, 25 May 1990.

29 Mike Welsh to Beazley, 7 July 1990, NAA: M3365, 7/8 Part 1.

30 Hutchinson to Beazley, 'Telecommunications: structural relationships and competition', 5 September 1990, NAA: M3365, 7/8 Part 5.

31 Roberts to Beazley, 29 June 1990, NAA: M3365, 7/8 Part 1.

32 D. M. Rowell to Beazley, 3 July 1990, NAA: M3365, 7/8 Part 1.

33 Alexander Rosser to Beazley, 4 July 1990, NAA: M3365, 7/8 Part 1.

34 Cutler, 'Notes of meeting with Treasurer, 20 June 1990', 21 June 1990, NAA: M3365, 7/8 Part 1.

35   See Michelle Grattan, 'Megacom rings Keating and gets static on the line', *Age*, 23 June 1990.

36   OTC, 'A competitive blueprint for Australian telecommunications', media release, 3 July 1990, NAA: M3365, 7/8 Part 1.

37   Chris Wallace and Roy Eccleston, 'Beazley plan splits cabinet', *Australian*, 24 July 1990.

38   Telecom, 'Why OTC is not the best or only viable platform for domestic competition', internal briefing note (5 August 1990), NAA: M3365, 7/8 Part 5. (Exclamation mark in original.)

39   T. A. Cutler, 'Notes of meeting with Treasurer, 20 July 1990', 20 July 1990, NAA: M3365, 7/8 Part 2.

40   Henry to Walters, 28 June 1990, NAA: M3365, 7/8 Part 1.

41   Keating, interview.

42   DOTAC, 'File note: Treasury/DT&C meeting on telecommunications market structures', 10 August 1990, NAA: M3365, 7/8 Part 5.

43   M. J. Hutchinson to Beazley, 'Carrier review: meeting between DT&C and Treasury to discuss duopoly versus open competition models', 13 August 1990, NAA: M3365, 7/11/2 Part 1.

44   Vanessa Fanning to Patrick Walters, 'Treasury minute on telecommunications reform', 3 August 1990, NAA: M3365, 7/11/1 Part 2.

45   Hutchinson to Beazley, 'Carrier review', 13 August 1990, NAA: M3365, 7/11/2 Part 1.

46   Fanning to Walters, 'Treasury minute on telecommunications reform', NAA: M3365, 7/11/1 Part 2.

47   See Fanning to Walters, 'Treasury minute on telecommunications reform', NAA: M3365, 7/11/1 Part 2.

48   DOTAC, 'File note: Treasury/DT&C meeting on telecommunications market structures', 10 August 1990, NAA: M3365, 7/8 Part 5

49   Fanning to Walters, 'Treasury minute on telecommunications reform', NAA: M3365, 7/11/1 Part 2.

50   Hutchinson to Beazley, 'Telecommunications: structural relationships and competition', 5 September 1990, NAA: M3365, 7/8 Part 5.

51   Keating, interview.

52   Keating's handwritten notes on his copy of 'McEwenism at its very worst', *Australian Financial Review* 16 August 1990, sighted by author.

53   Beazley, interview.

54   Terry Cutler to Walters, 5 August 1990, NAA: M3365, 7/8 Part 5.

55   Cutler, 'Notes of meeting with Treasurer, 20 June 1990', 21 June 1990, NAA: M3365, 7/8 Part 1; Cutler, 'Notes of meeting with Treasurer, 20 July 1990', 20 July 1990, NAA: M3365, 7/8 Part 2.

56   Walters to Beazley, 5 August 1990, NAA: M3365, 7/8 Part 5.

57   Harris, interview; Keating, interview.

58   Keating, interview.

59   'Beazley's megacom submission', *Australian Financial Review*, 14 August 1990.

60   Beazley, interview.

61 DOTAC, 'Carrier review', internal background paper 'not for distribution' [undated but likely July/August 1990], NAA: M3365, 7/8 Part 3.

62 'Beazley's megacom submission'.

63 Graham Evans, interview.

64 Beazley, interview; Cheah, interview; Costanzo, interview; Graham Evans, interview; Fanning, interview; Shaw, interview.

65 'Beazley's megacom submission'; Joanne Gray, 'Beazley relies heavily on CS First Boston analysis', *Australian Financial Review*, 15 August 1990.

66 'McEwenism at its very worst', *Australian Financial Review*, 16 August 1990.

67 Annotated original sighted by author.

68 Keating, interview.

69 'McEwenism at its very worst'.

70 Graham Evans, interview; Fanning, interview; Shaw, interview.

71 Preston to Evans, 24 August 1990, NAA: M3365, 7/8 Part 5.

72 See Tony Shaw to Beazley, 'Response to Treasury's coordination comments on the carrier structure', 28 August 1990, NAA: M3365, 7/8 Part 5.

73 Costanzo, interview.

74 Beale to Beazley, 'Cabinet submission—structural relationships among the three telecommunications carriers', 22 August 1990, NAA: M3365, 7/8 Part 5.

75 Fanning to Di Mildren, 'Press contact: Geoff Kitney', 31 August 1990, NAA: M3365, 7/11/1 Part 2. In interviews and correspondence, Graham Evans and Tony Shaw stated emphatically that Transport and Communications officials did not leak to the media at any stage during this period.

76 Costanzo to Beazley, 3 September 1990, NAA: M3365, 7/11/1 Part 2.

77 Gareth Evans, interview.

78 Roy Eccleston and Glenn Milne, 'Pressure grows to delay Telecom ruling', *Australian*, 31 July 1990.

79 Geoff Kitney, 'ALP sets date for conference on Telecom', *Australian Financial Review*, 14 August 1990.

80 Duffy, Dawkins and Kelly quoted in Wallace and Eccleston, 'Beazley plan splits cabinet'.

81 Steve Burrell, 'Centre-Left opposes plan for foreign Telecom rival', *Australian Financial Review*, 20 August 1990; Steve Burrell, 'Keating pushes for open slather', *Australian Financial Review*, 3 September 1990.

82 Roger Price, 'Telecommunications cabinet submission: comment by Roger Price M.P.' (23 August 1990), NAA: M3365, 7/8 Part 5.

83 Price quoted in Joanne Gray, 'Key Beazley man slams Megacom plan', *Australian Financial Review*, 10 September 1990. See also Graham Richardson, *Whatever It Takes* (Bantam Books, Sydney, 1994), 305–6.

84 Office of the Minister for Transport and Communications, *Telecommunications: Competition for Telecom*, 23 August 1990, NAA: M3365, 7/8 Part 5.

85 Mick Musumeci, media interview, ABC 'PM' program, 14 August 1990.

86 Saunderson quoted in Raiche, *History of Telecommunications Policy*, Chapter 4, pp. 7–8.

87 Brown in CPD (23 August 1990), 1460–2.

88 John Hewson in CPD (Reps) (23 August 1990), 1488–9.

89 Joanne Gray, 'Button opposes Beazley megacom plan', *Australian Financial Review*, 21 August 1990; Hawke in CPD (11 September 1990), 1533.

90 Hawke quoted in Tom Dusevic, 'Hawke hails and pushes party debate', *Australian Financial Review*, 23 August 1990.

91 Beazley, interview; Keating, interview; Hawke, *Hawke Memoirs*, 491.

92 Hawke, *Hawke Memoirs*, 490.

93 Michael Gordon, *Paul Keating: A Question of Leadership* (University of Queensland Press, St Lucia, 1993), 114.

94 Beazley, interview; Gareth Evans, interview; Keating, interview.

95 Graham Evans, interview; Keating, interview.

96 Costanzo, interview; Keating, interview.

97 See cabinet decision nos. 14405, 30 August 1990; 14408, 6 September 1990; and 14423, 10 September 1990, NAA: A14039, 7329.

98 Hutchinson to Beazley, 'Telecommunications: structural relationships and competition', 5 September 1990, NAA: M3365, 7/8 Part 5.

99 P. J. Cornish to Beazley, 5 September 1990, NAA: M3365, 7/4, Part 1.

100 Hutchinson to Beazley, 'Telecommunications: structural relationships and competition', 5 September 1990, NAA: M3365, 7/8 Part 5. For Beazley's view on full third-party resale, see M. J. Hutchinson to Beazley, 'Implementation of the new carrier arrangements', 25 September 1990, NAA: M3365, 7/11/1 Part 1.

101 Cabinet decision no. 14408, 6 September 1990, NAA: A14039, 7329.

102 Ferguson and Mansfield quoted in Geoff Kitney, 'Unions threaten to fight OTC sale', *Australian Financial Review*, 10 September 1990.

103 Costanzo, interview.

104 Hawke claims that Keating 'threw his pencil on the table and stormed out of the cabinet room describing us all as a lot of "fucking second-raters"' as defence minister Robert Ray called out, 'Go on Paul, take your bat and ball and go home.' Graham Richardson recalls that Keating 'threw his papers onto the desk, abused Beazley, me and the Cabinet in turn and stormed out, Robert Ray's comment "Spit the dummy" ringing in his ears.' See Hawke, *Hawke Memoirs*, 491–2; Richardson, *Whatever It Takes*, 307.

105 Keating quoted in Troy Bramston, *Paul Keating: The Big Picture Leader* (Scribe, Melbourne, 2016), 343.

106 Keating, interview.

107 Cabinet decision no. 14423, 10 September 1990, NAA: A14039, 7329.

108 Fanning to Beazley, 'Briefing for ACTU talks on carrier review', 10 September 1990, NAA: M3365, 7/8 Part 5.

109 Graham Evans, email to author, 12 October 2020.

110 Hoare to Beazley, 24 September 1990, NAA: M3365, 7/11/2 Part 1.

111 Kim Beazley, speech to Australian Labor Party Special National Conference (Canberra, 24 September 1990), 9–13.

112 FitzSimons, *Beazley*, 315.

113 Costanzo, interview; Fanning, interview.

114 Goss quoted in FitzSimons, *Beazley*, 315.

115 Richardson, *Whatever It Takes*, 305.

116 ALP, *Special National Conference* (Canberra, 24 September 1990), 4–5; Glenn Milne, 'Labor overturns its history', *Australian*, 25 September 1990.

117 Bob Hawke and Kim Beazley, joint news conference, Parliament House, Canberra, 24 September 1990.

118 Ted Plummer to Beazley, 29 October 1990, NAA: M3365, 7/4 Part 2.

119 Maddock, 'Microeconomic reform of telecommunications' in Forsyth (ed.), *Microeconomic Reform in Australia*, 255–6.

120 Paul Kelly, 'Hawke gains freedom to move', *Australian*, 25 September 1990.

121 Hawke in CPD (8 November 1990), 3596; Hawke, *Hawke Memoirs*, 492.

122 Beazley, speech to Australian Labor Party Special National Conference, 9; Kim Beazley, Foreword in *Micro-economic Reform: Progress, Telecommunications* (AGPS, Canberra, 1990).

123 Hutchinson to Beazley, 'Implementation of the new carrier arrangements', 25 September 1990, NAA: M3365, 7/11/1 Part 1; Raiche, *History of Telecommunications*, Chapter 5, p. 2.

124 Hutchinson to Beazley, 'Implementation of the new carrier arrangements', 25 September 1990, NAA: M3365, 7/11/1 Part 1; Cheah, interview; Costanzo, interview; Fanning, interview; Shaw, interview.

125 Graham Evans, email to author, 13 October 2020.

126 Hutchinson to Beazley, 'Implementation of the new carrier arrangements', 25 September 1990, NAA: M3365, 7/11/1 Part 1.

127 Hawke, *Hawke Memoirs*, 492.

128 Keating, interview.

129 Beazley, interview. See also Hutchinson to Beazley, 'Implementation of the new carrier arrangements', 25 September 1990, NAA: M3365, 7/11/1 Part 1.

130 See Hutchinson to Beazley, 'Carrier review', 13 August 1990, NAA: M3365, 7/11/2 Part 1; Hutchinson to Beazley, 'Telecommunications: structural relationships and competition', 5 September 1990, NAA: M3365, 7/8 Part 5; Hutchinson to Beazley, 'Implementation of the new carrier arrangements', 25 September 1990, NAA: M3365, 7/11/1 Part 1.

131 Cheah, interview; Costanzo, interview. The red book's formal title was *Micro-economic Reform: Progress: Telecommunications* (AGPS, Canberra, 1990).

132 Beazley, *Micro-economic Reform*, 2–15.

133 Hutchinson to Beazley, 'Implementation of the new carrier arrangements', 25 September 1990, NAA: M3365, 7/11/1 Part 1.

134 Dobes, interview.

135 Ian Beckett, 'Microeconomic reform and the transport and communications portfolio' in Jenny Stewart (ed.), *From Hawke to Keating: Australian Commonwealth Administration 1990–1993* (University of Canberra, 1994), 223; Raiche, *History of Telecommunications Policy*, Chapter 5, pp. 16–17.

136 Beazley to Davey, 9 November 1990, NAA: M3365, 7/4 Part 2.

137 Beazley to Alex Morokoff, 9 November 1990; and David Hoare, 9 November 1990, NAA: M3365, 7/4 Part 2.

138 Hutchinson to Beazley, 'Implementation of the new carrier arrangements', 25 September 1990, NAA: M3365, 7/11/1 Part 1.

139 Beazley in CPD (8 November 1990), 3651; Kim Beazley, 'The key steps towards successful implementation: a progress report and current assessment' in Bill Melody (ed.), *Implementing the New Telecommunications Policy: From Words to Deeds*, Proceedings of a CIRCIT conference (Melbourne, 15 March 1991), 12.

140 Alston in CPD (8 December 1990), 3773.

141 Willis to Hawke, 11 January 1991, NAA: M3365, 7/11/1 Part 1.

142 Beckett, 'Microeconomic reform and the transport and communications portfolio' in Stewart (ed.), *From Hawke to Keating*, 250.

143 Nevile, 'Politicians, media moguls and pay-TV', 63–74; Rodney Tiffen, 'The development of pay television in Australia', 6th World Media Economics Conference (Montréal, 12–15 May 2004), 6.

144 Cabinet submission no. 7329, 2 August 1990, NAA: A14039, 7329.

145 Michael Hutchinson to Beazley, 'Third PMTS licence—timing, structure and related issues', 22 January 1991, NAA: M3365, 7/11/1 Part 1.

146 Beazley, 'Key steps towards successful implementation' in Melody (ed.), *Implementing the New Telecommunications Policy*', 12–13.

147 Harris to Hawke, 22 March 1991. Original in Harris's possession and sighted by the author.

148 Peter White, 'NBN a repeat of AUSSAT fiasco', *Australian*, 25 February 2011.

149 Beckett, 'Microeconomic reform and the transport and communications portfolio' in Stewart (ed.), *From Hawke to Keating*', 250; Raiche, *History of Telecommunications Policy*, Chapter 5, p. 15.

150 Fanning, interview.

151 Cheah, interview; Costanzo, interview; Dobes, interview; Graham Evans, interview; Fanning, interview.

152 FitzSimons, *Beazley*, 322–3; Milne, 'Labor overturns its history'. The new entity established by merging Telecom and OTC was the Australian and Overseas Telecommunications Commission (AOTC), but Telecom and OTC continued to trade under their existing names. See Alston in CPD (4 June 1991), 4305.

153 Alston in CPD (4 June 1991), 4305; Sinclair in CPD (28 May 1991), 4115–16.

154 Warwick Smith in CPD (Reps) (28 May 1991), 4073–5.

155 See CPD (Senate) (20 June 1991), 5140–3.

156 Smith in CPD (28 May 1991), 4072–9.

157 Beazley in CPD (20 June 1991), 5140, 5144.

13. Lessons and Legacies

1 Kirby, Foreword in Armstrong (ed.), *Telecommunications Law*, xvii.

2 This section draws from John Doyle, 'NBN and the countdown to Telstra's final structural separation', *Australian Financial Review*, 15 June 2018; and Paul Fletcher, *Wired Brown Land? Telstra's Battle for Broadband* (UNSW Press, Sydney, 2009), chapters 1–2, 4 and 6.

3 Peter Leonard, 'The elusive mirage: competition regulation and telecommunications, 1997–2000', *Media Information Australia*, 96/1 (August 2000), 23–36.

4 Alston quoted in Fletcher, *Wired Brown Land*, 53.

5   Pamela Williams, *The Victory: The Inside Story of the Takeover of Australia* (Allen & Unwin, Sydney, 1997), 164–5.

6   Goot, 'Public opinion, privatisation and the electoral politics of Telstra', 219–20.

7   Williams, *Victory*, 281–3.

8   Coonan quoted in Fletcher, *Wired Brown Land*, 141.

9   Kevin Rudd, media conference on National Broadband Network, Canberra, 7 April 2009.

10 Kevin Rudd, 'New National Broadband Network', media release, 7 April 2009.

11 Rudd, media conference on National Broadband Network.

12 Conroy quoted in Phil Dobbie, 'The NBN is broken. Here's the fix', *Journal of Telecommunications and the Digital Economy*, 3/3 (August 2015).

13 NBN Co, 'Initial build complete, NBN Co announces next phase of network investment to meet future demand', media release, 23 September 2020.

14 Katy Gallagher (Minister for Finance) and Michelle Rowland (Minister for Communications) to Kate McKenzie (Chair, NBN Co), 22 July 2022, infrastructure. gov.au/sites/default/files/documents/nbn-co-sau-letter-to-nbn-co.pdf.

15 Andy Penn quoted in James Fernyhough, 'Telstra CEO Andy Penn warns: don't expect quick results', *Australian Financial Review*, 18 December 2018.

16 'Telstra Corporation, 'Telstra outlines steps to finalise its legal restructure', market release, 29 March 2022.

17 Penn quoted in Fernyhough, 'Telstra CEO Andy Penn warns'.

Bibliography

National Archives of Australia

Australian Post Office Commission of Inquiry, Submission Files, 1973–74, A4066.

Fraser Ministries, Cabinet Files, 1975–83, A10756.

Second, Third, Fourth and Fifth Fraser Ministries, Cabinet Submissions (with Decisions), 1975–83, A12909.

Fraser Ministries, Cabinet Memoranda, 1979–83, A12930.

Fraser Ministries, Cabinet Papers, 1976–79, A12933.

Second, Third, Fourth and Fifth Fraser Ministries, Folders of Cabinet Decisions, 1975–82, A13075.

Hawke Ministries, Cabinet Files, 1983–91, A11116.

First Hawke Ministry, Cabinet Submissions, 1983–84, A13977.

First Hawke Ministry, Cabinet Memoranda, 1983–84, A13978.

First, Second, Third and Fourth Hawke Ministries, Folders of Cabinet Decisions, 1983–91, A13979.

Second to Fourth Hawke Ministries, Submissions and Memoranda, 1984–91, A14039.

Department of the Prime Minister and Cabinet, Correspondence Files; Australian Postal and Telecommunications Union, Federal Executive, General Representations, 1978–87, A463.

Department of the Prime Minister and Cabinet, Correspondence Files; Australian Telecommunications Commission, Policy other than Finance, 1985–88; Review of Communications Regulation, 1987, A1209.

Review of Structural Arrangements (Carriers): ROSA, M3365.

Department of the Treasury, Correspondence Files, 1966–92, A9488.

Whitlam Ministries, Cabinet Submissions, 1972–75, A5915.

Whitlam Ministries, Folders of Decisions of Cabinet and Cabinet Committees, 1972–75, A5925.

E. G. Whitlam, Personal Papers, 1972–73, M503.

P. J. Keating Personal Collection

Annotated newspaper clippings, 1990.

Personal Interviews and Correspondence

Kim Beazley, interview, by telephone, 15 July 2015.

Neil Brown, interview, Melbourne, 19 December 2014.

Jim Carlton, interview, by telephone, 27 February 2014.

Chris Cheah, interview, Canberra, 2 April 2015.

Paddy Costanzo, interview, by telephone, 7 April 2015.

Robin Davey, email, 10 February 2015; interview, Canberra, 1 April 2015.

Leo Dobes, interview, Canberra, 31 March 2015.

Gareth Evans, interview, Melbourne, 10 February 2015.

Graham Evans, email, 14 May 2015; interview, Melbourne, 1 June 2015; email, 12 October 2020; email, 13 October 2020.

Vanessa Fanning, interview, Canberra, 1 April 2015.

Malcolm Fraser, interview, Melbourne, 4 February 2014.

Peter Harris, interview, Melbourne, 16 March 2015.

Paul Keating, interview, Sydney, 16 April 2015.

Tony Shaw, interview, Canberra, 1 April 2015.

Ian Sinclair, interview, Melbourne, 12 March 2014.

Tony Staley, interview, Melbourne, 3 March 2014.

Other Interviews

Coutts, Reg, published as Liz Fell, 'Interview with Reg Coutts', *Telecommunications Journal of Australia*, 53/2 (2003).

Musumeci, Mick, media interview, ABC 'PM' program, 25 May 1990.*

——, media interview, ABC 'PM' program, 14 August 1990.*

Hawke, Bob and Kim Beazley, joint news conference, Parliament House, Canberra, 24 September 1990, pmtranscripts.pmc.gov.au/release/transcript-8143.

Parliamentary Papers

Commonwealth Parliamentary Debates, House of Representatives, 1965–91.

Commonwealth Parliamentary Debates, Senate, 1968–91.

Reports and Submissions

Administrative and Clerical Officers' Association and Australian Postal and Telecommunications Union, *Joint Telecom Unions' Submission to Telecommunications Inquiry* (Melbourne, February 1982).

---

* Interview transcript previously available via parlinfo.aph.gov.au, now withheld due to copyright restrictions.

Anderson, Robert, *Report on the Business Management of the Postmaster-General's Department of the Commonwealth of Australia* (Commonwealth of Australia, August 1915).

Aussat, *Statutory Authorities and Government Business Enterprises: Paper by Aussat Pty Ltd* (August 1986), NAA: A1209, 1988/2742 Part 3.

Australian Electronic Industry Association, *The Role and Importance of the Australian Telecommunications Network to Local Equipment Suppliers* (Canberra, October 1987), NAA: A1209, 1987/1506 Part 3.

Australian Information Industry Association, *Opportunity and Efficiency – The Compelling Case for More Competition in the Telecommunications Environment* (October 1987), NAA: A1209, 1987/1506 Part 3.

Australian Telecommunications Commission, *Submission to Public Inquiry into Telecommunications Services in Australia* (Melbourne, February 1982).

———, 'Managing the new telecommunications era in Australia' (1983), NAA: A13977, 448.

Australian Telecommunications Employees' Association, 'A response by the Australian Telecommunications Employees Association to the proposed policy guidelines for statutory authorities and government business enterprises (The Green Paper)' (September 1986), NAA: A1209, 1988/2742 Part 3.

Australian Telecommunications Users Group, *Submission to the Public Inquiry into Telecommunications Services in Australia* (Sydney, February 1982).

———, *Telecommunications Policy: Increasing Efficiency Through Competition* (Sydney, February 1990).

———, 'Review of structural arrangements submission', 3 July 1990, NAA: M3365, 7/8 Part 1.

Beazley, Kim, *Micro-economic Reform: Progress, Telecommunications* (AGPS, Canberra, 1990).

Bond, Donald, *The Opportunity for Television Program Distribution in Australia Using Earth Satellites* (Television Corporation Limited, Sydney, 1977).

Bureau of Transport and Communications Economics, *The Cost of Telecom's Community Services Obligations*, report 64 (AGPS, Canberra, 1989).

———, *Financial Performance of Government Business Enterprises in the Transport and Communications Portfolio 1977–78 to 1988–89*, information paper 35 (AGPS, Canberra, 1990).

Business Telecommunications Services, *Submission to the Public Inquiry into Telecommunications Services in Australia* (Sydney, December 1981).

Button, John, *Submission to the Committee of Inquiry into Telecommunications in Australia* (December 1981).

———, *Supplementary Submission to the Committee of Inquiry into Telecommunications Services in Australia* (February 1982).

Commonwealth Government Task Force on the National Communications Satellite System, *Report on the National Communications Satellite System* (AGPS, Canberra, July 1978).

Davidson, Jim, *et al.*, *Report of the Committee of Inquiry into Telecommunications Services in Australia* (AGPS, Canberra, 1982).

Department of Communications, *Capital and Policy Requirements for the 1980s: Telecom Australia: A Report Prepared by McKinsey and Company* (AGPS, Canberra, 1981 [June 1980]).

———, *Selected Issues in Telecommunications Policy: A Submission to the Committee of Inquiry into Telecommunications Services in Australia* (Canberra, March 1982).

———, *Project: National Communications Satellite System* (AGPS, Canberra, 1982).

Department of the Treasury, *The Australian Post Office Commission of Inquiry: Submission by the Department of the Treasury* (Canberra, 1973), NAA: A4066, 434.

———, *Public Monopolies: Telecom and Australia Post: Submission to the Committee of Inquiry into Telecommunications Services in Australia and into the Monopoly Position of the Australian Postal Commission*, Treasury Economic Paper no. 10 (AGPS, Canberra, 1983).

Department of Urban and Regional Development, *Submission to the Australian Post Office Commission of Inquiry* (Canberra, 16 May 1973), NAA: A4066, 361.

Economic Planning Advisory Council, *Summary of BCA Response to Government Discussion Paper on Proposed Policy Guidelines for Statutory Authorities and GBEs* (AGPS, Canberra, 21 November 1986), NAA: A9488, I1985/29 Part 12.

Evans, Gareth, *Australian Telecommunications Services: A New Framework: Summary* (AGPS, Canberra, 1988).

———, *Reshaping the Transport and Communications Government Business Enterprises* (AGPS, Canberra, 1988).

Interdepartmental Working Group on Recommendations of the Australian Post Office Commission of Inquiry, *Report of the Interdepartmental Working Group* (3 October 1974), NAA: A5915, 1490.

National Communications Satellite System Working Group, *National Communications Satellite System: Working Group Report* (AGPS, Canberra, August 1979).

Office of the Minister for Transport and Communications, *Telecommunications: Competition for Telecom*, 23 August 1990, NAA: M3365, 7/8 Part 5.

Officials' Working Group on Communications Regulation, 'Telecommunications regulation: initial information paper', 27 November 1987, NAA: A14039, 5439.

Overseas Telecommunications Commission, *Policy Discussion Paper on Statutory Authorities and Government Business Enterprises: Response of the Overseas Telecommunications Commission (Australia) Board of Commissioners* (September 1986), NAA: A1209, 1988/2742 Part 3.

Postmaster-General's Department, *Community Telephone Plan 1960* (AGPS, Melbourne, 1960).

———, *Australian Post Office Commission of Inquiry: Submission by the Postmaster-General's Department*, I–VI (Canberra, 1973).

———, *Australian Post Office Commission of Inquiry: Statements by the Postmaster-General's Department on Submissions by Other Parties*, I–III (Canberra, 1974).

Price, Roger, 'Telecommunications cabinet submission: comment by Roger Price M.P.' (23 August 1990), NAA: M3365, 7/8 Part 5.

Royal Commission on Australian Government Administration, *Report* (AGPS, Canberra, 1976).

Task Force to Inquire into the Continuing Expenditure Policies of the Previous Government, *Review of the Continuing Expenditure Policies of the Previous Government* (AGPS, Canberra, 1973).

Telecom Australia, *National Satellite Communications System* (Melbourne, October 1977).

———, *Initial Response to Davidson Inquiry Recommendations* (January 1983), NAA: A13977, 448.

———, *Discussion Paper on Aspects of Telecom Australia's Non–Commercial Trading Activity* (Melbourne, 1987), NAA: A1209, 1987/1506 Part 3.

———, *Telecom's Outlook* (1987), NAA: A1209, 1987/1506 Part 3.

Vernon, James, James Kennedy and Bernard Callinan, *Report of the Commission of Inquiry into the Australian Post Office* (AGPS, Canberra, 1974).

Willis, Ralph, *Implementation of GBE Reforms and Telecommunications Pricing* (AGPS, Canberra, 1989).

Books, Book Chapters and Theses

Arena, Alex, 'What the government expects from the GBEs' in Mark Armstrong (ed.), *Telecommunications Law: Australian Perspectives* (Media Arm, Melbourne, 1990).

Armstrong, Mark, 'Introduction' in Elizabeth More and Glen Lewis (eds), *Australian Communications Technology and Policy* (Centre for Information Studies, Kuring-gai College of Advanced Education, Australian Communications Association, Australian Film and Radio School, Sydney, 1988).

———, 'The regulatory environment' in Mark Armstrong (ed.), *Telecommunications Law: Australian Perspectives* (Media Arm, Melbourne, 1990).

Ayres, Philip, *Malcolm Fraser: A Biography* (William Heinemann, Melbourne, 1987).

Barr, Trevor, *The Electronic Estate: New Communications Media and Australia* (Penguin, Melbourne, 1985).

Beckett, Ian, 'Microeconomic reform and the transport and communications portfolio' in Jenny Stewart (ed.), *From Hawke to Keating: Australian Commonwealth Administration 1990–1993* (University of Canberra, 1994).

———, 'To privatise or not?' in John Halligan and Roger Wettenhall (eds), *Hawke's Third Government: Australian Commonwealth Administration, 1987–1990* (University of Canberra, 1992).

Bramston, Troy, *Paul Keating: The Big Picture Leader* (Scribe, Melbourne, 2016).

Butlin, N. G., A. Barnard and J. J. Pincus, *Government and Capitalism: Public and Private Choice in Twentieth Century Australia* (George Allen & Unwin, Sydney, 1982).

Brown, Neil, *On the Other Hand: Sketches and Reflections from Political Life* (Poplar Press, Canberra, 1993).

Cuncliffe, Ian, 'AUSTEL: functions and powers' in Mark Armstrong (ed.), *Telecommunications Law: Australian Perspectives* (Media Arm, Melbourne, 1990).

d'Alpuget, Blanche, *Robert J. Hawke: A Biography* (Schwartz, Melbourne, 1982).

Davey, Paul, *Politics in the Blood: The Anthonys of Richmond* (UNSW Press, Sydney, 2008).

Davies, Anne, 'The origins of the Act' in Mark Armstrong (ed.), *Telecommunications Law: Australian Perspectives* (Media Arm, Melbourne, 1990).

Easson, Michael, 'Industrial relations policy' in Troy Bramston (ed.), *The Whitlam Legacy* (Federation Press, Sydney, 2013).

Evans, Gareth, *Inside the Hawke–Keating Government: A Cabinet Diary* (Melbourne University Press, 2014).

Fanning, Vanessa, 'Issues faced in drafting the regulatory legislation' in Mark Armstrong (ed.), *Telecommunications Law: Australian Perspectives* (Media Arm, Melbourne, 1990).

FitzSimons, Peter, *Beazley: A Biography* (HarperCollins, Sydney, 1998).

Fleming, Grant, David Merrett and Simon Ville, *The Big End of Town: Big Business and Corporate Leadership in Twentieth-Century Australia* (Cambridge University Press, New York, 2004).

Fletcher, Paul, *Wired Brown Land? Telstra's Battle for Broadband* (UNSW Press, Sydney, 2009).

Freudenberg, Graham, *A Certain Grandeur: Gough Whitlam in Politics* (Macmillan, Melbourne, 1977).

Gordon, Michael, *Paul Keating: A Question of Leadership* (University of Queensland Press, St Lucia, 1993).

Hancock, W. K., *Australia* (Jacaranda, Brisbane, 1961 [1930]).

Harcourt, Edgar, *Taming the Tyrant: The First One Hundred Years of Australia's International Telecommunications* (Allen & Unwin, Sydney, 1987).

Harper, John, *Monopoly and Competition in British Telecommunications: The Past, the Present and the Future* (Pinter, London, 1997).

Hawke, Bob, *The Hawke Memoirs* (William Heinemann, Melbourne, 1994).

Hocking, Jenny, *Gough Whitlam: A Moment in History* (Miegunyah Press, Melbourne, 2008).

Hutchinson, Michael, 'Restructuring Australia's telecommunications', in Anna Bodi, Anthony Newstead and Peter White (eds), *Telecommunications Management and Policy: Australian and International Perspectives* (Monash University, 1992).

Kelly, Paul, *The End of Certainty: Power, Politics and Business in Australia* (Allen & Unwin, Sydney, 1994).

——, 'Labor and globalisation' in Robert Manne (ed.), *The Australian Century: Political Struggle in the Building of a Nation* (Text, Melbourne, 1999).

——, 'The Whitlam legacy' in Troy Bramston (ed.), *The Whitlam Legacy* (Federation Press, Sydney, 2013).

Kirby, Michael, Foreword in Mark Armstrong (ed.), *Telecommunications Law: Australian Perspectives* (Media Arm, Melbourne, 1990).

Lindsay, David, 'Select legislative history of telecommunications' in Mark Armstrong (ed.), *Telecommunications Law: Australian Perspectives* (Media Arm, Melbourne, 1990).

Livingstone, K. T., *The Wired Nation Continent: The Communication Revolution and Federating Australia* (Oxford University Press, Melbourne, 1996).

Lloyd, C. J. and G. S. Reid, *Out of the Wilderness: The Return of Labor* (Cassell, Melbourne, 1974).

Maddock, Rodney, 'Microeconomic reform of telecommunications: the long march from duopoly to duopoly' in Peter Forsyth (ed.), *Microeconomic Reform in Australia* (Allen & Unwin, Sydney, 1992).

Manne, Robert, 'The Whitlam revolution' in Robert Manne (ed.), *The Australian Century: Political Struggle in the Building of a Nation* (Text, Melbourne, 1999).

Moyal, Ann, *Clear Across Australia: A History of Telecommunications* (Thomas Nelson, Melbourne, 1984).

Nethercote, J. R., 'Public service reform: its course and nature' in Alexander Kouzmin, J. R. Nethercote and Roger Wettenhall (eds), *Australian Commonwealth Administration 1983: Essays in Review* (Canberra College of Advanced Education, 1984).

——, 'Changing climate of public service' in Roger Wettenhall and J. R. Nethercote (eds), *Hawke's Second Government: Australian Commonwealth Administration, 1984–1987* (Canberra College of Advanced Education, 1988).

O'Mahony, John, 'Economic policy' in Troy Bramston (ed.), *The Whitlam Legacy* (Federation Press, Sydney, 2013).

Paltridge, S. R., 'Aussat: The Social Shaping of a Satellite System', PhD thesis (University of Wollongong, 1989).

Reid, Alan, *The Gorton Experiment* (Shakespeare Head Press, Sydney, 1971).

——, *The Whitlam Venture* (Hill of Content, Melbourne, 1976).

Reinecke, Ian and Julianne Schultz, *The Phone Book: The Future of Australia's Communications on the Line* (Penguin, Melbourne, 1983).

Richardson, Graham, *Whatever It Takes* (Bantam, Sydney, 1994).

Scott, Keith, *Gareth Evans* (Allen & Unwin, Sydney, 1999).

Waters, Frank, *Postal Unions and Politics: A History of the Amalgamated Postal Workers' Union of Australia* (University of Queensland Press, St Lucia, 1978).

Weller, Patrick, *Malcolm Fraser PM: A Study in Prime Ministerial Power* (Penguin, Melbourne, 1989).

Wettenhall, Roger, 'Statutory authorities' in Alexander Kouzmin, J. R. Nethercote and Roger Wettenhall (eds), *Australian Commonwealth Administration 1983: Essays in Review* (Canberra College of Advanced Education, 1984).

———, 'Statutory authorities' in J. R. Nethercote, Alexander Kouzmin and Roger Wettenhall (eds), *Australian Commonwealth Administration 1984: Essays in Review* (Canberra College of Advanced Education, 1985).

Wettenhall, Roger and Ian Beckett, 'Movements in the public enterprise and statutory authority sector' in John Halligan and Roger Wettenhall (eds), *Hawke's Third Government: Australian Commonwealth Administration, 1987–1990* (University of Canberra, 1992).

White, D. M. and D. A. Kemp (eds), *Malcolm Fraser on Australia* (Hill of Content, Melbourne, 1986).

White, Peter, 'Community service obligations' in Mark Armstrong (ed.), *Telecommunications Law: Australian Perspectives* (Media Arm, Melbourne, 1990).

Whitlam, Gough, *The Whitlam Government, 1972–1975* (Viking, Melbourne, 1985).

Peter Wilenski, 'Technological change and policy planning' in Elizabeth More and Glen Lewis (eds), *Australian Communications Technology and Policy* (Centre for Information Studies, Kuring-gai College of Advanced Education, Australian Communications Association, Australian Film and Radio School, Sydney, 1988).

Williams, Pamela, *The Victory: The Inside Story of the Takeover of Australia* (Allen & Unwin, Sydney, 1997).

Articles and Papers

'Beazley's megacom submission', *Australian Financial Review*, 14 August 1990.

'Don't call me – I'll call you', *Bulletin*, 22 January 1972.

'Establishment of separate posts and telecommunications corporations', *Queensland Postal Worker*, December 1974.

'Lionel Bowen: the model deputy', *ABC News* (1 April 2012), abc.net.au/news/2012-04-01/lionel-bowen-obit/3925846.

'McEwenism at its very worst', *Australian Financial Review*, 16 August 1990.

'New structure: fresh outlook?', *Age*, 26 April 1974.

'Postal losses must be faced', *Age*, 1 August 1974.

'Staley backs timed calls', *Age*, 5 February 1988.

Albon, Robert, 'A new age in telecommunications? An assessment of the May ministerial statement 1988', *ACC/Westpac Economic Discussion Papers*, 4 (December 1989).

———, 'Evaluating Telecom's cross-subsidies: political favours at a heavy cost', *Australian Economic Papers*, 30 (June 1991).

Aubin, Tracey, 'Mobile telephone "to cost $1bn"', *Australian*, 11 April 1990.

Austin, Paul, 'Telecom at heart of Macphee dispute', *Australian*, 23 April 1987.

———, 'Telecom viability "depends on freedom from controls"', *Australian*, 26 May 1987.

Austin, Paul and Tracey Aubin, 'Cabinet faces revolt over phone reform', *Australian*, 10 April 1990.

Barnes, Allan, 'Govt plans to split Post Office', *Age*, 25 April 1974.

Beazley, Kim, 'The key steps towards successful implementation: a progress report and current assessment' in Bill Melody (ed.), *Implementing the New Telecommunications Policy: From Words to Deeds*, Proceedings of a CIRCIT conference (Melbourne, 15 March 1991).

Bowers, Patrick, 'Fraser adamant: industrial chaos must stop', *Sydney Morning Herald*, 13 July 1979.

Brenchley, Fred, 'Lionel Bowen: Labor's "Mr. Fixit" is quietly moving up the ladder', *National Times*, 3–8 December 1973.

Brett, Judith, 'Fair share: country and city in Australia', *Quarterly Essay*, 42 (June 2011).

Brown, Allan, 'Golden bird or white elephant? Australia's Aussat satellite system', *Telecommunications Policy* (June 1991).

Brunetti, Edward, 'Public bodies need competition, says EPAC report', *Age*, 16 October 1986.

Burrell, Steve, 'Centre-Left opposes plan for foreign Telecom rival', *Australian Financial Review*, 20 August 1990.

———, 'Keating pushes for open slather', *Australian Financial Review*, 3 September 1990.

Carney, Shaun, 'Government will consider ending Telecom monopoly', *Age*, 4 September 1987.

Clark, Pilita, 'Caucus backlash on timed phones', *Sydney Morning Herald*, 18 December 1987.

Colebatch, Tim, 'Gibbs loves a challenge', *Age*, 7 June 1973.

Dare, Tim, 'A leap into the electronic future', *Sydney Morning Herald*, 24 January 1978.

Davies, Anne, 'Govt curbs Telecom deregulators', *Australian Financial Review*, 4 November 1987.

Dawson, Christopher, 'Industry that loses mail and money', *Sydney Morning Herald*, 3 May 1973.

de Silva, Janet, 'Deregulation plan lifts a few hackles', *Australian Financial Review*, 8 May 1987.

Dobbie, Phil, 'The NBN is broken. Here's the fix', *Journal of Telecommunications and the Digital Economy*, 3/3 (August 2015).

Doyle, John, 'Conceiving of Telecom: The Politics of Australian Telecommunications Reform, 1967–1972', *Australian Journal of Politics and History*, 61/2 (2015).

————, 'NBN and the countdown to Telstra's final structural separation', *Australian Financial Review*, 15 June 2018.

Doyle, Michael, 'Bans move on Telecom', *Age*, 4 October 1979.

Dusevic, Tom, 'Hawke hails and pushes party debate', *Australian Financial Review*, 23 August 1990.

Earl, Greg, 'Paul Keating's media masterstroke', *Australian Financial Review*, 23 February 1987.

————, 'Users' group steps up campaign against Telecom', *Australian Financial Review*, 11 May 1987.

Eccleston, Roy and Glenn Milne, 'Pressure grows to delay Telecom ruling', *Australian*, 31 July 1990.

Fernyhough, James, 'Telstra CEO Andy Penn warns: don't expect quick results', *Australian Financial Review*, 18 December 2018.

Fist, Stewart, 'AUSTEL – a legal minefield?', *Australian Communications* (August 1989).

Gerritsen, Rolf, 'The politics of microeconomic reform: structuring a general model', *Australian Journal of Public Administration*, 51/1 (March 1992).

Goot, Murray, 'Public opinion, privatisation and the electoral politics of Telstra', *Australian Journal of Politics and History*, 45/2 (1999).

Grattan, Michelle, 'Megacom rings Keating and gets static on the line', *Age*, 23 June 1990.

Gray, Joanne, 'Beazley relies heavily on CS First Boston analysis', *Australian Financial Review*, 15 August 1990.

————, 'Button opposes Beazley megacom plan', *Australian Financial Review*, 21 August 1990.

————, 'Key Beazley man slams Megacom plan', *Australian Financial Review*, 10 September 1990.

Greenlees, Donald, 'ALP gets in early for big sell-off', *Australian*, 14 August 1987.

Head, Beverley, 'Austel chief appeals for goodwill', *Australian Financial Review*, 24 April 1989.

————, 'Legal hurdles in Telecom reform', *Australian Financial Review*, 1 August 1990.

Heenan, Geoffrey, 'Regulation of the Australian telecommunications industry', *Economic Papers: A Journal of Applied Economics and Policy*, 8/4 (December 1989).

Hoare, Judith, 'Davidson report opens Telecom door', *Australian Financial Review*, 29 October 1982.

Housley, T. A., 'Communication in modern society', *Australian Journal of Public Administration*, 26/2 (June 1967).

Humphries, David, 'Labor's anchor through turbulent era', *Sydney Morning Herald*, 3 April 2012.

Hutchinson, Michael, 'Telecom structural separation clarified', *Australian Financial Review*, 19 June 2018.

Jones, B. F., 'The Post Office and the Community', *Australian Journal of Public Administration*, 26/2 (June 1967).

Kelly, Paul, 'Hawke gains freedom to move', *Australian*, 25 September 1990.

Kennedy, David, 'Union may block timed calls', *Sydney Morning Herald*, 16 December 1987.

Kitney, Geoff, 'Beazley wants Telecom-OTC merger', *Australian Financial Review*, 26 June 1990.

———, 'ALP sets date for conference on Telecom', *Australian Financial Review*, 14 August 1990.

———, 'Unions threaten to fight OTC sale', *Australian Financial Review*, 10 September 1990.

Langdale, John, 'Competition in the Australian telecommunications industry? The Davidson inquiry', *Australian Quarterly*, 54/2 (Winter 1982).

Leonard, Peter, 'Footprints down a narrow path: the regulation of AUSSAT', *Media Information Australia*, 58 (November 1990).

———, 'The elusive mirage: competition regulation and telecommunications, 1997–2000', *Media Information Australia*, 96/1 (August 2000).

Maiden, Tony, 'Managing a giant with clouded responsibilities', *Australian Financial Review*, 19 December 1972.

———, 'Customers must adapt to standards set by the line of least resistance', *Australian Financial Review*, 21 December 1972.

Maltby, George, 'Response to the proposed guidelines by the Overseas Telecommunications Commission', *Australian Journal of Public Administration*, 45/4 (December 1986).

Martin, Bronwen and Julietta Jameson, 'Taking on Telecom', *Business Review Weekly*, 29 May 1987.

McLean, Ian, *Telephone Pricing and Cross-Subsidization Under the PMG, 1901–1975*, Working Papers in Economic History, 27 (ANU, Canberra, September 1984).

Milne, Glenn, 'Aussat–OTC merger preferred', *Australian*, 2 July 1990.

———, 'Left warns Hawke: No asset sales', *Australian*, 9 July 1990.

———, 'Labor overturns its history', *Australian*, 25 September 1990.

Morgan, Hugh, 'A castle in France' in Hazel Ramsden (ed.), *Competition and Competitiveness in Telecommunications* (Centre of Policy Studies, Monash University, 5 August 1987).

Nevile, Ann, 'Politicians, media moguls and pay-TV: policy-making in Australia 1977–1995', *Australian Journal of Public Administration*, 59/2 (June 2000).

Raiche, Holly, *A History of Telecommunications Policy*, research paper (Faculty of Law, University of New South Wales, 1997).

Samuel, Peter, 'PMG charges set hot pace', *Bulletin*, 9 August 1975.

Schultz, Julianne, 'Deregulation by default or design', *Media, Culture and Society*, 7 (1985).

Scott, Keith, '9pc swing to the Liberals', *Canberra Times*, 7 February 1988.

Snow, Deborah, 'Telecom inquiry terms of reference revealed', *Australian Financial Review*, 7 September 1981.

———, 'Blueprint for Telecom's reduced role', *Australian Financial Review*, 29 October 1982.

Staley, Tony, 'Perspectives of some users' in Hazel Ramsden (ed.), *Competition and Competitiveness in Telecommunications* (Centre of Policy Studies, Monash University, 5 August 1987).

Tiffen, Rodney, 'The development of pay television in Australia', 6th World Media Conference (Montréal, 12–15 May 2004).

Toohey, Brian, 'Bureaucrats' wage splurge', *Australian Financial Review*, 18 July 1975.

Trengrove, C. D., *Telecommunications in Australia: Competition or Monopoly?*, Special Study, 4 (Centre of Policy Studies, Monash University, Melbourne, 1982).

Wallace, Chris and Roy Eccleston, 'Beazley plan splits cabinet', *Australian*, 24 July 1990.

Wallace, Chris and Ewin Hannan, 'NZ push for rival role over Telecom', *Australian*, 27 July 1990.

Walsh, G. P., 'Anderson, Sir Robert Murray (1865–1940)' *Australian Dictionary of Biography* (National Centre of Biography, ANU), adb.anu.edu.au/biography/anderson-sir-robert-murray-5021.

Wettenhall, Roger , 'The Post Office', *Current Affairs Bulletin*, 45/9 (23 March 1970).

———, 'Guidelines for statutory authorities', *Australian Journal of Public Administration*, 45/4 (December, 1986).

White, Peter, 'NBN a repeat of AUSSAT fiasco', *Australian*, 25 February 2011.

Young, Annette, 'Telecom might lose its monopoly: Duffy', *Age*, 5 May 1987.

Speeches and Media Statements

Anthony, Doug, 1972 election policy speech (Lismore, 20 November 1972).[†]

———, 'Protect Your Future', 1977 election policy speech.[†]

———, 1983 election policy speech (Sydney, 21 February 1983).[†]

Beazley, Kim, speech to Australian Labor Party Special National Conference (Canberra, 24 September 1990).

Fraser, Malcolm, 1977 election policy speech (21 November 1977).[†]

———, 'We're not waiting for the world', 1983 election policy speech (15 February 1983).[†]

Hawke, Bob, 1983 election policy speech (Sydney, 16 February 1983).[†]

———, 1984 election policy speech (Sydney, 13 November 1984).[†]

————, 1988 Garran Oration, published as R. J. L. Hawke, 'Challenges in public administration', *Australian Journal of Public Administration*, 48/1 (March 1989).

NBN Co, 'Initial build complete, NBN Co announces next phase of network investment to meet future demand', media release, 23 September 2020, nbnco. com.au/corporate-information/media-centre/media-statements/Initial-build-complete-NBNCo-announces-next-phase.

Overseas Telecommunications Commission, 'A competitive blueprint for Australian telecommunications', media release, 3 July 1990, NAA: M3365, 7/8 Part 1.

Rudd, Kevin, media conference on National Broadband Network, Canberra, 7 April 2009.[†]

————, 'New National Broadband Network', media release, 7 April 2009.[†]

Sinclair, Ian and Wal Fife, 'Telecom dispute', media statement, 11 June 1981, NAA: A13075, 15503.

Telstra Corporation, 'Telstra outlines steps to finalise its legal restructure', market release, 29 March 2022, telstra.com.au/aboutus/investors/announcements.

Whitlam, Gough, 'Into the Seventies with Labor', 1969 election policy speech (Sydney, 1 October 1969).[†]

————, 'It's time for leadership', 1972 election policy speech (Sydney, 13 November 1972).[†]

————, 'Report of the Commission of Inquiry into the Post Office', media release, 24 April 1974, pmtranscripts.pmc.gov.au/release/transcript-3220.

————, 1974 election policy speech (Sydney, 29 April 1974).[†]

————, 'A program for Australia's recovery', 1977 election policy speech (Sydney, 17 November 1977).[†]

Political Party Documents and Policies

Australian Labor Party, *Official Reports of the 27th Commonwealth Conference and Special Conference and the 28th Commonwealth Conference* (Melbourne, 1969).

————, *Platform, Constitution and Rules as Approved by the 33rd National Conference* (Adelaide, 1979).

————, *Platform, Constitution and Rules as Approved by the 35th National Conference* (Canberra, 1982).

————, *Platform, Resolutions and Rules as Approved by the 37th National Conference* (Hobart, 1986).

————, 1987 election policy statement (23 June 1987), australianpolitics.com/downloads/1987/87-06-23_policy-statement_hawke.pdf.

————, *Platform, Resolutions and Rules as Approved by the 38th National Conference* (Hobart, 1988).

————, *Special National Conference* (Canberra, 24 September 1990).

Liberal Party of Australia, *The Way Ahead with a Liberal Country Government* (Canberra, March 1974).

————, *The New Government Policies* (Canberra, 1976).[†]

————, '1983 policy speech supplementary statements' (Canberra, 1983).[†]

————, 'Get in front again', 1987 election policy statement (25 June 1987).[†]

Liberal and National Parties, *Communications Policy* (November 1984).[†]

National Party of Australia, 1987 election policy summary (Canberra, June 1987).[†]

[†] Copy of original document available via parlinfo.aph.gov.au.

Index

Abbott government, 209

ABC: as potential satellite user, 71, 77

ACCC, 205, 207

Accord, Prices and Incomes 1983, 123

ACTU: anti-privatisation campaign 1985, 107; attempt to limit telecommunications reform, 128; collaborates with Labor reform taskforce, 139, 153, 185, 188

Age newspaper: condemns PMG customer service, 38–9; criticises Coalition opposition to price increases, 44; supports satellite network, 2

Albanese government: commits to public ownership of NBN, 210

Allan, Ian, 11

ALP: approach to telecommunications debt, 47–8; attacks Coalition's politically motivated subsidies 1960s, 21; disputes Davidson report, 92; divided over Davidson inquiry, 85–6; equivocates over planned satellite network, 76; members reject timed local calls, 138–9; platform 1957, 1969, 17–18; platform 1986, 119; platform 1988, 143; proposes inquiry into PMG 1968–72, 21; proposes to split PMG's post and telecommunications services, 21–2; supports corporatisation of PMG, 18; wrangling over Beazley's plan, 180
See also caucus; Hawke government; Whitlam government

Alston, Richard, 151–2, 154, 163, 191–3, 206

Anderson inquiry 1915, 6–7

Anderson, Robert, 7, 9

Anthony, Doug, 16, 58, 95

Anthony, Larry, 14

anti-privatisation campaign, South Australia 1985, 107

APTU/APWU: campaigns against Public Service Board control of PMG, 17, 28–9, 39; favours corporatisation of PMG, 197; industrial action 1950s to 1970s, 17; membership numbers, 17, 133; shifts position on statutory corporation, 29; submission to Vernon commission, 29; Telecom censured by Fraser government for agreement with union, 66.
See also ATEA; telecommunications unions; Arndt, Rob; Slater, George; Waters, Frank

Arena, Alex, 147, 154

Armstrong, Mark, 150

Arndt, Rob, 102, 119

ASTEC, 101–2

ATEA: bids for coverage of Aussat technical staff, 102; campaigns alongside Labor 1983, 96; criticises John Button's submission to Davidson inquiry, 86; industrial action disrupts inter-city communications 1978, 61, 63–4; opposes Aussat privatisation, 171–2; opposes liberalisation, 126, 161–3; rejects timed local calls, 138; rejects weakening Telecom monopoly, 126; supports Beazley's model, 181, 185;

supports first telephone monopoly, 118–19
See also telecommunications unions

ATUG: establishment 1981, 62; makes submission to Davidson inquiry, 82–3; on securing competition in equipment market, 152; on slow pace of reform late 1980s, 153; opposes Telecom–OTC merger, 161, 169; proposes breakup of Telecom, 161, 165–6; questions Telecom's conformance with Trade Practices Act, 117–18, 134–5; supports Beazley's reforms, 193
See also Staley, Tony

Aussat, 98–108, 110, 112, 157–66, 168–72, 188–92, 199–200, 209–10: competition with Telecom and OTC restricted, 125; demand for capital, 106, 157, 159, 163; disruptive force in telecommunications, 77–8, 199; established 1981, 78; features in Coalition 1983 election policy, 95; financial crisis, 158–63; government agencies oppose Telecom takeover, 102; media reception of establishment, 73–4; merger with OTC proposed, 168–9; opposes Telecom merger, 102; part-privatisation proposed, 75, 98, 102–7, 120; part-privatisation resisted, 101–3, 107–8; powers constrained by Hawke government, 103–4, 200; privatisation proposed, 1, 5, 127, 134, 164, 169–72; privatisation opposed by unions and caucus, 171–2; prospective bidders emerge, 191–2; remains state-owned 1988, 146; review brought forward 1989, 157; sale to include pay TV, 191; Telecom defensive response to establishment 1981, 78; Telecom offers to take over Aussat, 99–100; Telecom takes 25 per cent stake, 103; Telecom stake jeopardises Aussat viability, 103–4, 108, 160; Telecom stake reacquired by government, 191
See also satellite proposals; White taskforce

Aussat Amendment Bill introduced, 191

Austel, 151, 154–5, 160–1, 163, 169, 189–90

Australian and Overseas Telecommunications Corporation Bill: passes 1991 with Australian Democrats' support, 193

Australian Conciliation and Arbitration Commission, 61, 102

Australian Democrats: oppose competition and privatisation in telecommunications, 92, 163, 193

Australian Electronic Industry Association, 134

Australian Financial Review: criticises Coalition opposition to raising charges, 44; critique of Davidson inquiry, 92; publishes competing papers by Beazley and Treasury, 176
See also Toohey, Brian

Australian Information Industry Association, 135

Australian Telecommunications Authority see Austel

Australian Telecommunications Commission see Telecom

Australian Telecommunications Development Association: protests at Telecom competing with private sector, 60

automatic telephone exchanges: growth in 1960s, 9

Barnard, Lance, 23, 52

Barton, Edmund, 7

Beale, Julian, 120

Beale, Roger, 179

Beazley, Kim, 3, 5, 130, 149, 154–5, 158–94, 201: appointed transport and communications minister 1990, 155, 158; Aussat crisis, 158–60, 162–3; backs Telecom–OTC merger, 170, 177; conflict with Keating, 169–70, 173–6,

183; envisages Telecom as 'national champion', 167–8, 178, 202; faces opposition to Aussat privatisation, 170–2; goes slow on third mobile licence, 192; moves to keep unions on side, 164, 170; negotiates with non-Labor parties to legislate reform, 186, 192–4; opposes structural separation of Telecom, 167; pitches to caucus transport and communications committee, 171, 173; reflects on how British Telecom 'screwed' Mercury Communications, 177; reviews merger and privatisation options, 163–8; steers reforms through Labor conference, 183, 185, 187; supports megacom, 165, 172–3, 175, 179; supports telecommunications duopoly, 174, 177; wants core government role in telecommunications, 176

Best, Robert, 7

Bishop, Reg, 40–3, 45–55: appointed postmaster-general 1974, 40; attacks Coalition subsidies, 55; attempts to reduce connection delays, 43; blamed for price increases, 54; presses government to respond to Vernon commission report, 40–7; proposes higher telecommunications and postal charges 1974, 42; reassures OTC workers, 52; reckons on continued ministerial influence on Telecom, 49; resists intervening in Telecom salary dispute, 53–4; rushes to pass corporatisation reforms 1975, 51; widens ministerial authority over Telecom, 51

Bjelke-Petersen, Joh: 'Joh for PM' campaign, 120

Block, David, 116

Bolkus, Nick, 180

Borthwick, David, 175

Bowen, Lionel, 23–5, 32–3, 41–7, 51–2, 102: appointed postmaster-general 1972, 23; appointed special minister of state 1974, 40; background, 23; chairs standing committee on PMG, 24; cuts rural subsidies, 32; joins with Reg Bishop to press for government response to Vernon report, 41–7; lambasts OTC, 52; represents postmaster-general in House of Representatives, 43–5; supports APWU, 28

Brack, Robert, 87, 106, 112, 114; as Telecom chair, 118

Brett, Richard, 119

broadband: demand for services grows from mid-2000s, 207; competing proposals for network advanced, 207–9

Brown, Neil, 120: as minister for post and telecommunications 1982–83, 56–7, 87, 92–6, 105; recommends competition in equipment installation, 94; rejects timed local calls, 93; responds to Davidson report, 92–4; supports NZ Labour telecommunications policy, 182

BTS, 62, 83, 91: calls for liberalisation of telecommunications, 75; submission to Davidson inquiry, 82–4; supports structural separation of Telecom, 82

Bulletin, 11, 54

Burdon, Stephen, 173

Bureau of Transport and Communications Economics, 140, 152, 155–7

Bureau of Transport Economics, 124, 128

Burgess, Phil, 207

Business Council of Australia: urges Hawke government to encourage telecommunications competition, 114

business telecommunications interests: complain about PMG, 27; complain about Telecom, 59–60; demand for services increases 1960s, 10; disadvantaged by high cost of intercity calls, 113–14; emergence of new telecommucations-specific interests 1970s, 58–63, 204; employ advanced telecommunications, 58–60; exposed to industrial action, 60–1; involved in

consultation on satellite, 75; support telecommunications liberalisation, 152–3
See also ATUG; BTS

Button, John: as industry minister, 134; as member of Structural Adjustment Committee, 124, 136; submission to Davidson inquiry draws harsh union response, 85–6

Cairns, Jim, 24, 52

Callinan, Bernard, 26, 35, 41

Cameron, Clyde, 24

Carlton, Jim, 81

caucus (ALP): forms telecommunications liaison committee, 130, 151, 163; influences Hawke government telecommunications policy, 140–53 *passim*, 181–2; opposes part-privatisation of Aussat, 98, 103; opposes structual separation of Telecom, 166; opposes timed local calls, 138; resists uniform financial guidelines, 111, 115; supports first telephone monopoly, 118–19; supports Telecom mobile monopoly, 163; supports Telecom–OTC merger, 168–71

Chadwick, Bert, 39

Childs, Bruce, 163

Coalition government (to 1972), 7–16, 20–21: introduces new rural subsidies 1970, 14–15; resists administrative reform 1960s, 13–15

Coalition parties: and Vernon commission report, 38; distrust Whitlam Labor's rural agenda, 49; emphasise ministerial control of Telecom, 50; express concern at Telecom's commercial orientation, 49; fight Whitlam Labor government plan for OTC, 48, 52, 198; incompatibility between business constituency needs and rural interests, 62–3, 74, 91–2, 198–9; legislative approach to Hawke government reforms, 202; policy on market liberalism 1983, 104–5; policy on telecommunications privatisation, 151–2, 181–2; position on Telecom stake in Aussat, 104; support telecommunications review 1987, 126; support corporatisation of Telecom and Australia Post 1975, 48–50; support liberalisation of equipment installation and maintenance, 133

Coleman, John, 74

Committee of Inquiry into Telecommunications Services in Australia *see* Davidson inquiry

Commission of Inquiry into the Australian Post Office, 25
See also Vernon commission

Committee for Economic Development of Australia: encourages telecommunications competition, 114

Commonwealth Bank: sets two-week deadline for Aussat capital raising, 162; threatens to withdraw Aussat support, 159

Commonwealth Government Task Force on the National Communications Satellite System *see* White taskforce

Communications, Department of (1980–87): 87, 97–8, 101, 107, 112–13
See also Post and Telecommunications, Department of; Transport and Communications, Department of

community service policy *see* universal service policy

Conciliation and Arbitration Commission, 61, 102

connection charges *see* telephone line rentals

Conroy, Stephen, 2, 209

Consumers' Telecommunications Network, 162

contract labour, 25, 27, 29, 50, 57, 64, 85, 198

Cooley, Alan, 54

Coombs, H. C.: leads inquiry into government expenditure, 30; forecasts increase in PMG need for Treasury funds, 16; opposes hidden subsidies and proposes higher connection charges, 31

Coombs taskforce, 16, 30–2

Coonan, Helen, 208

Costanzo, Paddy, 158–60, 164–5, 167–8, 170–1, 179, 183, 185, 192–3

Cotton, Bob, 21

Country Party: ALP attacks on, 33; influence over postmaster-general portfolio, 14; makes submission to Vernon commission, 27; opposes Coombs taskforce, 31–2; opposes increased telephone charges, 33; rejects PMG as statutory corporation, 27; responds to Vernon commission report, 38; supports cross-subsidies, 3, 9, 11, 14–15, 22, 43, 52, 196
See also Coalition parties; National Country Party; National Party

Country Women's Association, 27

Crean, Frank: anticipates inflationary pressures, 44; first budget 1973, 24, 32; warns of large budget deficit 1973, 24

cross-subsidies in telecommunications, 8, 14–15, 21, 37, 43, 71–2, 76, 84–6, 113–15, 118, 131–2, 196, 198–9, 202: and PMG on unfair effects, 28; and Vernon commission concerns about, 37; debate between Telecom and Treasury, 83–4; Fraser government rejects Davidson recommendations, 90–6; Hawke government rejects Davidson recommendations, 98–9; legislation proposed, 87; opacity of costs, 84; quantifying costs, 112–13, 131–4, 140, 149, 155, 172

CS First Boston: forecasts positive cashflow for OTC–Aussat merger, 168; predicts heavy capital demand, 163

Curtis, Jack, 47, 66–7, 72–3: prepares PMG submission to Vernon commission, 26;

promoted to Telecom managing director role, 53; warns that competition will jeopardise universal service, 76

Daly, Fred, 33

Darling Downs Housewives' and Homemakers' Association, 27

Datel (data transmission service), 58

Davey, Robin: as Austel chair, 154–5, 190

Davidson inquiry, 80–96, 105, 112, 126–8, 138: proposes structural separation of Telecom, 88; recommends full competition and direct funding of universal service, 88–91; report rejected, 90–6, 98–9, 200

Davidson, Charles, 14

Davidson, Jim: appointed to head Committee of Inquiry into Telecommunication Services in Australia, 82
See also Davidson inquiry

Dawkins, John, 97, 106, 124, 180: moves to develop performance measures, 110–11

Deakin, Alfred, 7

demand for telephones, 12–13, 18: boosted by low connection costs, 8–10, 30–1, 43

Dick, William, 82

direct dialling expands 1960s, 9

Dix, Bill, 191

Dobes, Leo, 190

Drake, James, 7

Duffy, Michael, 97–103, 117–19, 180; appointed communications minister 1983, 98; approves third satellite without cabinet sanction, 106; opposes Aussat part-privatisation, 101–2; opposes guidelines project, 110–14; proposes ruling out competition in equipment, 99; proposes Telecom takeover of Aussat, 102–3; reaches compromise with Finance on guidelines, 143; rejects Davidson recommendations, 99–100;

views influenced by Telecom, 98–9; warned of Telecom's Trade Practices Act breach, 117–19

Durack, Peter: emphasises community service in telecommunications, 49–50; opposes Telecom–OTC merger, 47, 52; fears wage blow-out at Telecom, 49

Duthie, Gil, 33

EPAC: calls for uneconomic services to be funded directly, 114

Elders agribusiness partners with Optus, 208

equipment manufacturers: and import competition, 133, 201; Country Party proposes protection through PMG purchases 27; Duffy supports protection 99, 104, 118–19; inquiry into sector, 82; Labor caucus telecommunications liaison committee supports transition assistance, 130; local content obligations protect manufacturers, 59, 99, 133–4; policy changes adjusted to ease transition, 130, 138–42; scale to be lifted by Telecom–OTC merger, 164, 168, 171, 176

ERC, 97–8, 103, 105–8

Ergas, Henry, 173

Evans, Gareth, 5, 103, 109–10, 117, 122–49, 153, 180, 182, 201: accommodates Labor caucus, 130; announces Telecom competition reforms 1988, 141–2; appointed transport and communications minister 1987, 122; becomes foreign affairs and trade minister, 149; directs Telecom to leave regulation to Austel, 147; focuses on Telecom corporatisation, 127; leads telecommunications review taskforce, 127–31, 137, 139–41; negotiates tailored corporatisation plans for telecommunication authorities, 144; proposes new independent telecommunications regulator, 141; proposes three-year transition to ending first telephone monopoly, 139–40

Evans, Graham, 3, 149, 156–7, 160, 164, 170, 177–9, 186, 189, 191: appointed secretary of Department of Transport and Communications 1988, 149; notes opposition to Telecom–OTC merger, 169; proposes various merger options, 168–9; remarks on resistance to structural reform, 130; says Telecom's structural separation 'unrealistic' without Telecom support, 166

Exicom, 184

Fanning, Vanessa, 150, 179, 185–6: recommends structural changes for Aussat, 159

Ferguson, Martin, 185

Fife, Wal, 67

Finance, Department of, 80, 97–8: advises against outright rejection of Davidson report, 100; develops efficiency and accountability guidelines, 109–15, 119, 124, 145; dismisses Telecom's estimate of cross-subsidy costs, 132–3; guidelines opposed by Duffy and Telecom, 110–14; opposes satellite, 74, 101; supports part-privatisation of Aussat, 102, 106–8; Walsh and Duffy reach accommodation on guidelines, 143

First telephone monopoly, 94, 128–9, 135: Brack defends monopoly, 118; breaches Trade Practices Act, 117–18, 123; cost to consumers, 139; excluded from Gareth Evans's competition review, 138–9, 150; Liberal Party proposes abolition, 120, 151

Fraser government, 62–96: confounded by conflict between business interests and rural base, 62–3, 74, 90–2, 198–200; emphasises improving rural services, 57; establishes Aussat, 78, 209–10; establishes national satellite system, 68–78; establishes inquiries into Telecom,

65, 79–82; focuses on industrial relations, 63–4, 66–7, 75–6, 203–4; limits Telecom management's industrial role, 66–8; opposes public sector 'crowding out' private enterprise, 60, 199; reasserts commitment to traditional telecommunications system 1983, 94–5 *See also* Davidson inquiry; satellite proposals

Fraser, Bernie, 122

Fraser, Malcolm: approached by Kerry Packer about satellite, 69; defends telecommunication cross-subsidies, 80; elected Liberal leader 1975, 48; expenditure cuts 1976, 56; hands-off management style, 56–7; objects to Telecom spending, 65

Freudenberg, Graham, 31–2

Gaudron, Mary, 61

Gerritsen, Rolf, 129

Gibbs, Bill, 41, 47, 53–4

Gillard government, 210

Gorton, John, 12, 16, 196

Gosewinckel, Graham, 103, 157, 159

Goss, Wayne, 187

GPO, Britain: structural changes, 13, 17, 19–20

Green, Fred, 53, 69

growth in telephone demand *see* demand growth

guidelines project *see* Finance, Department of

Hall, Steele, 40, 48; opposes ministerial control of Telecom, 51

Halton, Charles, 112

Hancock, W. K., 12

Hand, Gerry, 180

Harris, Peter, 160, 162; opposes delaying third mobile licence, 192–3; produces

paper on telecommunications reform, 165–6

Hawke government, 2, 97–215: adopts Beazley's reform package after fiery cabinet meeting 1990, 184–5; adopts new telecommunications liberalisation policy 1987, 4, 123; allows Telecom to take stake in Aussat, 101–4, 107–8; confronts economic difficulties 1984, 105; consolidates public service departments, 117, 122; defends telecommunications establishment 1984, 104; establishes Austel, 154–5; establishes Efficiency Scrutiny Unit, 116; gives low priority to telecommunications pre-1987, 106; includes telecommunications policy objectives in 1988 party platform, 143; moves to quantify cross-subsidies, 136, 140–1, 155–6; negotiates reform with Telecom, caucus and sector unions, 128–30, 133–4, 137–8, 144–5, 153, 164, 185–7, 201; officials divided over Davidson inquiry, 100; political and policy challenges posed by Aussat, 68, 78; produces telecommunications policy statement ('red book') 1990, 189; proposes part-privatisation of Aussat 1983, 98; responds to influence of international telecommunications reforms, 117; whole-of-government approach to reform, 124–6; *See also* Beazley, Kim; Duffy, Michael; Evans, Gareth; Willis, Ralph

Hawke, Bob: and ALP Economic Planning Committee 1967, 18; and 1978 telecommunications dispute, 61; announces public efficiency measures 1986, 115–17; appoints Gareth Evans as transport and communications minister 1987, 122–3; appoints Beazley as transport and communications minister 1990, 149, 158; claims credit for telecommunications reforms 1990, 189; commits to Telecom as monopoly carrier 1983, 96; involved in South Australian anti-privatisation campaign 1985, 107; mediates between Keating and Beazley, 183; presses Beazley to promote competition in telecommunications, 160; rules out privatising Telecom, 127; supports Beazley reform proposals, 182; tensions with Keating, 179–80; urged to push for comprehensive structural separation of Telecom, 165; uses opposition's privatisation agenda to galvanise support for Beazley's proposal, 182

Hayden, Bill, 24, 94, 149

Henry, Ken, 173, 176: blasts Beazley's 'national champion' plan, 174; proposes removing Aussat operating restrictions, 162

Hewson, John: adopts open competition policy, 177; attacks Beazley duopoly plan, 182

Hoare, David, 103, 170, 186, 191

Hogg, Bob, 180

Holmes à Court, Peter, 62, 75

Holt, Harold, 12, 196

Housley, Trevor, 11, 14

Howard government: attempts to limit Telstra's exercise of market power, 205; launches broadband plan 2007, 208; opens telecommunications sector to full competition, 207; protects Telstra's privileged market position to maximise sale price, 206; rejects Telstra's structural separation, 206–7

Howard, John: is target of anti-privatisation campaign, 107; sacks Ian McPhee as shadow communications minister, 120; supports direct funding of uneconomic services, 114

Howe, Brian, 180

Hughes Nationalist government, 8

Hulme, Alan, 12–14, 32, 35, 53, 146: emphasises PMG accountability, 13; financial reforms 1968 supported by ALP, 19; initiates area management strategy at PMG 1971/72, 15; introduces new rural subsidies 1970, 14; opposes ALP proposal for telecommunications review, 20–1; opposes PMG corporatisation, 21; pressed to increase rural subsidies, 14; supports existing institutional structures, 197; unhurried approach to reform, 15

Hutchinson, Mike, 170, 172, 175, 183–4, 190: ambivalent about Telecom–OTC merger, 184; proposes supra-board to oversee merger, 191

Hutchison Telecommunications Hong Kong: potential Aussat bidder, 191

industrial action, 17–19, 22: business responses to, 60–2, 203; effects on PMG, 11, 28–9, 38–9, 41; effects on Telecom, 139, 144–5; influence on government policies, 63–4, 66–7, 75, 80, 85, 153, 171, 185, 201, 203–4 *See also* ATEA; APWU/ATWU; telecommunications unions

Industrial Relations, Department of, 66, 102, 127, 148

Industries Assistance Commission, 122

Industry, Technology and Commerce, Department of, 114, 124, 136

Interdepartmental Working Group on Recommendations of the Australian Post Office Commission of Inquiry, 40, 45–7

Jones, Charlie, 77

Karbowiak, Tony, 82

Kater, Gregory, 35

Keating, Michael, 112, 115

Keating, Paul, 5, 97–8, 105, 108, 119, 181–2: ambivalent about Hawke's proposal for mega-departments, 117;

'banana republic' comment 1986, 105; claims credit for telecommunications duopoly decision 1990, 189; concerned to liberalise telecommunications, 109; conflict with Mel Ward, 129; disagrees with Beazley on proposed market structure, 173–6, 183; favours Telecom structural separation, 175–6, 183; lobbied by Packer against Telecom–Aussat merger, 102; meets Hawke and Beazley to thrash out differences, 183; opposes Telecom–OTC merger, 170, 173–82; public conflict with Beazley, 176–8, 182; 'spectacular tantrum' in cabinet 1990, 185; telecommunications 'not on radar' 1983–87, 106; tensions with Hawke, 158, 176; unsuccessfully challenges Hawke 1991, 193–4

Kelly, Paul, 107, 129, 188

Kelly, Ros, 154, 180

Kennedy, James, 26, 35

Kerin, John, 124

King, Malcolm, 82

Kirby, Michael, 1, 195

Kitney, Geoff, 179

Knott, John, 14

Labor party *see* ALP

Lane, Eber, 27, 30, 52

Lansdown, Robert, 74

Lawler, Peter, 47

LEK management consultants, 155–6

Liberal party: conflict between business efficiency and rural subsidies, 198–9; conflict between 'wets' and 'dries', 120; criticises Labor incrementalism, 151–3; does not prepare submission to Vernon commission, 27; releases new policy promising full competition as precursor to privatisation, 181; response to Vernon report reveals differences between urban and rural wings of party, 33, 38

See also Coalition parties

line rentals *see* telephone line rentals

long-distance calls increase 1960s, 9–10

MacBean, John, 126

Macphee, Ian, 120

Maddock, Rodney, 188

Maltby, George, 112

Mansfield, Bill, 185, 191

McClelland, Doug, 54

McEwen, Jack, 12, 16

McKinsey & Company: review of Telecom 1980, 59, 65

McLean, Ian, 171

McMahon, Billy, 11–13, 16, 196

Menzies government, 12, 26

Mercury Communications (UK), 92, 177

Messner, Tony, 126

Morgan, Hugh, 153

Moyal, Ann, 39, 57, 95

Murphy, Lionel, 24

Musumeci, Mick, 163, 172

National Broadband Network *see* NBN

National Country Party: backs Telecom against Davidson report recommentations, 92; concerned about Telecom's commercial orientation, 49; supports cross-subsidies during 1977 election campaign, 58

See also Country Party; National Party

National Party: renamed 1982, 120; less effective than telecommunications unions in defending rural constituencies, 203

See also Country Party; National Country Party

national satellite system *see* Aussat; satellite proposals

NBN, 2, 5, 73, 165, 202, 205, 208–11

New Zealand Labour government, 182: telecommunications competition reforms, 117, 172, 177

Nixon, Peter, 52

O'Grady, Frank, 14

O'Keefe, Neil, 130, 188

Office Equipment Industry Association: protests at Telecom competing with private sector, 60

Officials' Working Group on Communications Regulation, 127, 131–6

Optus, 192, 207–8

OTC, 160–6, 168–81, 184–91, 193, 202, 204: Coalition supports monopoly of international services, 105; competition not permitted with Telecom and Aussat, 125; established 1946, 25; incorporated as state-owned company, 146; involved in national satellite system planning, 70–1, 76; managing director and chairman resigns after unsanctioned pay deal, 147; merger with Aussat considered, 164; merger with Telecom debated 1990, 169–79, 181, 183; merger with Telecom proceeds, 190–1; opposes imposition of new performance metrics, 110, 112; opposes PMG/Telecom merger 1973–75, 29–30, 37, 39, 46–7, 52, 198; opposes Telecom merger 1990, 161, 172–4, 186–7; pressures Beazley for concessions, 186; proposed to privatise merged OTC–Aussat, 168; privatisation estimated to raise up to $3.9 billion 1990, 178; privatisation of OTC proposed by Liberal opposition, 120; profits increase 1960s, 25–6, 29; proposes consortium with Aussat and private interests, 173; struggles with PMG over satellite governance 1964, 25; Vernon commission supports continued autonomy, 35, 37–8

Overseas Telecommunications Users' Association, 39

PABXs, 58, 60, 64, 85, 94, 118, 135, 141

Packer, Kerry: lobbies to prevent Telecom supplying videotex services, 60; opposes ATEA coverage of Aussat staff, 102; promotes national satellite system, 69–70; scathing about Fraser government satellite plans, 78

packet switching, 66, 135, 140

Payne, Hugh, 29

Penn, Andy, 211

PMG: Australia's largest enterprise from 1950s, 10; capital expenditure, 8, 10, 30, 32, 42–4; corporatisation, 4, 37, 197; corporatisation supported by ALP, 18–22; customer service condemned 1974, 38–9; early inquiries into, 7–8; early tensions with OTC, 25–6; financial governance inadequate, 10–11, 19; established 1901, 6–7; expands network 1960s, 9–10, 16; financial flexibility granted 1967/68, 12–13; funding decided by parliament 1960s, 11; importance in rural life, 8–9; industrial disputes in, 11, 17, 19, 41; liable for interest to Treasury, 13, 15, 21, 24, 32, 47–8; management complains at lack of autonomy, 28; overwhelmed by rising demand 1960s, 9; predicts rising prices and losses 1973–76, 24; price rises 1967, 15; price rises deferred 1974, 42–4; price-setting subject to parliamentary approval 1960s, 11; reduced working hours, 42; retirement pensions indexed to inflation, 42; role developing Vernon commission terms of reference, 25; submissions to Vernon commission, 26–30; supportive response to Vernon commission, 39; subsidises rural network, 14–15, 30–2; uses insider knowledge to fortify monopoly, 195–6 See also Public Service Board; Vernon commission

Pollock, Bill, 67, 86–7, 92: produces PMG submission to Vernon commission, 26

Post and Telecommunications, Department of (1975–80), 53: involved in planning satellite system, 68–9, 72–4, 76 *See also* Communications, Department of; Transport and Communications, Department of

Post and Telegraph Act replaced, 41

Post and Telegraph Service: proposed spin-off from PMG 1968, 14

postal services, 10, 12–14, 17–18, 21: cross-subsidised by telecommunications, 8, 10, 21–2; history, 6–8; proposals to split PMG into separate post and telecommunications agencies, 21–2, 34–6

PREIA: opposes merger of OTC with new telecommunications authority, 39, 47; opposes OTC–Telecom merger, 172

Preston, A. J., 179

Price, Roger, 130, 163, 180–1, 188

privatisation *see under* Aussat; OTC; Telecom; Telstra

Public Service Board: ALP opposes Board remit over PMG, 18–20, 22; APWU opposes Board role, 17, 28–9; continued involvement in Telecom wages and conditions, 66; remit over PMG administration, 7–8, 10–11, 14–15, 25, 34 Whitlam government sidelines Board, 37, 39

Qantas, 106, 126, 185, 206

Racal Telecom, 173, 184 (later Vodafone, *q.v*)

Review of Commonwealth Functions ('razor gang') 1981, 79–80

Review of Structural Arrangements *see* ROSA

review of telecommunications 1987, 126

Richardson, Graham, 187

Roberts. Michael, 172–3

Robinson, Eric, 57, 75

Rolfe, Hylda, 113

ROSA, 157–76: officials keen to promote competition by structural separation of Telecom, 164–5

Rudd government: announces intention to build NBN 2009, 208–9

Rudd, Kevin, 207–9

rural communities: concerns not addressed in Vernon terms of reference, 25; depend on subsidised services, 8; submissions to Vernon commission, 26

rural interests: defended by telecommunications establishment and unions, 203; influence on communications policy, 202–3; satellites hoped to deliver high-quality services to rural areas, 68; subsidies stimulate demand for unprofitable services, 196–7 *See also* universal service policy

Russell, Don, 173

Ryan, Susan, 77

Samuel, Peter, 54

satellite proposals: Department of Post and Telecommunications reviews broadcasting potential, 68; emphasis on broadcasting, 70, 74; Kerry Packer proposes satellite system to Fraser, 69–70; media reception to plans for national system, 73–4; OTC struggles with PMG over satellite governance 1964, 25; planning for national system, 2, 4, 71–8; Telecom considers national system, 68, 70; Telecom excluded from planning system, 73, 76; *See also* Aussat

Satellite Communications Act 1984, 103–4, 107

Saunderson, John, 103, 130, 181: opposes weakening Telecom monopoly, 118–19

Schacht, Chris, 170

Sedgwick, Stephen, 115

Senate Standing Committee on Statutory Authority Financing, 109

Shaw, Tony, 128, 157, 168: builds avoidable cost model to quantify community service obligations, 155–6

Sims, Rod, 160

Sinclair, Ian, 3, 60, 64–7, 75–8, 80–1, 86–7, 92, 120, 193: announces Davidson inquiry, 80; appears before Vernon commission, 27; autonomy as minister for communications, 56; keen to attract private investment into telecommunications, 80

Slater, George, 28–9, 86

Smith, Jim, 66

Smith, Warwick, 192–4

Snedden, Billy, 38, 48

Snow, Deborah, 81

Spigelman, Jim, 30

Staley, Tony, 1–2, 74–5: appointed minister for post and telecommunications 1977, 56; as ATUG chair, 118, 126, 138, 152–3; bars Telecom from competing with private suppliers for some advanced telecommunications equipment, 60, 87; becomes disillusioned with Telecom, 71–3; does contingency planning for network disruption, 63; enthusiastic about satellite system, 2, 68–9; excludes Telecom from satellite planning, 71–2; initially prefers Telecom to operate satellite network, 71, 199

Stewart, Frank, 33

Stone, John, 30, 145

Street, Tony, 61

Structural Adjustment Committee, 122, 124–41, 144–8: directs departments to develop competition scenarios and investigate Telecom's universal service, 136; opts for independent telecommunications regulator,

134; public servants advise greater competition, 144; substantially accepts Gareth Evans's corporatisation measures, 146

structural separation proposals, 5, 82, 88, 93, 164–7, 175, 179, 183, 189, 206–9

Tanner, Lindsay, 207

Task Force to Inquire into the Continuing Expenditure Policies of the Previous Government see Coombs taskforce

technological change, 4–5, 123: challenge to PMG, 20; Davidson inquiry on, 87–9; delivers improved services 1960s, 9–10; emphasis on data services mid-1970s, 58; growth of broadband demand, 207 See also specific technologies: automatic telephone exchanges; direct dial telecommunications; PABXs; packet switching; videotex

Telecom administration: corporatisation, 48, 127, 137, 144–6, 151; departmental committee approval required for work agreements under Fraser government, 66–7; disputes over industrial coordination, 144–5, 147–8; employs contractors in key exchanges to preempt industrial action, 64; inaugurated July 1975, 52; ministerial approval required for supply contracts under Fraser, 87; ministerial sign-off required for community service plans under Hawke, 141; OTC merger debated 1990, 169–79, 181, 183; OTC merger proposed for inauguration 1975, 37, 39, 46–7, 52, 198; OTC merger proceeds, 190–1; removed from Public Service Board control 1975, 48–9; responds to Davidson report, 92; responds to Hawke government competition reforms, 128, 187; restrained from abusing market power under 1989 reforms, 150; review of classifications 1975, 53–4; to remain a statutory authority under 1988 reform plan, 146

Telecom, economics of: borrowing limit increased 1981, 65; cannot meet rising demand, 199; capital expenditure high, 65, 86, 147; capital works focused on traditional telecommunications, 66; compromise on tax liability 1983, 97–8; increases prices 1975, 53–4; issues securities to raise capital 1976, 57–8; plans to enter private-sector markets for PABXs 1979, 60; reduces dependence on Treasury, 57–8; required to repay debt under Hawke, 105–6; takes on historical debt 1975, 47

Telecom market power: advanced services protected from competition, 140; businesses blocked from setting up private networks, 118; competition not permitted with OTC and Aussat, 125; complaints about, 73, 203; difficulties distinguishing reserved and competitive services, 150; Duffy focuses on dominant interests, 99; duopoly set five-year deadline, 183, 189; fails to satisfy demand for business services, 82; Hutchinson offers 'devastating' assessment of anti-competitive behaviour, 172; keeps network 'deliberately backward' to discourage market entrants, 167; leverages scale to influence telecommunications policy, 204; local content obligations protect equipment manufacturers, 134; monopoly of information on cross-subsidy costs discourages policy reform, 91, 196; monopoly of inter-city links provides huge profits, 72, 83, 85, 113–4; monopoly power scrutinised 1987, 108; offers to surrender standards-setting role 1983, 94, but later revokes offer, 99; questions raised about dual role in regulating and providing services, 123; refuses regulatory approvals to thwart innovative services, 135; regulates equipment permitted to connect to network, 59; regulatory powers to be curtailed, 125; tensions with Fraser government, 66; warns of end to universal service if loses inter-city monopoly, 129; warns of rising prices if monopoly ended, 84

Telecom privatisation: competition viewed as a safeguard against privatisation, 187; debated by ALP 1988, 126; Hugh Morgan calls for, 153; Coalition opposition proposes, 181–2; public opinion of, 127; ruled out by Hawke and Gareth Evans, 127
See also Aussat; first telephone monopoly; OTC; structural separation; universal service policy

Telecommunications Act 1975, 89, 118

Telecommunications Act 1989, 150

Telecommunications Act 1997, 205

Telecommunications Bill 1991 passes, 193
See also Australian and Overseas Telecommunications Corporation Bill

telecommunications unions, 5, 11, 96, 99: disrupt telecommunications, 61–4; fear job losses, 133; influence ALP policy, 18–19, 86, 197–8, 201; influence Aussat–Telecom deal, 101–3; make submission to Vernon commission, 26, 28–9; oppose Aussat part-privatisation, 102; oppose new mobile licence, 163; oppose private-sector involvement in telecommunications, 85; oppose weakening of Telecom first phone monopoly, 118–20, 128–30, 138–9; pleased at sidelining of Public Service Board, 39; resist change from latter 1970s, 203; support Telecom/OTC merger, 161, 170; threaten industrial action if services privatised, 85; threaten split in ALP, 184–5
See also APTU/APWU; ATEA

telephone line rentals: business subsidises consumers 1960s, 8; city subsidises country, 8, 11, 28, 31; country raised to city rates 1973, 32; Davidson inquiry recommends raising rates, 90; increase in rates 1974, 42, 44; low rates boost demand, 8–10, 30–1, 43; rates set below cost 1960s, 10, 30–1

Telstra, 2, 151, 202, 205–9: positions for NBN Co privatisation, 211; privatisation opposed 1996, 206

Thatcher government, 116

Thatcher, Margaret: introduces competition in British telecommunications 1980, 91–2

timed local calls, 90, 92–6, 120, 138–9

Toohey, Brian, 54

Trade Practices Commission, 117–18, 141, 154: advocates telecommunications competition, 75

Transport and Communications, Department of, 124–53, 155–8: ambivalent about Telecom-OTC merger, 184; concerns about Aussat saleability, 175; develops reform work program, 124–8; prepares for review of carriers, 157; supports delaying third mobile licence, 192
See also Communications, Department of; Post and Telecommunications, Department of; Evans, Graham; Fanning, Vanessa; Hutchinson, Mike; Shaw, Tony; Wilenski, Peter

Treasury, Department of: charges interest on PMG funds, 13, 15, 21, 24, 32; debates PMG financial controls, 12–13, 28; pushes for private investment in satellite, 74–5, 102, 106–8; questions Telecom debt and tax liabilities, 45–6, 97–8; questions Telecom estimate of cross-subsidies cost, 132; reduces Telecom funding, 57–8; supports open competition in telecommunications, 174–9; supports uniform performance metrics, 109–15, 143–4; targets Telecom cross-subsidies as economic barrier, 83–4, 113–4

Trujillo, Sol, 207

unions, telecommunications *see* APTU/APWU; ATEA; PREIA; telecommunications unions

universal service policy, 2, 8, 11–12, 27–8, 43, 49, 196, 198, 204: Bureau of Transport and Communications Economics engaged to cost policy 1988, 140; Coalition sceptical of Whitlam government rural policies, 49–50; competition deferred until community service quantified, 131–4, 140; costs quantified under Ralph Willis, 149; Davidson inquiry recommends direct funding, 89, 91–2; depends on cross-subsidies, 85–6, 99, 113–15, 131–2, 191; Fraser government attempts to reconcile universal service with looser restrictions, 91–6; Hawke government codifies Universal Service Obligation, 190; restricted to basic telephony, 133; Telecom engages consultants to quantify community service costs, 155; Telecom resists quantifying costs, 172; universal service viewed as compatible with competition, 5, 155–6, 184–5, 201–2; Whitlam argues for direct subsidies, 20
See also Coalition government (to 1972); Country Party; cross-subsidies in telecommunications; National Country Party; National Party

Unsworth, Barrie, 138

Urban and Regional Development, Department of, 27

Uren, Tom, 24

Vernon commission, 26–9, 33: opposes extreme cross-subsidies, 37; proposes revised accounting practices in telecommunications, 42; proposes separation of post and telecommunications, 34; public responses to report, 37–9, 48–9; report, 34–7, 43, 198; Whitlam government response, 37, 40, 42, 45–52

See also Interdepartmental Working Group on Recommendations of the Australian Post Office Commission of Inquiry

Vernon, James: appointed as royal commissioner 1973, 26; declines invitation to chair Telecom or Australia Post, 41; supports OTC remaining stand-alone enterprise, 35, 38, 46

Victorian Employers' Association: calls for PMG to operate more commercially, 15

videotex, 58, 87, 100; Telecom barred from entering market, 60, 87

Viner, Ian, 64

Vodafone: begins operating in Australia 1993, 194
See also Racal Telecom

Walsh, Peter, 97, 106, 110–12, 114–16, 124, 143–6

Walters, Patrick, 159, 174, 176

Ward, Mel, 118, 128–9, 163, 173–4

Waters, Frank, 17, 28

Webb, Harry, 18, 20

White taskforce, 69–71, 74

White, Harold, 47, 69–70, 74; as chair of ATUG, 62; campaigns against planned abolition of OTC, 39

Whitlam government, 23–55, 195, 197–8, 202–3: attacks cross-subsidies, 4, 43; establishes Vernon commission, 24; fails to acknowledge likely pressure on PMG wages and costs, 49, 198; ministers' inflammatory approach to rural concerns, 33, 198; rebalances telecommunications charges, 31–2, 42–3, 89–91, 197

Whitlam opposition, 18–22, 58, 203: argues that uneconomic communication services should be supported by subvention, 20–1, 27; proposes that postal services be placed under a separate agency from telecommunications, 21–2;

repudiates bipartisan consensus on telecommunications 1967, 2–4, 195

Whitlam, Gough, 12, 16, 19–22, 89–90, 197–8: aims to corporatise PMG, 17–19; announces double-dissolution election 1974, 34; appoints Coombs taskforce, 31; cites PMG failings in attack on Coalition economic management 1972, 22; committed to administrative reform, 18, 197; determined to see OTC merge with Telecom, 37, 46–7, 52; supports user-pays principles in telecommunications, 4, 18, 25, 43, 197; wins office 1972, 23

Wilenski, Peter, 123–4, 129–30, 149

Willesee, Don, 24

Willis, Ralph, 5, 97, 119, 130, 150–8, 191, 201: appointed minister for transport and communications 1988, 149; calls for improved public-sector productivity, 116; establishes ROSA (Review of Structural Arrangements) 1989, 157; member of Structural Adjustment Committee, 124; supports avoidable cost model to calculate Telecom's community service obligations, 149, 156

About the Author

John Doyle held strategy and regulatory roles at Optus from the late 1990s to the early 2010s and was also a board director of the telecommunications sector's primary industry body, Communications Alliance. He subsequently completed a PhD on the politics of telecommunications reform at La Trobe University, for which he received the Rhys Isaac Prize for best thesis in the humanities and social sciences, and where he is now an adjunct research fellow.

Ingram Content Group Australia Pty Ltd
Printed in Australia
AUHW021216290323
376242AU00012B/59